CHINA POP

How Soap Operas,

Tabloids,

and Bestsellers

Are Transforming

a Culture

Jianying Zha

THE NEW PRESS
NEW YORK

THE NEW PRESS

Published in the United States by The New Press, New York
Distributed by Perseus Distribution

Library of Congress Cataloging-in-Publication Data

Zha, Jianying.
    China pop: how soap operas, tabloids, and bestsellers are transforming a culture /
Jianying Zha.
        p.cm.
    ISBN 978-1-56584-250-2
    1. Mass media—Social aspects—China. 2. Social change—China.
    1. Title.
    P92.C5Z43 1995
    302.23'0951—dc20   94-43004   CIP

Portions of chapter 1 appeared in substantially different form in *The Voice Literary
Supplement*. Chapters 2 and 7 appeared in slightly different form in *Transition*. Chapter 3
appeared in slightly different form in *The Antioch Review*. Chapter 4 appeared in slightly
different form in *Sight and Sound*. Portions of chapter 5 appeared in substantially different
form in *The Nation* and *Public Culture*.

The New Press was established in 1990 as a not-for-profit alternative to the
large, commercial publishing houses currently dominating the book publishing
industry. The New Press operates in the public interest rather than for private
gain, and is committed to publishing, in innovative ways, works of educational,
cultural, and community value that are often deemed insufficiently profitable.

www.thenewpress.com

Book design by Ann Antoshak

Printed in the United States ofAmerica

9 8 7 6 5 4

To Ben

CONTENTS

ACKNOWLEDGMENTS

I HAVE encountered so much kindness, encouragement, and help in the course of researching and writing this book that I cannot possibly thank everyone. I would, however, like to single out a few people here. A hundred flowers to Henry Finder, formerly an editor at *Transition* and now at *The New Yorker,* who, ever since publishing my first piece in English on the basis of a blind submission, has offered invaluable criticism and advice on everything I wrote, often through line-by-line editing. Without him, this book would not have been possible. To André Schiffrin, my publisher and editor, for his belief in this book from the beginning, and insightful comments all the way through. To Molly Friedrich, my agent, for her staunch support and smart feedback on all the chapters. To Lore Segal, my mentor, for her generous friendship and time to read and criticize. To Jane Kramer, whose wonderful essays on Europe and personal encouragement of my writing have both been inspiring. To C. T. Hsia, my teacher at Columbia University, who urged me to branch out from the academy and into bilingual writing. To Leo Ou-fan Lee, my bicultural, bilingual fellow traveler, who criticized and cheered me on. To the many people who helped me with their useful responses on different parts of the manuscripts: Ackbar Abbas, Vincent Crapanzano, Manthia Diawara, Dilip Gaonkar, Mingxia Li, Ping-hui Liao, Barry Schechter, Leonard Schwartz, Michael Warner. To these three fine people at The New Press: Ted Byfield, Grace Farrell, and Matthew Weiland. To Gayle Feldman, who introduced me to Molly. To the editors who respectively worked with me and printed portions of this book in their magazines: Carol Breckenridge, of *Public Culture,* Philip Dodd, of *Sight and Sound,* Robert Fogarty, of *Antioch Review,* Reginald Gibbons, of *TriQuarterly,* Scott L. Malcomson, of *The Voice Literary Supplement,* Micah Sifry, of *The Nation,* and Michael Vazquez, of *Transition.*

My special thanks to the Rockefeller Foundation for funding a China Program for which I have been serving as a coordinator; this provided me with numerous opportunities to visit Beijing and Hong Kong. Thanks are also due to Bernard Weissbourd, Chairman of the Center for Transcultural Studies in Chicago, whose international vision and generosity have been instrumental to my work and research.

ACKNOWLEDGMENTS

Of course, I am deeply indebted to all those in China whose trust and cooperation have been indispensable. Sometimes, for safety reasons, their names have been changed in this book. But at least I can express my special gratitude here to several principal interviewees: Zheng Wanlong, Ma Guoxin, Chen Kaige, Chen Xilin, Jia Pingwa, and Chan Koon-Chung.

My final thanks and salute must go to Benjamin Lee, my husband, to whom this book is dedicated. He has been my toughest reader and critic. Without his love, support, understanding, indulgence, cooking, and cleaning, I would not have started or finished this project.

CHINA POP

I

AFTER AN ICON

THERE ARE many clichés about China. Often, they circulate with the aid of famous icons: the Great Wall, the Chinese box, Mao, the smiling panda, and so on. The latest is Tiananmen Square. Since 1989, Tiananmen has dominated our fantasy about China like a massive, dark, bloody cloud. Despite a continuous trickle of coverage about China's economic reforms and the more recent interest in the booming Asia market, Tiananmen persists. The images of tanks, blood, and the small statue of Liberty crumbling to dust still haunt us. In the minds of the Western public, China's face is forever tarnished: once again, the distant giant has lapsed into its repressive, backward pattern, which all the money and the cheap labor markets cannot quite redeem.

Like all clichés, this one, partly perpetuated by media sound bites and daily newspaper reports, contains a measure of truth. Still, by framing China around a set of simple political facts and images, it reduces a complicated, constantly changing reality to a sweeping dichotomy and a black-and-white picture. So instead of the mad, conformist China of Mao Zedong's epoch, or the lovable pandalike China of the early Deng Xiaoping's reign, we now have a China with a totalitarian government on the one hand and a runaway free market on the other. A new puzzle, to be sure, but seen through a pair of old lenses.

A closer look at China from multiple angles would yield a more complex, more ambiguous picture. China is going through an unprecedented transition. This process, sometimes called "the third way" or "the Chinese way," in contrast to the Soviet model, is ridden with contradictions, ambiguities, and often impossible dilemmas. To understand it beyond clichés requires openness and patience. To observe it close-up and meticulously, one may have to give up the grandeur of the panoramic view and resist the temptation of easy abstractions and conclusions.

Few would disagree that such an approach is useful. This book is my effort to portray present-day China in a multi-faceted, minute fashion. Broadly, the book is about the changes that have taken place after Tiananmen, the moods that have hung over Beijing, and the ethos of those individuals whose lives have been caught in the throes of rapid social transition. In particular, it is about people in the Chinese culture industry, how their beliefs, friendships, and survival abilities have been tested by or have adjusted to the intrigues of cultural politics and the new needs of commercialism. At a personal level, this is also a book about my Chinese friends, about our mutual and separate passages from the past to the present, from the romance and ironies of revolution to the realism and challenges of cosmopolitanism. All the chapters are set in the years after Tiananmen, except for "A City without Walls," the chapter about Beijing's urban transformation, where I widen the focus to give more historical background to China's long struggle for modernization. A central concern in this book is China's ongoing cultural transition. The book opens with "Yearnings," a story about the making of a wildly controversial television soap opera right after Tiananmen, and ends with "Islanders," a portrait of a Hong Kong corporation arriving recently in mainland China to open joint-venture businesses on the cultural front. The chapters in between—which cover topics ranging from urban planning, filmmaking, the news business, art, and eating, to pornography and sexual politics—all deal in different ways with the changing environments in which culture is being produced and consumed in China. Through these stories and portraits, I hope to evoke the tension-fraught atmosphere of the current Chinese cultural scene, to chronicle how cultural productions are being commercialized and professionalized in a semicommunist, third world country, and how such processes have complicated, profound implications for the future of Chinese society.

To the extent that the choices of events and characters in this book reflect my personal interests and subjective portrayal, an autobiographical sketch here may be in order. Born and raised in Beijing, I grew up in the chaotic years of the Cultural Revolution, and was among the first lucky batch to obtain a college education right afterward: I arrived on the campus of Beijing University straight from a year of "reeducation" farm labor with the peasants. In 1981, I came to America at the age of twenty-one, and after five and half years of graduate school in South Carolina and New York, I went back to China in 1987 with a dissertation grant and hopes of reconnecting with my roots. In the following two years of living there, I started a moderately successful career writing Chinese fiction, and became increasingly involved in China's lively cultural trends and intellectual circles. By the time the students arrived in Tiananmen, I was coediting an elite Beijing magazine with a group of high-profile Chinese writers and working at a temporary job at the *New York Times*'s Beijing bureau.

Tiananmen brought all that to a halt. After witnessing the June 4th massacre, I returned to the United States. Since then, my working life has been spent in both China and America. Since 1990, my job as a China program coordinator at an independent research center in Chicago has enabled me to visit China regularly. I have been able to stay in my mother's apartment in Beijing for weeks, sometimes months, in order to conduct research and interviews. In the past two years, I've been writing a regular column of commentary on Beijing for a leading Hong Kong monthly. I am married to a Chinese-American and have made a home in Chicago while writing in both Chinese and English.

Given these circumstances, I cannot claim to be a total outsider or insider in either cultural scene. Instead, I have split identities, loyalties to peoples and values on both sides of the Pacific Ocean. My usual reply to questions regarding where exactly I locate myself mentally and culturally has been: I have one foot in China, one foot in America, and my head is somewhere in between, probably resting in Hong Kong.

This flighty image of myself as a brave cosmopolitan straddling vast cultural spaces and continents, however, hardly tells anything about how it actually feels to be in that position. Through researching and writing this book, I've learned that, for me at least, the life of seemingly glamorous intercontinental jet trips and the freedom of not being totally bound by one single nation and culture come at a high price. I still cringe to think of the anguish and sometimes galling confusions it has brought me—of constantly having to juggle, question, and clarify my multiple personas and voices, my mixed emotions and dual perspectives. To a lot of the people in China I talked with or interviewed and eventually wrote about in this book, I was a friend, a journalist, a fellow writer, a drinking and bantering buddy, just another Chinese, an alienated Chinese, an overseas Chinese, a half-and-half, or all of the above. I made a safe, easy confidante, sometimes, because I no longer live there; at other times, because all that shared background and history count for a lot, I was still considered "one of our own." This, obviously, presents advantages and pitfalls. This special kind of trust, camaraderie, and involvement are fraught with tensions. They have frequently forced me to face at least two subsequent issues: on the one hand, I must take special care to avoid damaging the lives of those living in China; on the other, I must maintain sufficient distance from them in order to paint reasonably fair and balanced pictures of their lives.

Most of the central figures in this book are what we might call "intellectuals." Although in China the term is used casually for anyone with a college diploma, I use it here to refer to a range of educated, urban professionals, including writers, architects, filmmakers, artists, critics, and publishers. It would be easy to explain and justify my decision to focus on them by pointing out the traditionally important role intellectuals have played in Chinese public life, and how, as the country's best and brightest, their stories would shed light on China's current situation in a singularly interesting way. While this is generally true, the eloquence of other groups of people, the intricacies of other life stories certainly have an equal claim to attention and would have an equal hold on me, were it not for my own personal fascination and, in many cases, familiarity and ease with this particular cast of characters. Some of my interviewees in this book are acquaintances going back years, some are friends or colleagues of friends. Networks, background, connections, and friendships are often crucial in any line of work in China, and considering the degree to which people are still subject to official surveillance, such personal trust and ease understandably help a good deal in obtaining frank, in-depth exchanges on whatever subjects Chinese deem "sensitive." I should make clear, however, that my goal in this book is not to give an all-encompassing picture of contemporary China. The large Chinese population made up of peasants and workers would be of central concern in such a general portrayal. Instead, I have focused on the big cities, the intellectuals, and the culture industry, in order to capture the spirit of the emerging cosmopolitanism that is helping to pull China into a global culture.

I have grown accustomed to my ambivalent feelings about China: I confront them every time I go there. Sometimes Beijing is like a skin disease: my itch and feelings for her are intensely bitter and tender, full of the sort of violence that marks convoluted, poorly examined passion. The city becomes nearly unbearable whenever I stay there for more than a few weeks—the itch get worse and worse, tormenting me until I bleed. I take to the wildest mood swings, overreact to things and people; then, to breathe more freely, to regain my balance and rationality, I have to flee. America enables me to take a more clear and dispassionate view, to put what I bring back from China into perspective. It allows me to grow some new skin.

But it does not take long for me to feel China's spell again. The old itch returns, and I start longing to go back, fantasizing about all that chaotic grit, all that raw, uncouth, yet somehow refreshing thirst for a better life. Writing my column for Hong Kong and overseas Chinese readers, socializing with scores of exiled or visiting Chinese friends who regularly drop in and out of my tranquil, orderly life in the States, I start missing the pleasures of being immersed in my native tongue and hanging out with pals in the old and new local joints in Beijing. I wonder what new Beijing slang and blackly humorous jokes are going around, and how my friends have been getting on since I last saw them. Before long, I need to hop onto a plane and plunge into the next cycle of swings. Deep down, I know I am addicted to them.

Perhaps this is partially why so many of my principal characters in this book have turned out to be those beleaguered individuals balanced and torn between different eras, lives, and factions, whose struggles and choices have made such deep impressions on me. Meeting them has marked the many high points of my journeys. Drawn as I am to those who cross frontiers, who embrace and negotiate with multiple scenes and settings in life, whose loyalties, motivations, and roots are therefore often the subject of controversy, these people are, in some ways, my brothers and sisters. Most of them do not have the privilege I have, of leaving. They have to fight it out where they are and take the full brunt of the fire. I am humbled by the tough complexities of their situations, moved by the spirit and poignancy of their stories. In a sense, they are cosmopolitans ahead of their times.

IN THE past few years, so many of the people I know in China have shed their old skins and picked up new lives.

Songzi's story is but one in a hundred. A bright young scientist in a military weaponry research institute in Beijing, Songzi was one of the many members of China's elite who got heavily involved in the 1989 protest movement. He phoned me several times a day, wildly excited and hopeful, feeding me with the latest news from the Square or the freshest rumor about the army and the politburo from his circle of well-connected friends. He was the first to inform me of the martial law; and before I heard the first gunshot, Songzi had called from the west side of the city, telling me in a hollow voice that the killing had begun. He was a loyal friend. On that fateful day after the massacre, when all transportation broke down in Beijing, he offered to help with my departure. Risking sniper shots and armed soldiers with their eyes glazed from the heat of killing, he biked beside me in the rain until a gypsy cab finally agreed to take me over to the airport.

When I saw him again nearly two years later, Songzi was half transformed. He had developed a new passion: he'd been playing mah jong for the past two years. "The population of mah jong players in China is huge," he informed me: "Great way to kill time." He had been idle, taking a prolonged sick leave from work. He made sharp jokes about himself ("Those armored personnel carriers we researched really worked!"), threw scathing remarks at those who turned to making money, and said that anyone who wasn't thinking of leaving the country must be sick—and that he himself was only too sick to leave. He became someone who killed the fun instantly at a dinner party. Tiananmen had crushed the idealism out of him so badly, it was painful to look at him.

Yet I was more startled by his next transformation. One day during my 1992 visit to Beijing, Songzi turned up in my mother's apartment in a three-piece suit and glossy leather shoes, a beeper on his belt, and a broad grin on his face. "I'm a businessman now!" he announced. In an easy manner, he told me astonishing tales about how he and his colleagues at the military research institute used their privileges to sell oil for a profit, how he and a partner made a pile with phony ad campaigns ("Chinese consumers are so gullible!"), and about swindling and smuggling everywhere. He helped his wife bribe her way through the railway officials so that she got on the famous trans-Siberian with large sacks of goods (liquor, silk, down jackets), which she sold in Moscow for a good profit. The trans-Siberian trains, he said, were filled with smugglers and traders—Chinese, Russians, Hungarians, Romanians, everybody was out to make a buck and hoping, with luck and flair, to strike a fortune. "Call it joining the international trade!" Songzi declared cheerfully. "No need to corrupt the Party, it's all rotten from within. Even the Party officials at our institute are busy making a buck for themselves. I'd be a fool if I still refused to come to my senses. The thugs with blood on their hands will get it in the end. But until then, I'd better move along and get some dough myself. I don't enjoy money making—my idea of a great time is lying in bed with a good book on a rainy day. But what choice do I have?"

One of my classmates at Beijing University who had been a noted avant-garde literary critic in the eighties went through a similar transformation. In 1989, she marched in support of the students; in 1991, she became a private saleswoman. She still retained her state job at a literary institute, which required her to report to the office only once a week; the rest of the time she spent in her little vendor room in a downtown shopping plaza, selling women's clothing: colorful jackets, leather coats, sweaters. She and her partner hung a large Pierre Cardin poster above the racks, and called their store "Eve's Dream." The immediate reasons that got her into the private sector had to do with inflation, the cost of living, boredom, and depression at her state job, where her hard-line boss ordered her to collect "black materials"—compromising information—about fellow Chinese intellectuals. Like Songzi, though, she too had a theory about her new life. "We intellectuals had been too alienated," she told me. "We knew nothing about Chinese reality at a very basic, daily-life level. We didn't understand what an ordinary person wanted or how society functioned at the bottom level." When I pointed out that she still kept her copies of Foucault and Lacan by her bed, she shrugged: "I read them sometimes, before going to sleep. I don't find it contradictory— selling clothes by day and reading theory at night. Actually, they both have to do with certain fundamental needs and impulses in life." Since then, she has moved from job to job, working for an advertising company at one point, traveling to South America to look into investment opportunities at another. I notice lifestyle changes about her: she wears more stylish clothes, more subtle makeup, and races around town in cabs rather than on buses. With her new life on the fast track, I wonder if she still finds time to read Foucault and Lacan.

One of my old friends, a Beijing magazine editor and art commentator, took off to the southern city of Shenzhen after his magazine, a reformist forum, was shut down in the wake of Tiananmen. In the freewheeling "Special Economic Zone," he went into stock speculation, made a lot of money, lost half of it, turned himself into an expert on the subject, and wrote a column for a business newsletter. Nowadays, he helps to produce television variety shows, and is on the lookout for an opportunity to start his own magazine with his own money.

So many novelists I know of have teamed up in recent years to write soaps and sitcoms for television. Some of them have sold manuscripts at literary auctions, a new venue set up to publicize and sell "serious literature" to rich entrepreneurs. One newspaper article intoned, "Our literati should abandon their traditional condescension toward business. A new era calls for new literati."

An investigative reporter friend, fed up with the endless official inquiries into his involvement in Tiananmen, simply quit his old job and opened his own business consulting agency. I have been to his slick, computerized office suites in one of Beijing's extravagant new highrises. Half of his employees, he tells me, are teachers who were purged after Tiananmen. Amid the brisk telecommunication buzz, they now look like calm, competent professionals in a private firm. Among his many plans for expansion, my friend says, his ultimate dream is to open a private university: "Independent, high-quality education is so important in China." And he believes this can be done in the foreseeable future.

My half-brother, a former Red Guard* from an elite Beijing prep school who, at seventeen, answered Mao's calls to "change heaven and earth"† and

---

* That is, a member of the radical student organization—the Red Guards—that sprang up in Chinese middle schools and universities during the Cultural Revolution.

† "To change heaven and earth" was a popular slogan during the Cultural Revolution; it is a quotation from Mao's high-flown speech that urged China's educated youth to go to the countryside and join the peasants in improving China's agricultural production.

ended up spending the ensuing twenty-one years in an impoverished farm county in Inner Mongolia, returned to Beijing in the spring of 1989. He went straight to Tiananmen Square and predicted that "the people will win this time." Nowadays, he devotes his energies to getting bank loans, opening new factories, and starting business ventures. Some of his peasant pals from Inner Mongolia have followed his trail to the capital city, and he has turned them into trusted foremen in his new factories. Politics remains his passion, and he is still convinced that freedom and democracy will come to China, and that some people must give their life for these ideals; but capital and financial status, he now realizes, are the sort of credentials he'll need to have a voice in the future. Now and then, we'd have a drink between his business banquets and trips. Listening to him lapse into long, impassioned speeches about human rights and the multiparty system, and knowing that another of his factories has turned out unprofitable and that large debts are piling up on his back, I can't help feeling the irony of his life. It's the story of a man who seems always half a step ahead of his time, and half a step behind it.

STORIES OF this sort may have a familiar ring to us by now. Since the ending of the Cold War, the struggles among the former communist countries to transform centrally planned, Soviet-style economies into market economies have created in these societies many of the same tensions and a similar ethos. Cultural communities disintegrate, lifestyles change, uncertainties about the future linger. There is a pervasive sense of the loss of illusions and innocence and a quiet mourning of failed utopian ideals—but such elegiac sentiments are quickly suppressed in the onslaught of new realities. With the exception of the ethnic war zones, in large sections of Eastern Europe and the former Soviet Union, as in China, commercialization, accompanied by the rise of popular culture and consumerism, has been a common phenomenon. Privatization, concurring with globalization, has had an intense impact on economic structures and people's lives.

Profound cultural differences aside, though, China's post–Cold War social transition is marked by a singularly important factor that sets it apart from all others: the revolution failed in 1989, and the Communist Party stays on to guide and control the reform process.

This is a crucial fact in efforts to understand the peculiar complexities and ironies of China's current situation. It produces a half-baked, sheepish, defensive, cynical, masked, stealthy, and often comic atmosphere in which China's reform zigzags ahead. Instead of dramatic, exhilarating breakdowns of old regimes, as occurred in Eastern Europe and Russia, what we witness in China is a slow, soft, and messy meltdown of the old structure. I would whimsically refer to this as "the Whopper effect": there is an impure, junky, hybrid quality in nearly all spheres of the present Chinese life—culture, politics, attitudes, ideology. This is not romantic, not a picturesque scene for the camera. It's too blurry, too slippery, often shamelessly vulgar. Who can blame the CBS, ABC, and NBC anchors for not having rushed back since Tiananmen? To some, it might be akin to filming a merry, grotesque banquet on the ruins of a slaughterhouse.

If the post-Tiananmen China provides no heartwarming, soul-cleansing catharsis as triumphant revolts for freedom and democracy would, nor does it then offer, to the consternation of some prophets, the starkly bleak picture of protracted oppression and depression which often comes after a brutal crackdown. Under the cloud of political dishonor, China has gone right on with its noisy march toward economic prosperity, all cheered on by the same old drumroll of "socialism with Chinese characteristics." In Eastern Europe and Russia, there was a powerful sense of the dawning of a new era. Chilly or warm, it was "the morning after," history turning a new page. In China, again, there was no such luck when it came to clear-cut lines.

China has been moving on according to its own curious logic. As the government repeatedly defies international condemnation over its human rights abuses, as it drones on about China's uniqueness and refuses to be "cowed by outside pressures," it *has* been "cowed" by internal pressures in ways that have surprised many and eluded easy definition. The Party has not, of course, allowed democracy in China; but then almost everyone now agrees that the Chinese never cared much for Western-style democracy, and that, in any case, no Chinese—not even the Tiananmen students—really understood what democracy was. The Party is not granting more political freedom, but it has granted more economic freedom, which everyone knows cannot be restricted simply to economics. Talking about Tiananmen, a Chinese lawyer friend said: "When a million people went to the streets, they couldn't possibly be motivated just by some abstract idea. It's got to be related to self-interest. Why, democracy was irrelevant, the real issues were inflation and injustice! Prices had been climbing, and people were angry at not getting a fair chance to make more money like those high sons and daughters of the Party leaders." A veteran Beijing journalist summed it up for me this way: "Tiananmen forced the Party into a corner: improve living standards or step down." And he shrugged off the hard-line rhetoric: "Of course the Party talks tough. It has a duck's mouth, which stays tough even when the body gets all cooked through. Don't ever expect it to publicly admit any mistakes—how could it rule after losing face like that? But, in reality, old Deng knew the economy was the key. He has opened it up, and as a result China has made more progress than we demanded at Tiananmen Square."

This is a sentiment echoed by a lot of Chinese. Even some of the most passionate rebels of 1989 seem to have learned their lesson. A media reporter, who had played an active part in the Tiananmen protests, confessed to me over a mug of beer in the spring of 1993: "It's like getting a hard punch in the face from your father. Very hard to get over. Only by and by do you realize he's your father after all. And there is nothing you can do but slowly chip away at that hard socialist wall."

As passions dissipated, other disturbing factors about 1989 also surfaced. More and more people noticed, for example, how the ultraradical wing of the students, speaking the purist language of blood and sacrifice, eventually got the upper hand at Tiananmen Square, how their apparent extremism panicked the state's gerontocracy. In a last-ditch confrontation, passion and force, not reason and moderation, dominated; and ironically, the moderate, more mature dissident leaders got the longest sentences in the postmassacre trials. What's more, in the wake of one highly publicized event, a generation of prodemocratic struggles paid a heavy price. For a whole decade, a fragile yet lively Chinese version of civil society (semi-independent, democratizing publications and organizations) had been quietly building up bases within or on the margins of the official structure; after Tiananmen, most of them were suspended or purged. Facts like these gradually led many Chinese to regard Tiananmen as the tragic offspring of the decade-long prodemocracy movement—a stillborn that kills its mother in birth. And then, the news about how the exiles have been running their affairs abroad sent home another sobering message. With students and intellectual leaders endlessly fighting among themselves and embezzling funds, those in China turned increasingly harsh toward their former comrades: if the dissidents had won in 1989 and taken the country into their hands, things would be much worse today. Perhaps, after all, the rebels were themselves products of communism, the students children of Mao, and they could not but fight for new ideals in the old way, with mass rallies, slogan chanting, factionalism, and corruption. A heritage of decades could not go away in one romantic season; it is likely to run through its course through the veins of generations.

This prevalent sense of futility about direct political action has, I think, to do both with the tight-lid official control and this kind of somber reassessment of the past events. And as a "spring wind of marketization" blew across the land and other pressing matters beckoned, people got busy with them.

For the time being at least, a silent pact seems to exist between the old emperor and his people: I rule, you prosper, and let's forget all else.

From all the evidence, the Chinese population has been playing by this rule. So far, the result should please Deng: the Party is still running the country, the country is enjoying a boom, and the boom is eroding the memories of the past tragedies. Nobody save for the exiles and a few isolated individuals, it appears, is brooding over the fading of memory.

MY MOTHER and I visit my father's spot at Babaoshan, the most prestigious cemetery in China because of the large numbers of top-ranking Party leaders buried here. People fight over it, yearning for the distinction, I suppose, of spending their afterlife among eminent figures. My father had said he couldn't care less about such things since he was an atheist, but he ended up here anyway, because of his rank.

Babaoshan is a pain in the neck to visit: inconveniently located—a long bus and train ride to the outskirts of Beijing, then a long walk on the dirt road—and always crowded. It is especially so on this day, April 5, the annual memorial day when the Chinese sweep the graves of their ancestors and honor their dead. My mother and I have been squeezed in crowds all the way through our train ride, and the cemetery is almost like a circus. People push, shove, and trip over bumpy stony objects everywhere. The loudspeakers blast away regulations: *no pushing, no shoving, no loud talking, no inappropriate gathering or loitering.* Wherever you turn, there is a loudspeaker propped up, banging you over the head with these rules, repeated again and again and again. It just won't let go. I hurriedly glance at the photograph of my father's face: he too is pinched in there among a full wall of people, and the space is so tight I can't even find a nook to place the single white lily I've brought him.

"Still a police state!" my mother says angrily as we leave in haste. "No peace and quiet even for the dead." I feel numb. All the way home on the train, I am seized by a sudden flash of memory about my tearful quarrel with my father in 1979, when I turned twenty. During the first "Beijing Spring"—China's political thaw, our Prague Spring—Wei Jingsheng, the most prominent dissident emerging from the then exuberant "Democracy Wall Movement," was sentenced to fifteen years in jail. The government said Wei leaked secret military information to foreigners, but all of us knew his real "crime": he called Deng a dictator and demanded freedom of speech. My father believed the government. We had never before argued so furiously, flinging words at each other like knives. I remember sitting alone in a broken bamboo chair afterward, and starting to cry. It was the beginning of our split: my father had been my idol and had doted on me, but the generation gap got deeper and deeper over the years, and the wound would never heal.

The last quarrel that erupted between us was during the Tiananmen protest. Both he and I had been going out every day, separately, to "check out the situation"; at dinner, we'd talk a bit about it. My mother and brother were sympathetic to the students; my father thought both the government and the students were wrong-headed. I was much too hot-headed to listen to that. The argument quickly became overheated, and it was my brother, who, by calmly pointing out some logical flaws in both my father's reasoning and my muddled declarations, managed to quiet down all of us. I also felt terribly disappointed to see my father carrying on with his long, merry morning rituals of exercising and dancing at a nearby park rather than becoming obsessed, as I was, with "the great historical moment." How ironic this is, I thought bitterly, for an old communist who himself had been a leader of student protests against the reactionary government of his time! One day, a young scholar brought an open statement sympathetic to the students and asked if my father would sign on. Many eminent scholars had signed already. My father refused. Watching the disappointed young scholar leave, I couldn't help saying, "Dad, did you notice Hu Sheng's signature on it?" Hu Sheng was the head of the academy where my father was a senior scholar. He looked at me and said simply, "Yes, but I don't agree with the statement." Late one night, as we sat reading opposite each other in the family living room, for some reason I can no longer recall my father remarked, a bit chagrined, about how much we disagreed these days. Feeling completely cold toward him at that moment, I said without looking up, "Yeah, but who cares?" He threw a newspaper at my face, and I saw that he had turned white. A few days later, I left China. That was the last time I saw him.

My father visited the Soviet Union and four Eastern European countries before his death: he was in Berlin when the wall came down, in Prague when Vaclav Havel was inaugurated. In Moscow and Leningrad and Kiev, he got a sense that communism was not doing too well. After the trip, he told my mother: "I think my difference with our daughter boils down to this: she believes culture will save China, I believe the economy will." There was reconciliation in his tone. He wrote me a letter full of interesting perceptions about his journey. Impressed, I wrote back, praising the intelligence of his observations. Later, my mother told me how pleased he had been by my rare acknowledgment. Weeks after that exchange, he died.

In some ways, my relationship with my father is not unlike what happened between the Tiananmen students and the government. Most of the time, he and I were able to live with our differences and maintain a friendly rapport. If I differed from him on something but spoke of it in a reasonable, respectful manner, he'd usually listen or at least not feel offended. Sometimes he'd even give some credit to my position. But a confrontation was a different matter: carried away by pride and passion, we'd start getting narrow-eyed, each stubbornly bent on being right, and we'd jump and bark, tearing at each other and squaring off like two pit bulls. And I'd always end up feeling crushed, since my father would never back off when he felt his authority was being challenged in an unacceptable way. On the other hand, in a very important sense, there was nothing in common between my father and the Chinese regime. Throughout his life, my father had been both an idealist and a rationalist; he was as proud of his Marxist beliefs as his analytical skills. The last time he floundered in his rationality was in 1989: with firm conviction he had argued that the Chinese communist army would never open fire on its own people—that would be completely against its ideals. On June 4, he was stunned into silence.

MEMORY. DO the Chinese have a short national memory? On a breezy, balmy spring day in 1991, as I slowly pedaled my bike past Tiananmen Square, my eyes gazing toward the vast, empty space and the stern-looking monuments—the Monument of People's Heroes and Mao's mausoleum—at the distant south end, this question keeps ringing in my head.

In terms of space, Tiananmen is the largest square in the world: arrow-straight lines, no curve, no tree, not a single bench or stretch of shade in sight. It is unapologetically humorless, devoid of any signs of human comfort, warmth, or playfulness which seem "natural" in central urban plazas. The Square, in any case, was not designed for such idle pleasures; it served as the converging center for parades, rallies, the masses paying tribute to the state. And the state was usually personified in one single great leader, the modern version of a great Chinese emperor. In a sense, what the world saw there in the spring of 1989 was rather incongruous: the Square was taken over, usurped, and converted to a purpose utterly contrary to its original mission. It was turned into a grounds for prodemocracy protests, for individualistic carnivals, or, from the perspective of the Chinese government, for antistate activities. So the Square had to be salvaged, and any powerful state must show that it can reclaim its own property. Today, the only reminder of those "abnormal" days is the armed People's Liberation Army guards lining the edges of the Square. Order is restored. Buses, bicycles, and people pass by without slowing down. Nobody lingers or even casts a glance at the Square. Why should they? The moment order is restored, the Square is deserted.

But what about memory? Have people really forgotten those euphoric days in 1989? Buoyed by the idealism of peaceful protests on Tiananmen Square, the city in those days had floated on an ocean of goodwill and generosity. Amazingly, public manners transformed overnight: people stopped pushing, shoving, and yelling; strangers smiled broadly to one another on the streets, flashing a V sign or discussing, civilly, the problems of society. Taxi drivers gave free rides to students, small shop vendors donated money for the hunger strikers. Even the thieves, I remember, were said to be so touched by the spirit of nobility and solidarity that they stopped stealing. Later on, thousands of ordinary Beijing citizens volunteered to pacify the soldiers sent in to reinforce martial law at gunpoint. I saw with my own eyes how some of the armored personnel carriers were stopped by gray-haired grandmothers who lay down on the streets.

When I first returned in early 1991, the people of Beijing seemed both list-less and guarded in public. At social occasions, I felt the hidden strain con-stantly: so many people were looking over their shoulders, and some choked up at mere mention of Tiananmen. I still remember a dinner party at a friend's apartment. For a moment the subject turned to the then rampant rumors about a big earthquake approaching Beijing. Someone joked that he hoped at least the center of the quake would be right under Li Peng's feet. Premier Li was the most hated figure in Beijing, the focus of blame for the Tiananmen massacre. But another said that in the event of such a great earth-quake, Li Peng would surely be picked up by a helicopter beforehand—that's the privilege of those high officials. "Well, I guess there's just no way to kill him, then!" the first guy said despondently, laughing. The entire room fell into a long, charged silence.

Since 1992, the atmosphere has changed dramatically. With Deng's water-shed speech early that year granting wider, faster, and deeper marketization, people seemed to wake up from a long, depressing slumber and suddenly saw a whole world of opportunities opened up to them. Some were con-fused, some panicked, but many sprang into action. Commercialization exploded onto Beijing like a great tide, shaking up old structures, breaking down old habits and alliances, smashing old illusions and romanticisms. The city started to churn again. Hong Kong and Taiwan influences grew quickly. Trade and commerce seized the popular imagination. "Jump into the sea!" ("Xia hai!") was the new slogan of the day—the "sea" of business and trade. For the brave, young, and agile swimmers, a new, exciting horizon came into view; for some others, new fright and horror set in. The city has turned into a giant bubbling pot with everyone pushing and shoving, trying to get a piece of the action. Energies, hopes, dreams—the exuberance has returned. But it is different from 1989: in some fundamental sense, Beijingers have never looked and felt so alone. Distressed by the ways friendships have changed, Songzi once asked me: "What would an American do if he gave an idea to a friend, and the friend took the idea and made a lot of money out of it? Would he charge his friend for it?"

Many looked up with envy to my editor-turned-stock-expert friend as a quick success story: others were just starting off, and he was already loaded with money and business contacts. One night, having missed the last bus, as we left a mutual friend's place he gave me a ride home on the back seat of his bicycle. Peddling along a deserted lane, he reminded me that we had biked together along this same route back in 1989. Then, suddenly, he confessed how much he missed those days, how he had been seized with nostalgia periodically. "It's usually at night. They'd come back to me in a flash: the magazines, the salon gatherings, the long debates late into the night—it was all so exciting. There was a sense of a community; people were joining forces and making things happen. We didn't realize it then, but that was the best time of our lives."

"There is no time for aimless chats," a young Beijing video artist in his early twenties told me, "because these days time means money, and action is more important than words. Only those stuck in the old mindset would sit around chatting about old times."

"The country is haunted by ghosts," a writer in his early forties muses quietly after explaining some intricate signs from ancient Chinese cosmology. His novellas about the Cultural Revolution were famous in the 1980s. "You can tell by looking through the *qi*, the air in the Chinese sky. So many wronged souls are floating around. They have to be appeased somehow, or one day they'll drag us all down."

MEMORY HAS generational gaps. My generation of Chinese, born in the fifties and sixties, were considered the Red children. "Born and raised under the red flag" and "flowers of the motherland" were two typical, proud phrases of that time to sum up our incredible good luck. Our rite of passage was the Cultural Revolution, our coming-of-age experience political fanaticism—screaming mass rallies, delirious faith in the Great Helmsman Chairman Mao, brainwashing propaganda as education. Conformism on the one hand, social anarchy on the other—such were the staple foods of our youth. We were packed onto a crazy red train, and plunged headlong toward violent disillusionment.

We are fated, perhaps, to carry a burden of memory not only heavier than those our younger siblings will carry, but it is probably heavier than those of our parents: many from their generation took their faith and its glory to their graves, whereas we lost ours before reaching middle age. We are the golden children who went astray, the delicious promise that turned sour, the little angels who somehow grew horns on our heads. Our lesson about history is that it should never be repeated. It's an important lesson to keep in mind— but how can we reasonably expect others to carry this burden or feel the same way about our past? After all, hadn't we bitterly resented our parents for cling-ing to their own history? Our younger siblings have little recollection of the Cultural Revolution. Our children will have no memory of Tiananmen. They may read about these events in the history books, see them in films, hear sto-ries about them at dinner tables. So we hope. But they probably won't share our intensity about them. They will have a lightness of spirit about life that doesn't come naturally to us. Or so we hope.

Still, the question about the collective Chinese memory lingers and gnaws.

This is a country where nobody confesses sins. Massive destructions have occurred, atrocities have been committed, millions have died of starvation and persecution, children have turned in their parents, husbands have denounced wives, people have sold friendships for a casual nod from a Party secretary—yet it has *never* been popular to acknowledge openly the wrongs you have done to others. The venerable form of "self-criticism" is practiced only when individuals apologize to the Party: you may say you're sorry to the system, even if you aren't really sorry. Other forms of confession or self-analy-sis, however, are neither encouraged nor expected. In fact, it's hard to talk about psychological issues in Chinese—the language just isn't well-equipped with words and expressions to discuss your inner demons. The common atti-tude is to leave the demons alone.

Let bygones be bygones. Let's look ahead. This is not just the Party's motto to fool the population; it is, many feel, something that the population needs very badly to do. There are too many skeletons in everyone's closet; once you started opening one, there's no telling where things would end. People might have to hang themselves, or go after one another's jugular again. A witch-hunt might ensue, and then it would all be over. The past might take over the present and the future—the country might turn into a giant graveyard, a fresh battleground. You can count on the Chinese to bear misery stoically, but don't count on their restraint when you give them a break. This is an ancient people, but their emotional age is supposed to be infantile. "The national psychology is so immature!" a famous Chinese filmmaker once lamented to me. "That's why the Chinese still need a wise emperor sitting at the top."

So, no matter how cynical it is, there is practical wisdom in the Party's policy of keeping the lid on tight and keeping the national imagination fixed on the present. Just look at Bosnia, and look at the former Soviet Union—aren't they lessons enough for remembering too much of the past, fixating too keenly on settling old scores and turning history upside down? The result is a slaughterhouse, a mess. The Chinese know better. Let's stay together. Let's move right on.

OF COURSE, "looking ahead" cannot work as a policy unless there is something ahead to look toward. This something has turned out to be a large dollar sign. Thus, a nationally popular pun has the "looking ahead" replaced with "looking at money." By a happy coincidence, the two phrases happen to sound exactly the same in Chinese: both phrases are pronounced *xiang qian kan*. It is hard to imagine a more revealing confusion.

Naked greed for money, raw selfishness, complete disregard for moral principles, destruction of the environment, nihilism, vulgarity, corruption, injustice: we hear these laments and criticisms constantly about the new Chinese reality, from elite cultural critics as well as ordinary citizens, especially those who have been left out of the new economic boom. Such charges point sharply to the dark side of China's post-Tiananmen development, but sometimes they are biased and moralistic, focusing exclusively on the black stains on a large canvas with rich, ever-shifting textures. Caught in an unprecedented messy transition, China today is full of phenomena with complex, sometimes unpredictable implications for the future. The accusations become even more problematic when they take a moral high ground that conceals their source: the speaker's own discomfort and dilemma in the new reality.

Mr. Xu, father of one of my close Beijing friends, has grown bitterly rancorous about the ways China has changed under Deng. An upper-middle-level administrative cadre recently retired, Mr. Xu left his job with a strong sense of pride for his upright record as well as the social status and material benefits with which the Party rewarded him for his service. Nowadays, though, what with inflation and the sudden emergence of a class of nouveaux riches, Mr. Xu's social status and income level have both plunged comparatively. He grumbles, howls, gives unwanted lectures to his wife and son over corruption, injustice, and every evil that is plaguing the Chinese society. A lot of what he says is true. However, it is equally true that at the root of his perception lies something deep and simple. "In the seventies," my friend explained to me, "my old man drank liquor every evening with several side dishes, and at least one was meat. It was a luxury few could afford then. He still drinks every evening, but usually with just one side dish, sometimes only peanuts or pickled turnip. He can't go to any of the new fancy restaurants that those rich young men so ostentatiously frequent. How can he not feel a sense of loss?"

I know a lot of people who feel a deep sense of loss in today's China. My older relatives, for example, aunts and uncles, find themselves in a lot similar to Mr. Xu's. My high school buddies, too, are workers stranded in low-skilled jobs at moribund state factories which can no longer provide them with the salary increases or bonuses needed to accommodate the ever-higher cost and standard of living. The same is true of my intellectual and artistic friends, who experience intense culture shock in their home territory, who struggle to find their bearings in the frantic and entangled commercialization of politics and culture. I've heard them talking about loss; I've also heard them talking about gains, and hope.

Perhaps it is precisely because so much in the post-Tiananmen China makes one feel ambivalent that we need to be very cautious about our judgments and conclusions.

The fear of Chinese nationalism is a case in point. With the "Asian model" of economic growth combined with political and intellectual control, it is up for grabs when or whether China will ever see a Western-style cosmopolitanism thrive. In fact, as the communist ideology gradually becomes an empty shell, nationalism is increasingly being used by the Chinese officialdom to hold the country together. Indeed, because of its historical link to independence from Western dominance, nationalism still has a positive appeal in China. Watching China's ambitious military buildup, many in the West have begun to feel alarmed by surging Chinese nationalism. Manipulated by vicious politicians, the consequences could be disastrous for future world peace.

And domestically, the Chinese economy is growing pell-mell. Uneven development, perhaps inevitable in periods of rapid growth, propels widespread social discontent as well as a further weakening of central control. Fears of chaos and instability run deep in the Chinese mind, troubling leaders and ordinary citizens alike. In a crisis situation, then, it is easy to see how the rallying power of nationalistic rhetorics could be used to serve despots and justify violence.

Certain counterfactors, on the other hand, should not be overlooked. The kind of nationalism that leads to xenophobia and wars, I think, usually works best on wounded pride, a heightened sense of ethnic identity, and powerful yearnings for collective belonging. But China may be passing through a historical moment in which economic restructuring and commercialism have bred and consolidated so much self-interest and interregional economic dependency, have driven so many wedges between the private, the collective, and the national, that nationalist language is slowly losing its potency. It is becoming harder and harder to sell the grandiose nationalism that demands a substantial personal or collective price.

China's bid for hosting the Olympics in the year 2000 is a good example. When the Chinese public displayed its support for the government's campaign, many in the West took it as a sign of rising Chinese nationalism; few saw the undercurrent. I happened to be in Beijing and Shanghai before and after China lost its Olympics bid: while I did hear progovernment, patriotic discussions—curiously, this happened mostly among the intellectuals—I also heard plenty of remarks *against* China's bid. Assigned by the central government to host the expensive 1993 East Asia Games, the municipal government of Shanghai had to raise funds locally, and all ordinary residents were required to donate. Since the chairman of the Olympics Committee attended the games' opening ceremony, the people of Shanghai viewed the whole thing as Beijing putting on a pre-Olympics showcase to prove China's financial and organizational strength. Absolutely everyone I talked to in Shanghai was against it, laughed at it openly, and cursed the government in private. Publicly, though, the city was cleaned up, poor laborers from the nearby provinces were ordered out of Shanghai for the week of the games, and the local media dutifully blared wholehearted support and propaganda.

Hypocritical support was no less visible in Beijing. Pro-Olympics slogans, billboards, and media propaganda covered the capital for a whole year; but privately, at homes and dinner tables and banquets, a lot of Beijingers talked about the Olympics as "mainly a face thing for the government." Sarcastic tales about the staged public shows and secret official bribes for the visiting Olympics delegates spread through the local grapevine. Many people worried that if China won the bid, the state would spend wildly on building big, showy stadiums and expressways rather than the residential housing and commercial spaces the city truly needed. The Western press reported about the Chinese crowd gathering on Tiananmen Square before the Olympics announcement, anxiously waiting to celebrate China's victory. Afterward, though, many Beijingers told me they felt relieved that it went to Sydney, and that "they're in a better condition to do it than we are."

Commercialism and private sector prosperity have surely created new problems in China, but they have also helped to dissipate some of the old anger and frustrations. As life gets easier and people become richer, they may also grow more self-confident and less bitter. Further, they may be more skeptical about ideological propaganda and less eager to jump on an extremist bandwagon. And, hopefully, the past century of destructive wars and policies, so often carried out in the name of nationalist ideologies, have taught the Chinese an important lesson.

Luan—chaos, disorder—is another widely dreaded scenario about China, the flipside of nationalistic Chinese aggression. Just imagine the refugee spillover were there a governmental or social breakdown, the world might be submerged by it! This is to say nothing of the economic and political consequences of a breakup of the immense Chinese market.

But chaos is also a double-edged sword. On the one hand, it is dangerous and, under certain circumstances, it can result in the disintegration of the nation or rampant social anarchy, as during the Cultural Revolution; on the other hand, chaos can be extremely creative. The present chaotic state of affairs in China has certainly helped to loosen the rigidity of old structures, hierarchies, and attitudes, and to inspire new productive energies and resourceful initiatives. The lack of clearly defined rules, orders, and laws is common during early stages of economic transformation, which many entrepreneurs—Chinese and non-Chinese, regional governments and cultural producers—have taken advantage of. A great number of private ventures have been set up under a thin disguise of public or collective ownership. Capitalist investors from Hong Kong, Taiwan, and America came in through joint ventures. Many regional governments, especially in the prosperous south, have been playing economic and political games with the central government, shrewdly moving regional economies and social lives toward a more open, liberal, and international direction. The cultural scene—aspects of which are the substance of this book—has become more diversified. Born in the cracks between the old and the new, the official and the popular, the elite and the commercial, the Chinese and the international, a lot of literary and artistic works after Tiananmen have turned out to be a mixed breed, and the debates about them have been more open, more polyphonic. These changing sensibilities and the new emphasis upon the value of everyday life over politics have as much to do with the society's inner needs as with outside influences and imported models from Hong Kong, Taiwan, and America. This economic and cultural hybridization has played a significant role in eroding the tyranny of the old monolithic ideology. It is also helping to breed a new generation of Chinese who are more interested in lifestyle than revolution.

After a century of tumultuous wars and revolution at great human cost, China appears to have finally turned to the path of *hepingyanbian*, "peaceful evolution." In her long struggle for modernity, this is a profoundly important shift. For the more optimistic champions of gradualist reform, Tiananmen may represent the tragic last gasp of the radical, revolutionary approach to changing China. The current path requires its own human toll and a good deal of compromise and deferment, yet many believe that, in the long run, this way of change will bring more substantial gains at a lower cost of human sacrifice.

At present, the slow transformation from "communism, Chinese style" to "market economy, socialist style" remains fluid, shifting, its future uncertain. China will probably remain a *sibuxiang* for a long time, a bizarre, hybrid animal neither horse nor donkey, neither here nor there. The people in this book are part and parcel of this extremely complex, frequently ironic process. Hopefully, their stories will convey a sense of this dynamic, fascinating time.

2

YEARNINGS

TEACHER BEI is a buxom, sixty-three-year-old retired elementary school teacher who lives in a prefabricated apartment in the east side of Beijing. I call her "Teacher Bei," instead of "Aunt Bei" as Chinese normally call somebody her age, because of a warning from the friend who introduced us: It is very important, he said, to make her feel that she belongs to the educated class and is someone with culture. Teacher Bei was so pleased by our visit and got to talking so much that she skipped her nap and made a big pot of tea. She made us a delicious lunch in her spotless, drab living room, but she herself only nibbled. "I haven't had such a good time since *Yearning*," she admitted.

She says she has always been prone to depression. She has a history of breakdowns—the first one when she was twenty-five and married off against her will. Maybe this is why she always finds the gloom of Beijing's harsh winters so difficult. Last year, though, she didn't mind the winter because *Yearning* was on television just about every night. Two stations were showing it on different evenings, and she watched them both. "A good show gets better the second time," she says. She would shop, clean, wash, cook, and do what she could for herself and her husband (which was not that much at all), then get ready for the evening. She has two sons, both married, living away. They only drop by once in a while. "They are good children, as filial and respectful as anybody's, but they're always busy and have their own families to worry about now," Teacher Bei tells me stoically, not wanting to complain about what is obvious in her old age: the boredom, the emptiness, the marriage that never would have lasted were it not for the children.

Her husband, old Tang, is a railway engineer, half deaf from an accident but still working part-time. They have long lived in separate rooms; nowadays they hardly talk to each other. But in the months when *Yearning* was on, their household was almost conjugal. Every evening at six-thirty, Tang would arrive from work and find dinner ready on a tray and his wife settled into a puffy lounge chair in front of the television, ready for *Yearning*. He would join her, sitting doggedly through the show, his eyes fixed on the screen even though half of the dialogue was lost on him. "It was bliss," Teacher Bei admits, sounding wistful. "Why can't they make a show like that more often? I guess it must be hard to come up with a story so complicated and gripping."

Yearning was a fifty-part Chinese television serial, in a genre that the Chinese television people call "indoor drama" because it is mostly shot with studio-made indoor scenes. The Chinese title, *Kewang*, literally means "a desire like thirst." Desire is a central theme of the show, which covers the lives of two Beijing families during the years of the Cultural Revolution and the eighties reforms. In normal times, according to normal social customs in China, they are not the kind of families who would care much to mix or socialize with one another: the Lius are simple workers living in a traditional courtyard house, whereas the Wangs are sophisticated intellectuals living in a modern apartment. However, the Cultural Revolution struck a heavy blow to the Wang family's fortunes, creating a chance for their son, a forlorn, sappy, soft young man of the type the Chinese call a "Little White Face," to meet the daughter of the Liu family. Of course, they get married, not out of love so much as a desire for the qualities of the opposite class: he for the simplicities of a heart of gold, she for the charm of being "cultured." From there on, despite the omnipresent Chairman Mao portraits on the walls of both homes, the Cultural Revolution and larger political events remain a blurry, under-examined background. Instead, the show focuses on daily family life and various romantic relationships.

At the heart of the story is Huifang, daughter of the Liu family, whose saintly presence quietly dominates and holds the moral high ground above the clatter of worldly events. Also central to the drama is a little girl whom the Liu family accidentally picks up: Huifang raises her through all manner of hardship, only to find out that she is the baby abandoned by the Wang family. Huifang is forever patient, kind, and giving—what Americans would call a goody-goody—yet she has the worst luck in the world. By the end of the show, she is divorced from her ungrateful husband, hit by a car, paralyzed and bedridden, and has to give back the adopted daughter so dear to her. In the true spirit of a long, drawn-out melodrama, *Yearning* entices its viewers with a fairly convoluted plot, conveniently linked by unlikely twists and turns, a good dose of tearjerking scenes, and a large gallery of characters from a broad spectrum of life.

There was little advertising for *Yearning* when it first aired in Nanjing in November 1990. The first few episodes attracted little attention, but by the end of the month just about anybody who cared anything about what's happening in China knew that the country was in for a "*Yearning* craze." By January 1991, all the major television stations had picked up the show. The number of stations quickly climbed to over one hundred, and the reception rate was unusually high. In the greater Beijing area, for instance, the rating was 27 percent, surpassing all previous foreign hits. In Yanshan, an oil and chemical industrial town with a population of over one hundred thousand, the audience share was a stunning 98 percent.

Thousands of letters and phone calls flooded the stations daily. Demands were made with a good deal of fervor: people wanted *Yearning* on their television every night, and as many episodes as possible. Those who missed the earlier portion begged for a replay. Startled networks responded quickly. The time slot for the show increased, and reruns began even before the first run had ended—which helped to fan the flames and give the show more publicity. In some heavily populated cities such as Nanjing and Wuhan, the streets were deserted whenever *Yearning* was on. A department store in Hubei province broke its sales record: over fifteen hundred television sets were sold while *Yearning* was on the air. In Wuhan, a scheduled power cut occurred in the middle of one episode; instead of sitting in the dark or going to bed as they had always done, an angry crowd surrounded the power plant and put so much pressure on the mayor that he ordered the power back on immediately.

People talked about *Yearning* everywhere—in the crowded commuter buses, on the streets, in the factories, offices, stores, and at family dinner tables. You could hear people humming the show's theme music in the narrow, deep lanes of Beijing and Nanjing. The audio track was packaged quickly into eighteen cassette versions, all of which sold like hot cakes. By the time the crew took its promotion tour for the show around the country, the main actors were already household names and the crew was mobbed by huge crowds everywhere. In some instances, the crew's arrival caused monumental traffic jams, de facto strikes, and work stoppages.

According to one report, the crew received such a spectacular welcome in Nanjing that the only other comparable turnout in the history of the city was when Chairman Mao first visited there decades ago. Fans waved banners and posters, some wept openly in front of the main actress, who had become, for them, a symbol of the virtuous victim; some even threatened to beat up the main actor, the embodiment of the selfish villain. Male viewers said that they yearned for a wife like Huifang; female viewers said that she was like a lovely sister to them. Everybody said that *Yearning* had brought out the best in them and made them understand better what it meant to be Chinese and how deeply rooted they all were in the Chinese values of family and human relations—and how all of this made them yearn for *Yearning* every night.

The press also jumped in. All sorts of stories about the series were rushed into print in every possible form: behind-the-scenes reports, on-the-spot interviews, profiles, special columns, analytical essays, letters from the audience, statements from the writers and actors. For months, the promotions raged on fantastically, heating up a public already gripped by the show. Amid the flood of literature on *Yearning*, a three-hundred-page book topped all others: from collecting the pieces to editing, laying it out, printing, and binding, the entire book was processed in sixteen days. And how could a title like *The Shock Waves of Yearning*, with a glossy cover photo of the demurely smiling star, fail to stop the heart of a *Yearning* fan browsing at a bookstall?

Such excitement had not stirred in China since Tiananmen.

BY THE time Teacher Bei was watching *Yearning* for the second time (it was soon to be shown a third time, and she along with many others would watch it a third time), a certain standing member of the Politburo was also watching it at home. On January 8, 1991, this Politburo member, Comrade Li Ruihuan— who had risen from his first job as a carpenter to become overseer of national ideology—met with the *Yearning* crew. It was in a reception room inside Zhongnanhai, the Chinese Communist Party headquarters, nuzzled against the red walls of the Forbidden Palace.

Li Ruihuan was clearly in a very good mood. He congratulated the crew on its success and called it "a worthy model for our literary and artistic workers." It is a lesson for us, he said, that a television drama depicting ordinary life could elicit such a warm *and* positive response from society. It tells us that an artistic work must entertain first, or it is useless to talk about educating people with it. The influence we exert must be subtle, imperceptible, and the people should be influenced without being conscious of it. In order to make the socialist principles and moral virtues acceptable to the broad masses, we must learn to use the forms that the masses favor. What he meant by socialist principles and moral virtues was "new types of human relations"—honesty, tolerance, harmony, and mutual help among the people. These, he said, were precisely what *Yearning* had portrayed so well.

On the following day, all the major Chinese newspapers reported Li's remarks on the front page.

Li Ruihuan had been assigned the job of ideology control right after the massacre at Tiananmen. It was an important promotion because, in the Chinese Communist Party's brutal history of power struggles, ideology was deployed like the army: both were used as weapons of control and intensely fought over. Intellectuals, writers, and artists were watchful, for here was the new boss of the political campaigns and the ideological policies that had the power to advance or destroy their careers, to still their pens, even to rob them of their livelihoods. The promotion of Li Ruihuan, the well-liked mayor of Tianjin with a reputation of being a down-to-earth, no-nonsense man on economic matters, was itself a significant political signal.

The mechanism of control in these areas is extremely complex. The centralized party structure has its people in every small office, building itself up level by level all the way to the central party committee. But in the last ten years, it has been weakened from both within and without: independent research associations, political and artistic salons, and joint ventures that crisscross institutions and countries had grown and provided the Chinese with something like an alternative, parallel structure. Still, nobody seemed to doubt that Li, at the top rung of the party structure, would be a most valuable player in the game. He was called into a Beijing fraught with tension, where the victorious but nervous hard-liners were trying to reclaim as many controlling posts as possible after the crackdown at Tiananmen.

Li surprised everyone with his first move. With energy, spunk, and a good deal of charisma, he launched a campaign against pornography. He went everywhere, and everywhere he went he talked about "sweeping out the pornographic literature and trade poisoning our society." His speeches were filled with a conviction that pornography was the chief evil of bourgeois liberalism and the chief object of his rectification campaign. He vowed to stamp out pornography and called on every leader to join him in this important battle. Other issues tended to sound abstract or muddled in Li's speeches—obscured by the heated antipornography rhetoric. The hard-liners didn't know what to say about this, since pornography was definitely a disease of Western liberalism and bourgeois decadence, and antipornography was surely a politically correct line. The intellectuals smiled knowingly and relaxed a little. Seasoned by decades of party campaigns, Chinese intellectuals, especially those above thirty-five, possess a keen political consciousness: they can read between the lines of a party document or a party leader's speech—which to an outsider or novice in Chinese politics may seem like dull, standard party lines worded in dull, standard party jargon—and detect at a glance signs of a new political shift. Even at private gatherings, discussing and speculating on the latest party policies is a perverse fixation among elder, educated Chinese. As for the ideologically minded cadres at various levels, the correct interpretation and response to signals and messages from above is an automatic reflex. Some intellectuals began to find Li quite appealing, for a politician;

some even worried that his style might be a bit too flamboyant, too bold, that such a style would backfire all too easily, that he wouldn't last very long—there had been plenty of instances like this in the history of Chinese Communist Party politics.

Others who saw in the former carpenter a born statesman, shrewd and crafty in the games of politics, liked to cite a widely known story about Li Ruihuan's actions during the critical period of the students' movement in 1989. The students of Tianjin, a big city only two hours away from Beijing by train, had been agitated by the hunger strike on Tiananmen Square and wanted to join forces. Many other cities were already swept up by local student demonstrations. Li Ruihuan, then mayor of Tianjin, quietly offered free train fares to those who wanted to go to Beijing. With the stream of students flowing to Beijing—to rock someone else's boat—and his conciliatory speeches about the importance of keeping up Tianjin's economic production, Li managed to preserve peace in his own territory. There were also other rumors about Li's personal friendship with Deng, for whom Li had made home furniture with his own hands. This is playing politics Chinese style: with clever maneuvers and personal ties, you can go far, sometimes very far, in China's political arena.

Whatever Li Ruihuan's political prospects might be, he was a powerful figure and his words carried a formidable weight among the intelligentsia. Thus, the fact that Li Ruihuan had so graced *Yearning* with his warm endorsement seemed to indicate that the top leadership was well disposed toward the show. The large number of party VIPs accompanying Li to the Zhongnanhai reception included even leaders from the Beijing municipal party committee, a notoriously conservative bastion much hated for its active role in cracking down on the students at Tiananmen. Among them was Li Tieying, the education chief in the Politburo, whose image had been tarnished among educated Chinese because he took a firm stance alongside the hard-liners when the students went on their hunger strike. Li Tieying, as the papers reported the following day, used the occasion to talk about the need for "an in-depth campaign against cynicism about our country." Of course, he himself was hardly exempt from the charge of cynicism, after an embarrassing incident on television a few days after the Tiananmen massacre. It was one of those public political performances for politics: Li Tieying had been conducting a group of school children through a famous propaganda song, "Socialism Is Good," but the camera, fixing on his face, revealed that the conductor himself couldn't sing the song. His vaguely moving lips didn't match the words: a sinister ritual had been turned into a laughable farce.

Despite all the standard propaganda lines, however, the general tone of the reception was clearly conciliatory, for Li Ruihuan's was the dominant voice. Li's remarks, highlighted in some papers by boldface print, were punctuated by telltale words like "harmony," "unity," "tolerance," and "prosperity." He kept saying things like: "Under socialism, everybody shares the same fundamental interests." Any Chinese with a degree of political sensitivity could see what was going on: Li was using *Yearning* to push his moderate line, to imply the need for political relief. While the hard-liners had been drumming about deepening the campaign of repression, using phrases like "live-or-die ideological struggles" to describe the post-Tiananmen situation, here was Li Ruihuan saying, basically, "Comrades, let's look at the bright side of the picture, let's focus on positive values."

WHEN *YEARNING* was first televised, some of China's writers and intellectuals tuned in too. At least here was something watchable, some of it even enjoyable. True, the story slowed down and the lines got repetitive, but the plot was absorbing enough, the tone not too didactic, and there was even some decent acting. The Wang family—and the intellectuals in general—didn't come out too well, but there was no need to take it so seriously. After all, it was only a soap opera. Their innocent enjoyment didn't last long, though, because it soon became clear that *Yearning* was not being seen as simple light-hearted entertainment. Apart from the enthusiasm of the general public, officials from every level were following Li Ruihuan's cue and showering praises on the show. "They were wrapping the show up in a royal robe," a writer later told me. There was no question that the series was being exploited by a wide spectrum of officials, all of them lauding an aspect of the show to justify their particular approach to politics, or to illustrate their own theory of the Chinese national character.

The person who led the cheers within the literary community was a Mongolian by the name of Marlaqinfu, author of several undistinguished novels in the fifties and at the time party chief of the Chinese Writers Association. He dashed off an essay gloating over the public enthusiasm for *Yearning* as if it had been his personal victory. The show's success was living proof, declared Marlaqinfu, of how socialist realism is still vital in China and, what was more, how literature and art prosper after bourgeois influences have been cleaned away.

This kind of touting, so obviously opportunistic, was nevertheless joined by some other writers' more earnest, heartfelt appreciation of *Yearning*. These were the writers who, in the initial thaw after the Cultural Revolution, had won fame overnight, when a newly liberated literature assumed the prodigious role of moral spokesman for a people long silenced, and when writers became celebrities on the basis of a single "taboo-breaking," "truth-telling" story. Most of their works, though serious and courageous, had no style to speak of, let alone any breathtaking technique; they practiced a tiresome realism lacking the sophistication and depth that marked the great works of classical Chinese fiction and European realism. In the ensuing years, several waves of younger writers exploded onto the scene, dazzling the reader with their stylistic and narrative energy. They spearheaded an avant-garde movement infatuated with style, especially the styles of Western modernism. Their drive for new styles so overwhelmed literary circles that, suddenly, all previous writings seemed unimaginative, outdated, and irrelevant. In the meantime, nurtured by economic reform, commercial publishing was booming. It wasn't much of a fight: the majority of readers didn't have to be won over by sensational reportage and easy, entertaining materials—they rejoiced in them. Snubbed by elite critics and dropped by the general public, a great number of "outdated," "serious" writers, their memory of yesterday's glory still fresh, either had gone on producing works that were thoroughly ignored, or had stopped writing completely.

It was not surprising, then, that *Yearning*'s phenomenal success should excite them. As they saw it, here was a work done in a manner of good old realism, a show that depicted unambiguous, solid characters, gave them authentic, down-to-earth dialogue, followed an absorbing plot, and involved the audience emotionally with the dramatic fate of the characters. And it worked! The audience laughed and cried with it! What could be more precious, more satisfying to a writer than such a vital reaction? Chen Jiangong, a Beijing writer whose fiction was rather popular in the early eighties and who has been suffering a creative block since then, sounded almost grateful in a rave review of *Yearning:* in his view, the series owed its success to the good literary quality of its script—and by "good literary quality" he meant the solid creation of lifelike characters, from which Chinese writers had strayed. He was voicing the frustrations of an entire generation of writers for whom the popularity of *Yearning* had stirred the hope that perhaps their writing careers were not over yet.

Those who considered themselves members of the literary avant-garde, on the other hand, regarded *Yearning* with unreserved disgust. In their eyes, everything about the show was offensive—its official status of "model product" and "campaign fruit," its crude, derogatory portrayal of the intellectuals, its vulgar, melodramatic style, and its celebration, in the service of party politics, of old Chinese values such as self-sacrifice and endurance (versus mod-

ern, Western values such as individualism and initiative). Beyond their antag-
onism toward the government — and they would have found whatever the
current regime promoted repulsive, even if it were promoted by a moderate
politician such as Li Ruihuan — the contempt for mass culture ran quite deep
in the minds of these elite and elitist intellectuals. Most of them never bothered to watch *Yearning;* it was enough to condemn the show by its reputation,
and for its success.

Yet in their sneer one could easily detect a certain embarrassment. After all,
Yearning had been a great showcase for the state: the Chinese people may
have followed the students and the elite intellectuals to Tiananmen Square,
but now these same people were suddenly reunited with the government.
Their love of *Yearning* stood in jarring contrast to their indifference toward
the avant-garde scene, which by this time was suffering a rapid, cheerless dete-
rioration: works continued to be published, but the movement had lost its
steam, and nobody seemed to care. Another disconcerting thing about the
series was that one of its seven script writers, Wang Shuo, happened to be a
young novelist who was not only tremendously popular among urban youths
and common folk in Beijing but also respected, if grudgingly, by many elite
critics. Puzzled by this man's role in *Yearning,* one such critic could not refrain
from telling me that Wang Shuo was merely "playing" with television, earning
a few easy bucks, and that he could not be responsible for such a gross product. "What about Zheng Wanlong?" I asked — about another widely
acclaimed writer who was involved in developing the script. The critic's face
fell. He was not at all ready to absolve Zheng the way he tried to excuse Wang.
Frowning, he said coldly: "Oh, *he* sold out. I have no respect for writers like
that. It's unforgivable."

I T W A S unclear if the producers of *Yearning* at the Beijing Television Art
Center (BTAC) fully understood the complexities of their show's reception.
Soul-searching was not the order of the day: swept up as they were by the
wild cheering, the center and the *Yearning* crew were too busy savoring a long-
coveted, hard-won success. It was as if a dream had suddenly come true, a
passionate yearning at long last fulfilled. Hadn't they always wanted to make
the first great all-Chinese "indoor drama"?

Indoor drama is as new as China's television culture itself, which, by
Western standards, is quite primitive. Up to the end of the Cultural Revolution
in 1976, the sight of a small black-and-white television in a Chinese living
room had been a sure sign of luxury and privilege. To most Chinese families,
not having a television set was no loss: for decades, the government had

banned foreign movies and television shows, except for a dozen or so from "socialist brother countries"—movies like *Lenin in October* from the Soviet Union. Local productions were pathetically few.

It was only in the last ten years, beginning with Deng's reform and open policies, that television began to enter the living rooms of ordinary Chinese families. Given China's still-backward economy and standard of living, the increase of television sales has been quite remarkable: by the end of 1990, the country could already boast about 166 million sets installed in people's homes. This means that as of this writing, whether in urban or rural China, one of every six or seven Chinese owns a television set. By the calculations of some television experts, China should have some two thousand episodes of television dramas each year to fill up the available time slots.

The reality has been a far cry from the demand. One problem has been the government's low funding. Since Chinese television is totally state controlled, the networks expect absolute financial support from the government; but the government, under the banner of reform, has decided on a peculiar form of decentralization—it reduces funds without reducing control. By one reporter's account, the state gives roughly two billion yuan (about $364 million) to TV networks each year, which in 1990 averaged out to less than $2.20 for each TV set in the country. From this meager sum must come the salaries of every network employee, funds for basic infrastructure maintenance and development, and so on. Advertising has been explored in recent years, but for the majority of networks, government funds still make up the main portion of the budget.

Furthermore, there was a common tendency (or, in the words of some critics, a "disease") among Chinese television producers which made the money problem far worse. In pursuit of elaborate cinematic effects, they liked to make expensive shows—"the cinemazation of television." Many television workers were originally trained to make movies with poor technique and a propensity for grandeur, under the widespread conviction that, since film is the highest form of visual art, the closer a television drama is to a film, the more respectable it becomes. But it boils down to one fact: the absence of professionalism—and to one result: squandered money.

The young people at BTAC, though, got fed up with the situation. Around 1986 and 1987, when a couple of long soaps from Mexico and Brazil became huge hits in China, a Japanese one made a big splash, and a host of indoor dramas began to swarm into the mainland from Taiwan and Hong Kong, the younger BTAC employees became restive, even ashamed. "What's happening with our TV productions?" was the question everybody was asking. "Why can't we make something decent ourselves?" Typically, when they saw it in terms of China losing face, their blood boiled. Lu Xiaowei, who was later to be the director of *Yearning*, openly admitted that he was driven by a sense of honor, and that he wanted to "prove it" when he got the job assignment to direct the series. BTAC's chief literary editor, Li Xiaoming, who was to become the show's chief script writer, did not emphasize the issue of face, but he said his fingers became itchy as he watched those imported indoor dramas and thought how easy it would be to make a mainland Chinese version. "All the main scenes were shot indoors; you could tell at one glance that they didn't cost much." To him, the issue was whether you were a true TV professional: if you were, you should know the strength and limits of the media and the field, which means that you should focus on low-budget indoor dramas rather than waste time and money on grandiose outdoor epics.

The center's leaders were thinking the same thing. In fact, they were already steering the center in that direction when, in 1988, they built a new studio at the foot of Mt. Fragrant, a scenic area on the outskirts of Beijing. The center rented a basketball stadium on the site, which was owned by the athletic division of a military unit, and transformed it into a film studio. The renovation cost 1.8 million yuan. Mr. Chen Changben, then the head of the Beijing Broadcasting Enterprise Bureau, of which the center is a subsidiary, had approved the budget himself and let everybody know that it was for developing the center's own indoor dramas. It was the biggest single investment made during Chen's office term: it sucked up so much money that the center had nothing left with which to develop any other program that year, and skepticism was in the air. Was it wise to pour so much money into a project that was merely a "concept"?

By the end of 1988, however, the new studio was a fait accompli. The pressure was higher than ever. To prove that they had chosen the right path, the center needed to produce a show—the *first* show—that would get high ratings, or else. So everybody, in particular Mr. Chen, whose career was at stake because of the studio controversy, was anxious about one thing: they had to find the right kind of script.

At first they settled on a script named *Muslim Funeral*, but the director walked into the office with an impossible demand—he wanted a trip to London to get the exterior scenes right—which killed the project on the spot. "That was the funeral for the *Funeral* project," said Li Xiaoming, a script editor. Since no one else had come up with a script and there was no time to sit waiting, the center had to create one on its own. Zheng Xiaolong, the center's young deputy director, and Li Xiaoming decided to get help from their buddies: they called the writers they knew, and everybody became excited and hopeful when Wang Shuo and Zheng Wanlong agreed to participate.

On a dark, snowy day late in the winter of 1988, at a suite in Beijing's Hotel Jimen, the first script session began. There were five people: the novelists Zheng and Wang, script editor Li Xiaoming, BTAC deputy director Zheng Xiaolong, and Chen Changben—whose reward for staking his reputation on this effort would be a promotion to vice minister of culture. Talk, talk, talk was all they did for two days locked up in that suite. There would be more sessions to come. Later on they would use writer's slang to describe what they had done during their sessions: *cuan gu shi*, "assembling a story," a phrase that unmistakably conveys the flavor of an industrial workshop—it conjures up an image of a literary factory producing stories on assembly lines. And that was how their script was put together. The five men had very little raw material to start with: Zheng Xiaolong brought in a newspaper report about a divorced working mother raising her deaf son, and Zheng Wanlong had an idea about an abandoned baby. They ironed out the plotlines by talking together, and each threw in his own ideas. With the help of notes from the discussions, Li Xiaoming wrote up a detailed outline of the story. They met again to go over the outline, revising and filling in more details. After that, they voted that Li Xiaoming should write a full script.

Li lacked the literary prestige enjoyed by the two novelists; his professional ambition revolved around the center and television, and he was the most experienced of the five in terms of writing for that medium. Taking the discussion notes home, he worked like a machine for five months (writing an average of nearly ten thousand words per day) and came out with a script roughly amounting to a fifteen-hundred-page book. This, moreover, was the spring of 1989, the demonstrations for democracy were rolling on the streets of Beijing, and the world was watching the events unfolding on Tiananmen Square with tense fascination. But Li was aware of nothing except the ticking of a clock on his desk. He cut himself off from all social contacts and worked himself to the point of exhaustion—his writing hand would tremble long after he turned in the script. The center had approved the outline, and a shooting crew had been formed when Li was only half done. It was a frantic gamble: the center poured in about two years' worth of their development funding for TV shows (about 1.2 million yuan) in order to strike up the interior scenes for *Yearning*. Nearly empty handed, they had to ask the actors to accept low pay. As though inspired by the spirit of the gamble, all of them agreed. The shooting began before Li completed the script. For a last-minute polish on his draft, the center hired two other writers, both unknown hacks, to work closely with the crew on location.

As I leafed through piles of reports on the shooting of *Yearning*, I came to see quite clearly the earnestness with which the crew worked. Nearly every report contains some touching tale about how hard the crew toiled, the primitive working conditions, the shockingly low pay (the highest paid actor, a well-known senior stage actor, received only 100 yuan—$20—per episode), and the crew's dedication to the show. The speed of the shooting was as astonishing as the speed of the writing: all fifty episodes were completed within ten months, an average of six days per episode. The director and actors worked under the same time pressure: sometimes, a section of script or director's instructions had to be rushed to the rehearsal room as soon as it was finished, and the actors often practiced their parts with copies still warm from the Xerox machine. Later, the crew would talk about all this with pride, reporters would write about it with admiration, the public would read it with unending wonder, and party leaders would hail it as a triumph of collective socialist idealism.

What slipped from public attention, however, was the new way of writing: it differed not only from the writer working in the solitude of his own imagination and experience but even from the more recent (though no less traditional) collaboration between a script writer and a director. This was writing as a joint venture, as a group collaboration, a collective enterprise. This mode is something that people in the West may feel perfectly jaded about—what isn't teamwork nowadays on television?—but in China it's totally new. Moreover, what further complicates this innovation is the fact that it involved serious novelists and professional hacks, and even a high-ranking party official! What enabled them to tuck away their egos and negotiate their differences? What sort of understanding bound them together?

By all accounts, the collaboration had been remarkably smooth, but what struck me in particular was their stringently practical attitude, their way of assessing the job at hand. The script sessions had been unabashedly audience oriented: under the pressures of commercial success, "please the audience or perish" had been the one sentiment all shared as soon as they came on board. Later on, a reporter asked Li Xiaoming whether *Yearning* was a conscious reversal of the Chinese avant-garde movement, which by definition had to assume a hostile posture vis-à-vis the mainstream audience. Li's reply was unequivocal: No, definitely not. However, his further remarks reveal that the posture *Yearning* assumed toward the audience had everything to do with a new sense of professionalism. He explained, for example, that he himself used to love all the modernist fiction and films—which, in China, means avant-garde, more or less—but that after he turned thirty his taste underwent a change and, more and more, he turned to pop culture. He was fascinated by Jin Yong, the Hong Kong master of kung fu novels, and he admired the craftsmanship evident in many Taiwanese best-sellers and popular TV shows. He went on to say:

> I know these works are not first-class literature. But what's the first thing in television? It's mass media, it's entertainment. If there is such a thing as the art of television, it could only be the art of popular entertainment. Television writers have no right to talk about "improving the taste of the audience." It's ridiculous to produce avant-garde shows on TV, because the channel is switched right away. In the meantime, everybody loves the soap operas from Taiwan. One may pronounce a thousand times how shallow and crude these shows are, but it will change nothing: the audience will stay tuned and stick to their tastes. If you're a television writer, and you know that the majority of your Chinese audience had to save up for years in order to buy a TV set, then you'd better come to terms with them. So in the end I ask myself: Is our audience so shallow? And I feel I can't simply say yes. Writing for them, I must treat them as my equals, as people I like.

What Li spelled out was an attitude shared by *Yearning*'s writers. The two novelists may have been far more cynical than Li about the taste of the average audience, but they too knew from the outset the goals and terms of the show. To get the job done, they could not make any mistakes about who their audiences were, what they liked, and how to give them what they liked. The writers also made good use of previous hit shows in China. Those from Taiwan, for instance, were often family dramas, and to play up themes of family unity in difficult times, they set up a standard plot scheme—the search for a lost child. Popular soaps from Mexico and Brazil, on the other hand, usually had involuted love relationships, and these elements became a core of the ongoing drama.

These reference points helped the writers to chart the basic course for *Yearning*. They decided, for example, that their show must be about the family and moral values with which the majority of its audience could identify. They also decided that the central character must be a virtuous, filial woman, who would appeal to the sentiments of the elderly, a considerable portion of TV's regular audience in China—and they wanted her to be a woman in the prime of her beauty, with qualities that would fulfill the desires of all Chinese men. (The five men made no bones about the male angle of the show, even though it turned out to be a little too complex to be simply sexist.) In the initial sessions, the five called their heroine, quite fittingly, "the oriental woman." In fact, they applied this "typecasting" method to almost all the main characters, making up temporary code names for each one. The heroine's husband, for example, was "the sappy intellectual," his sister was "the shrew," and the heroine's childhood friend and shy admirer was "the silent pursuer." They gave this working method a name: *shenghuo huanyuan fa*, "the methodology of restoring life."

With sparks of glee in his eyes, Zheng Wanlong later explained, "We molded a character first from a simple idea, then added flesh and blood to it, until it looked like a real-life character." Wang Shuo sounded more tongue-in-cheek: "It means we tortured all these characters, making everyone suffer. We made sure all the good guys had a heart of gold, but we made them as unlucky as possible; and the bad guys are as bad as you can imagine—that's the sure way to a good drama." In fact, Li Xiaoming was so pleased with the accuracy of their calculations and the smoothness of their cooperation that he later nostalgically recalled the sessions as "casual and fun . . . like the chat General Patton had with Montgomery in the washroom." They were on top of their game: everybody knew they were drawing up ridiculous caricatures, yet they all understood that in order to win at the game, they had to treat these caricatures seriously. The finished script left no overt trace of cynicism. The code names were replaced by real names, warm and authentic, and the dialogue sounded earnest; nobody, surely not the "average Chinese" having a good cry in front of the television after a hard day's work, could hear the muffled chuckles behind the scenes—and, even if viewers could, why would they care whether the writers were sincere? A Chinese proverb sums this up nicely: If the fish likes what's on the hook, well then, fishing is fair play.

In the end, though, the show was so successful that everybody felt compelled to pass judgment on it. Some therefore pronounced that *Yearning* was a perfect example of writers coldly manipulating an audience; some went further, saying, in a tone of indignation, that these writers had "licked the ass" of the working class, on the one hand, and of the government, on the other. Some even suspect that the show was really a scheme organized by the ministry of culture after the Tiananmen massacre. Others, as we have heard, declared *Yearning* to be a new masterpiece of realism, triumphant proof that socially concerned writers could—and still can—engage the masses. With equal conviction, everybody heaped his or her own one-line judgment on the show, and nobody felt that they had to pay attention to what the script writers themselves said. What they had to say was simple enough: all they wanted was to write a popular show, and to do that they had no choice but to play by the rules of the game. Yet amid the clamor of judgments, as time went by, they themselves found it hard to believe that this was really all there was to it.

ZHENG WANLONG now says that the whole thing was absurd. "What do you think my friends in exile would think of me getting mixed up in a model TV serial?" he asked me from behind the shroud of thick smoke from four hours of his chain-smoking. A fortyish, dark-skinned man, Zheng never went to college and had been a model factory worker and a low-level party bureaucrat until his fiction began to win critical acclaim ten years ago. A number of the critics who praised his fiction live in exile now. Since I knew some of them, and knew what they would say, I hesitated. He said, "Wouldn't they say that I have totally degenerated?" Without waiting for my reply, he shrugged and said: "Well, all my life, throughout my writing career, I have never degenerated. Let me taste just once what it feels like to degenerate."

In fact, the success of *Yearning* has transformed not only Zheng's image among his intellectual friends but, even more miraculously, his political fate. It was widely suspected that Zheng had something to do with organizing demonstrations and petitions in May 1989—even that he had held up huge banners on the front lines. Serious trouble was in store for him. After the military crackdown on June 4, 1989, the Party moved on to a pervasive campaign of "facts verification." Every party member, especially in Beijing, was required to report his or her own activities during the democracy movement—whether one had gone to the Square, marched or signed any petitions, whether one had been sympathetic toward the movement, and what one thinks of it now, if one's "level of thinking and understanding" has improved after studying Deng's speeches and party documents regarding the "counterrevolutionary rebellion," and so on. This process of "facts verification" is normally referred in Chinese conversation as *jiang qing chu*, "making things clear"; but when an investigation deals with a million people on the streets, and thousands daily on the world's largest square, there is really no way to make things clear at all. Many people simply denied that they had done anything in May and June—and, anyway, they said, now they were taking the "correct stance" alongside the Party. In most such cases, so long as nobody came up with hard proof to the contrary, that was the end of it.

A friend of mine, a college teacher who had marched, designed humorous posters, and written slogans, flatly denied everything he had done. "You see, I was lying, and they probably knew I was lying, but they didn't mind my lies," he told me glibly, with no trace of shame or guilt on his face. "It saved me some trouble, and it saved them some work, so both sides are happy, and both sides are cynical. Thirty years ago the party wanted us to believe in it, now the party just wants us to *say* that we believe in it. And, what's more, so long as they need us intellectuals to do some work, they'd rather close one eye and pretend that things weren't really that bad."

Zheng, however, could not disentangle himself quite so easily. What with certain complications about his signature on a certain petition, and his status as a prominent writer and vice editor in chief of a large publishing house, it was not so easy to "close one eye" to him. So when things didn't become "clear," a special task force was formed, its task being to interrogate him daily. Members of this task force consisted of various political work cadres from the security and personnel divisions of Zheng's publishing house; among the perks they received was a car put at their disposal. The investigation went on for almost a year. For months, Zheng had to answer meticulous questions about everything—for instance, where had he been on a certain hour of a certain day, with whom, for how long, by what type of vehicle he had gotten there, and what he did there, what he saw, and so on and so forth. "That's when you find how inadequate your own memory is and how much they know about you," Zheng now says, smiling. "Well, they know much more than you think. For example, I said that on a certain morning around nine o'clock I had left home by bicycle. One of them would be taking this down in his notebook, while the other checked *his* notebook and frowned: 'Are you sure about this?' he would say this looking into my eyes. 'According to our record here, you left at 8:15 that morning by bus.' That's the sort of thing that puts you in a cold sweat and makes your head throb, trying to recall every fucking little detail." In order not to complicate the situation and get more people entangled, Zheng simply stopped visiting or receiving friends. He also stopped writing letters and making phone calls. "Now I know what it means to be a hermit in a big city," he said, shaking his head, and laughed cheerfully.

Zheng can laugh, though, because his year of bad luck has turned into a new round of celebrity with *Yearning*. When his name appeared as a group of official censors screened the working copy, one of them asked if this Zheng was the writer from that publishing house; when this was confirmed, the official looked thoughtful for a moment, but the screening went on without further questions. From that moment on, the investigation of Zheng fizzled out. Since then, journalists have been flocking to Zheng's apartment and interrogating him about his role in the series. Because of *Yearning*, anything he says has news value and will find its way into a deliciously gossipy story; reporters reverently quote casual remarks he makes about writing, not because they care about his views on such things, but because of the fan club–like curiosity the show has inspired. One Beijing writer told me when I arrived there, "For a whole year Zheng was a criminal hiding in his hole; now he's once more a *xiang bo bo*"—a piece of sweet bread, which in Beijing slang refers to somebody who is hotly pursued. Zheng, though, says, "It's absurd," shaking his head, visibly pleased and a bit dazed by the turn of things for him. "First I felt like a hunted dog—then all of a sudden the search light switched, but I'm still a hunted dog!"

Deep down in his mind, Zheng later confessed to me, there is still something else that has been haunting him. It is, to put it simply, the phantom of literary glory. A few years ago, a young Chinese critic made the comment— which immediately became a favorite line to quote at literary parties—"The dog of innovation chases Chinese writers so hard they don't even have time to pause by the road and take a piss." He was not exaggerating. Coming out of the party's tight grip and a literary vacuum of three decades, anxious and ambitious young Chinese writers have raced frantically to make up for the past and catch up with the future. The West was the inevitable goal, with Latin America (with such glittering names as García Marquez and Borges) showing the way. In a short period of ten years, writers and critics hastily embraced and abandoned one style, theory, trend, movement, -ism after another. Of a scene that changed with numbing frequency, a famous writer wrote famously (and I translate his wordplay poorly),

> Oh, fickle is the vogue of literature
> Each beauty has but a few days to bloom!

Zheng had been one of the leading figures in one of these trends, the "Search for Roots" movement of around 1985. The movement's writers were supposedly held together by their conviction that Chinese literature would "go to the world" only through "regionalism," so all of its writer's typically set their writings in a specific locale. They usually chose peripheral territories and were drawn to the barrenly remote or lavishly mythical. Zheng's locale, for instance, had been a mountain tribe people in the old Manchurian region, and he had come out with a charming collection of stories serialized under the title *Exotic Tales from a Faraway Land*. After a short bloom, however, his career, like that of a good number of writers in the movement, soon withered. He churned out a few more short stories, but they generated no response from critics, who by then were preoccupied with the new crop of blossoms bursting onto the scene. There was much rancor among the outdated writers. They might still enjoy fame, status, even material privileges, such as a monthly salary from the Writers Association or a spacious apartment, but the limelight was turned away from them by the trendy young critics who dominated the scene.

It was not easy to deal with these critics who considered the previous trends as products of a "prefiction period," and who could spew torrents of their newly acquired Western theories to intertextualize, to deconstruct, to postmodernize, as they wrote the sort of article that seemed to have been produced by alien computer programs. It was as though these critics had inserted foreign computer chips into their heads (a Lacanian chip, for instance, or a Foucauldian chip), for what flew from their pens read less like literary analysis—at least to the poor outdated writers—than garbled messages. But, alas, it was precisely their bizarreness and alienness that gave the scene a fresh turn and gave them authority. They were, in a way, the radical chic in Chinese writing.

The chase, however, took another turn ("Another dog in the hunt!" Zheng would probably say). While the literary critics busily dropped certain writers and picked up others, somebody else got busy with literature: the "average reader," who, with cheerful composure, dropped serious literature and picked up entertainment. Poetry went first, then serious fiction, then entire batches of literary journals and magazines. Years ago, when underground poetry inspired a whole generation of social protest, there was a joke about the poetry-writing craze in the country: "The population of poets in Shanghai is sixty thousand." By 1989, a second line was added: "The population of poetry readers in Shanghai is also sixty thousand." The students on Tiananmen Square did scribble a few poems on their posters, but most poetry magazines in China have now returned to their small-time mimeograph form. *Today*, the most influential underground literary magazine twelve years ago, has been revived abroad after Tiananmen. Supported by various foundations and donors, the quality of its graphics and Hong Kong printing is far superior to its earlier stencil copies, but the magazine is banned inside mainland China and clearly operates from the periphery. The main writers live in exile in Europe and North America, and most of its poetry lost its vanguard spirit long ago.

WITH ECONOMIC reform came consumerism. Once the door to the West opened, even a government notorious for control could not keep up with the number of things and thoughts flooding the country. Foucault and Lacan slipped in, along with Sydney Sheldon and Madonna. *Rambo* was a hit, as was Hong Kong pornography, though with no publicity. Milton Friedman and Lee Iaccoca arrived with the stock market and foreign cars; Holiday Inn came with Deutsche Bank. Kentucky Fried Chicken opened, with air-conditioning, on a street southeast of Tiananmen Square, and in May of 1989 it made a snug place for the Tiananmen-goers to discuss over wings and soda the "boiling situation on the Square." Dinner at the new Maxim's is too expensive for all but the wealthiest Chinese, but other restaurants hosted private parties where foreigners mix with locals and fledgling rock 'n' roll bands perform.

All of this faced a China that was only just beginning, gingerly, to renew its contact with the world and to negotiate the boundaries between the state and a market. This flirtation with capitalism was uneasy: China after Mao was not at all like China in the first decades of the twentieth century, when the Western capitalists, aided by gunboat diplomacy, forced their way into port towns such as Shanghai and built them up quite freely. In the post-1949 Chinese discourse, this process has been called "colonization" and Shanghai the "imperialist adventurers' paradise." But that was in the "old society," a totally different era.

The Chinese are in the habit of calling all the "dark years" from the Opium War in 1840 up to the communist victory in 1949 "old society," and they like to bracket the preceding two thousand years with the term "feudal." But then Mao came up with the vision that, in the first half of this century—in the "old society"—feudalism bled into the republic while imperialism bled into feudalism, called this period "the semifeudal, semicolonial old China." It was one of those brilliantly disastrous visions that Mao would concoct in a moment of great clarity, and the phrase, of course, would show up in every contemporary Chinese history book. By thus sealing off one of the most interestingly uncertain periods of Chinese history with a phrase of all-encompassing simplicity, the Chairman had given citizens of the "new society" the confidence to rest assured in the triumphant new course the nation was taking.

After Mao died, Deng and his protégé Zhao Ziyang (now in disgrace since the massacre) pushed reform. Compared to Mao, there is very little romance in Deng, very little that is not cautious and pragmatic. And the flair of his right-hand man, Premier Zhao—decked out like a CEO in his well-tailored suit and tie and sporting a golf club—was a good complement to Deng. This difference in personalities was partly what lured the West to believe that here, at last, was a man and a country it could do business with. Deng, however, was by no means above the habit of bestowing "correct" names upon things, processes, or historical periods, nor could the Party resist naming the new era Deng was ushering in. And, to be fair, why relinquish such a good old Party tradition: it exercises linguistic control over a murky reality, and it appeals to the national character.

Yet Mao proved to be a hard act to follow in the naming business. It was clear that, with all the new things coming into the country and bleeding into the system, one could no longer simply call it "socialism." In China's nascent state of reform, doubts and anguish were hanging heavy in the air: socialism seemed to be splintering into so many directions but refusing to coalesce into a new clear image. After much fretting, Deng had to decide: instead of hatching a new egg, though, he took a characteristic half step by redecorating the old one. The new term turned out to be "preliminary phase of socialism," and Deng had, inevitably, a slogan to go with it—"construct a socialism with Chinese characteristics!" Despite these phrases' smell of compromise, they were picked up everywhere in the country, and they made people feel more comfortable.

In reality, nobody was quite sure what all these patchwork slogans meant. The reformers in the Party thought themselves to be cautiously infusing a measure of capitalist blood to revitalize an ailing socialist body, but it wasn't clear to anyone what the result would be, practically or ideologically. The new entrepreneurs saw a budding market and knew they were allowed to make a pile of money fast, but it wasn't clear how long this policy would last. State workers knew their incomes were dropping, and they had to pick up second, usually private, jobs to make ends meet—but they held on to their state jobs, because it wasn't clear if the private sectors would collapse.

"Nothing is clear," said one of Zhao Ziyang's top economic advisers two days after the student demonstrations began in April 1989. Over lunch with an American reporter, he explained: "You see, China is a big experimentation field right now. Nobody knows exactly where we are going or what will happen next. It's like crossing a river by groping along the stones." He spoke rather contemptuously of the students on the Square: "It won't amount to anything big. It is as if a two-year-old insists on having what a twenty-year-old has. Democracy? It's premature. China is not ready for it." As it turned out, he was both right and wrong. History has turned a bloody chapter since then. The regime has once more tightened its grip, but the clock has not been turned back completely. The market, small and restricted as it is, has proven to be a wedge driven deep into the system, stronger than political movements, yet unclear in its implications. The coastal towns continue to prosper, in what some would call the "south China economic miracle." Even in Beijing, business is bustling. And for the time being at least, the populace, with all the apparent reasons to be disgruntled, appears to care for nothing but money and good cheer.

What is happening in China? What will happen next? Nobody knows still, and few have the heart to predict. Chinese intellectuals were so crushed by the

45

fiasco at Tiananmen that they feel they have lost even the power to describe China—and how can they put things in perspective if they can't describe them? When, in 1990, a group of exiled Chinese intellectuals read Vaclav Havel's essay "The Power of the Powerless," they came upon the term "post-totalitarian society," which, they felt, perfectly described the system in China. Later, a Chinese avant-garde critic, Mengke, came up with another theory: he said perhaps one could describe China's present reality as "postmodernism with Chinese characteristics." Mengke—who has had some exposure to Western postmodern theories during his two years of exile in Chicago—has been working on a project he calls "deconstructing Mao-style discourse." However, another avant-garde critic who stayed on in China says that such applications of Western terms are frivolous and really don't help to illuminate the messy situation there. How can one say China is experiencing postmodernism, he asks, when it hasn't even experienced modernism? If one must use a Western term, it would be just as easy to describe what is going on in China as "primitive accumulation with Chinese characteristics," except that quoting Marx isn't so trendy in China anymore.

No matter how differently one describes the present situation, however, every Chinese intellectual is waking up to one common fact: no longer is the government the only thing they must deal with. Now they must reckon with forces of commercialism. They can't kid themselves anymore: the days of huge readerships are gone, along with the feeling that a writer is the beloved and needed spokesman of the people and the conscience of society.

In the past, a debate over a short story occasionally had the power to unite or divide the whole nation. No longer. Political strictures have slackened, not so much because the government became enlightened, but because it seems to have lost the knack and efficiency to tighten the screws to the desired degree. There are more opportunities to make money. As a result people seem to be too absorbed in daily life to care about what goes on in literature. If they read something, they do so for relaxation and amusement, not to "vent griev-ances" or "purify the soul." Reportage had been popular for a while, as it exposed social and political problems in much more direct and sensational ways than did fiction; but it, too, has waned quickly after the Tiananmen crackdown. Experimental literature stays in print, but because few read or understand it—neither the average reader, nor the officials, not even a "criti-cal mass" among university students—its impact is minimal.

"On one side, you have all those arrogant writers taking their fiction so seriously—touch one word in their manuscripts and they threaten to sue you," my friend Wu Ping, an editor from a major Beijing publishing house, once complained to me. "On the other side"—referring to recent cuts in state subsidies for publishing houses, which has caused the houses to look for other ways to sustain themselves—"you have these private book distributors. Most of them come from nowhere. I mean, they've never been to college and don't sound educated, but they are arrogant too, because they've got the market. That means they've got *you*. Profit was never an issue before. It didn't matter whether the books and magazines you printed got sold or not—now it does. Since printing serious literature almost always loses money, you've got to make money elsewhere. That means you've got to turn to the private distributors, because they know what kind of books sell, and they have networks of book vendors and other outlets. They don't come to you; you go to them, begging."

Wu is a graduate from Beijing University, China's number-one university, whose reputation is synonymous with intellectual elitism. Such a background did not prepare her to act humble and sweet toward these private distributors. She felt humiliated in front of them: "They are very condescending, treating you like a poor bookworm who is totally out of sync with reality. What can I do but lick their boots? I'm sent to them because the house needs money for the staff's annual bonus, and for printing the serious books that nobody will buy. Once when I told my boss that the distributors wanted more kung fu novels, he thought for a while and said to me: 'You know, why don't you get a couple of such novels from the vendors, use them for reference and write one yourself; I'll give you a month leave.' I stared at him in disbelief, but he was serious!"

Such experiences, Wu says, gradually led her to a different attitude toward literature and publishing. Wu used to write short stories herself; although critics ignored them and friends thought them too soft, Wu would be the last to concede that her own writing had anything to do with "popular literature." Since then, however, she has turned willingly to writing sellable work, including kung fu novels, murder stories, and reporting on a 1989 exhibition of nude paintings in Beijing's Museum of Fine Arts—which itself was an effort to make money (and indeed it broke the museum's boxoffice record). Wu still feels uneasy about doing "pop stuff," but she clearly does not see any prospects for the other camp: "The avant-garde can put on airs and write what they think is revolutionizing Chinese literature, but in reality nobody outside their small circle cares."

The scorn is mutual. When I talked to an "avant-garde" critic about the issue of popular literature and the attitude of literary people like Wu, his response was quick and haughty: "People like her never had a chance to make it in serious literature anyway. The talent just isn't there. So all this put-down of the 'avant-gardes' and 'small circles' in the name of popular opinion is sour grapes, at bottom. As for what the masses think of literature," he continued, his eyebrows arched sarcastically, "it's never been a great concern for me. The masses are stupid and have no taste. Why should I produce garbage just because they like to read garbage?"

And up until the time of Tiananmen, the Chinese avant-garde did hold its ground vigorously. One of the leading young critics in Shanghai, Wu Liang, published two essays late in 1988 defending "experimental fiction." The titles sounded like manifestos: "Salon or Bestseller: No Middle Road" and "The True Avant-Gardist Marches Ahead as He Always Will." This was a tragic heroism cornered by reality, though: sales of literary journals were dropping steadily, and it was useless to deny that literature was becoming a quaint commodity. If one did not market it in a more desirable package, it would simply sit on the shelves.

Not everybody, to be sure, is ready to agree with Wu Liang that there is really no middle road. For example, the editors of one literary monthly in a northeast province, hard up for funds, have abandoned the magazine's straight-faced seriousness and tried a new formula. They reserve all the serious, experimental pieces for their odd-numbered issues, while packing their even-numbered issues as tight bombs of sensational material decked out with lurid sex goddesses on the cover. So far, they have done well enough, but they are an exception. Most people in the publishing business have not mustered up the courage—or the ingenuity—to do anything like this. They fret, complain, mince a step or two, and for the most part watch their sales slump.

THE TRUTH is, the Chinese do need more entertainment. Beijing, the nation's political and cultural capital, is sad proof of how dull life still can be for the majority of its residents. As part of the propaganda showcase of reform and openness, the government has funneled a great deal of money—both its own and outside investments—into the city over the past ten years, resulting in massive construction of joint-venture hotels, office buildings, restaurants and shops, as well as more imported cars, more tourists, and more traveling businessmen from the provinces and abroad. Despite all the commercial hubbub, however, the city remains largely provincial and boring. In the daytime, streets are crowded and business is lively in stores and restaurants, but most restaurants and shops close at seven or eight in the evening, and by ten o'clock even the major avenues are deserted. Some Japanese-style karaokes are open late, but the entrance fee often runs as high as 15 percent of an average person's monthly salary. The bars and cafés in the big hotels cater mainly to foreigners and the city's small number of nouveaux riche, but ordinary Chinese are shut out either by snooty doormen or by the steep prices of drinks. In any case, bar-hopping has never been a great Chinese tradition.

Older people like to reminisce about the pleasures of great teahouses in the old society, where people sipped tea and chatted while enjoying all kinds of artistic performances. Nowadays, the only teahouse of that nature in Beijing is Lao She Teahouse, a tourist attraction much too expensive and formal for local commoners to walk in and relax. There are small neighborhood tea-houses scattered around the city, but few live up to the old standards. They don't draw good business from the older generation, and they're just not the right cup of tea for the young.

The urban youngsters may prefer to go to rock concerts, but the only pop-ular Chinese rock star, Cui Jian, has always drawn so many cops to his con-certs that any "unsuitable" display of zeal is sure to be snuffed out quickly by the law. Movies aren't much of an alternative: most Chinese productions are poorly made, whereas most foreign movies are either too costly or too "unhealthy" for the government to bring in. Theater is, at present, an almost extinct art since most plays are either banned by the state or ignored by the public. The museums in Beijing are shabby and dull; great classical paintings are mostly hidden in the backrooms for "protection" (of the art—and of the people, from "reactionary art"), and few people care about the contemporary art scene. The police, on the other hand, care a great deal: at the opening of the first Chinese modernist art exhibition in February 1989, where a young woman artist finished her piece of work by shooting at it with a pistol, they showed up in full riot gear. The city holds several festival fairs throughout the year in the parks, but to people like Teacher Bei, who remembers the variety of exciting fairs in the old society, today's fairs seem like a sham. "I went to one of the biggest last year, and left in twenty minutes," she told me. "It was so boring." The way she sees it, the basic difference between old society and new society is this: you have more economic security in the new society, but you had more fun in the old one.

So for the millions who work for the state six days a week for a meager salary, there is almost nothing to do in the evenings except stay at home and watch television. Precisely because so many people can count on nothing but television for daily entertainment, it has been the butt of constant public ridicule. Everybody has something bad to say about Chinese television. The domestic news really involves nothing more than Party meetings, leaders cut-ting the ribbon at the opening ceremonies or planting trees for greening cam-paigns and the like; the international news is so brief that it ends before you get ready for it; stand-up comedians are seldom funny (they laugh more than you do); soap operas and sitcoms put you to sleep . . . the complaints could go on and on.

And then *Yearning* arrived. If millions of Chinese, especially those living in the dour northern cities, found it soothing and charming to watch a soap opera that offered them a recognizable slice of daily lives as mundane and banal as their own as well as the unpredictable ups and downs of political and social fate, such as they themselves had experienced over the past few decades, who can blame them for their earnest and sorely needed pleasures, or for their intense identification with the characters in the show?

ZHENG WANLONG says that while he was investigated by the special task force and lived like a hermit for a whole year, he had time to contemplate the whole business of writing. He asked himself what it meant to be a writer and a member of the intelligentsia in a country like China. In a grave voice, he says to me: "The problem with us is that a lot of us took ourselves too seriously. We were too uptight; we thought we were too good, too deep to write just for the ordinary little guys." When I tell him that a Chinese writer's ideal reader is either the Nobel Prize committee or the politburo, he laughs, his face lighting up as though we have just reached some important mutual understanding. We discuss Milan Kundera, whose novels have been very popular among literary Chinese. Zheng says he doesn't like a lot of the values Kundera wants to restore. I mention the word "center" and Zheng jumps up, all excited. "That's a word I've been looking for!" Looking back, he says, Chinese writers and intellectuals have been too caught up with the center, with history painted on a huge canvas; this is true even of "depoliticizing" literary trends such as the Search for Roots movement, which for Zheng remains the hallmark of his career.

Zheng's reflections in some ways echo the sentiments felt by many Chinese students overseas. Talking about the difficulties of the exiled Chinese intellectuals after Tiananmen, Renqiu Yu, who now teaches history at an American university, wondered if these exiles had ever been "misfits" back home. "If you really think about it," he mused, "they have all done very well in China. They knew the system there, where the doors and traps were, they played the game comfortably with that knowledge, and had a sense of superiority and power. And they all flourished. Whereas here, left as individuals to scramble for themselves, they feel their role has diminished to nothing."

In the wake of Tiananmen, however, some Chinese intellectuals at home have begun to rethink the question of intellectual elitism. It occurs to them now that the rise of such elitism in recent years in China may have much to do with the politics of the state. In order to curb and degrade the intellectuals, the state has exploited a pseudo-populism: "Serve the people" and "Workers and peasants are the best teachers of the intellectuals" typify the phrases chanted over and over again. To fight the state, the intellectuals started promoting elitism. Yet this tactic seems to be the flipside of what the state promotes, for the pattern of thinking is similar, merely inverted. Before, the party was the vanguard; now, the intellectuals are. It shows just how much the intellectuals are tied up with the game of the center.

Zheng feels the Chinese intellectuals' elitism has become for the most part a ridiculously self-inflated mentality, a sort of hollow delusion. "We think we're great and dignified, and the national destiny weighs heavy on our shoulders, but one morning we wake up and find out we are nobody, and we are absolutely vulnerable and insignificant in the eyes of others." He doesn't explain who he means by "others," but I think of a story I heard recently about a very famous Chinese painter who, sitting among the guests at a banquet in honor of a senior Party leader, was referred to by the leader as "the fellow who draws."

Many people have asked why so many educated Chinese share the belief and the hope that, ultimately, what they say and what they write can in some way affect, whether by destabilizing or enlightening, the central power. It has to do, in part, with the Chinese tradition of the rural gentry serving the imperial state. The system of *ke ju*, the imperial state exams for the selection of civil officials, had long cultivated the notion that the most desirable goal of education is to rise high in officialdom. Under the communist reign since 1949, the state had further tightened its grip on the intellectuals while systematically destroying every intermediate institution that supported and generated independent cultural and political criticism. Yet the majority of the intellectuals identified with the party's ideology and willingly cooperated. Certainly, there were individual cases of resistance, but examining the broader picture, China cannot boast a rich history of independent thinking and independent intellectual critique of the state.

Maybe it's unfair to castigate intellectuals for being so obsessed with a power center that rules over them with such deep suspicion and contempt. When culture and tradition have been cut off for generations, what's left for intellectuals to reach back and hold on to? For years, the mainland Chinese intellectuals have been talking about "reconstructing culture," and now they talk about "writing in a time of crisis." A lot of them feel they have fallen through the cracks of history and have nowhere to go. Singapore, which Deng admires immensely, scares the hell out of them: political control combined with economic prosperity. If that's where China is headed, what will the intellectuals do? After ten years of fighting for reform, they find themselves the victims of both politics and the market. They are poor, wretched, and ignored. What is more, they seem mainly to have themselves to blame: why did they collaborate? Why couldn't they see better?

I ask Zheng what he has learned from his contemplations on writing. He says he now feels that the writers ought to think less of the fate of the state but more about how to make their work readable and accessible to the little guys. "Why always focus on the Big Pain? I want to write about joy, the small joys of daily life." Writing *Yearning*, he says, was for himself a break away from the *haute couture* mentality. "I don't mind the vulgarity of it. That's what we wanted—a vulgar show. But there is vitality in vulgarity. We start from the low and, who knows, maybe later on there will be hope." Then he adds, "Perhaps the whole old path had been wrong from the beginning."

Does he really believe what he says? Or is it all a matter of bad faith, the defensiveness of a guilty conscience? Or is he maybe gloating over his new popularity, and wants to put a slick gloss over it? Or is he simply confused? Is that smile on his face nervous, resigned, elated, expectant, or affected? Perhaps it's a bit of everything. Every time we talk, questions like these flash through my mind.

In the meantime, the show goes on. Chinese consulates in the U.S. distribute videotapes of *Yearning* to Chinese students in various American campuses, promoting it as "a very positive text." The official Chinese Federation of Women, on the other hand, deeply regrets the popularity of the show, saying its submissive heroine has managed singlehandedly to lay waste to forty years of their work on women's rights. Wang Shuo announced that he was plunging into writing a series of popular romances. "I'll hire hacks to write the sequels if the first ones turn out successful." He told me this not so much as a secret plan but as a practical joke, his boyish face shining with impish glee. "For this kind of job, you don't need much brainpower, all you really need is wristpower. The other hook is: Chinese always fall for anything labeled 'the first.' Now that we've done 'the first all-Chinese indoor drama,' you've got to come up with some other 'firsts'—'the first suspense soap,' say, or 'the first love-talk soap.' I'm betting on the love-talk, and I'm going to call it something like"—here his voice went tender, more girlish, purring—"'No Choice in Loving You.'"

Zheng Xiaolong, BTAC's young entrepreneurial director, was already busy with their next production. This time, it was to be a fast-paced urban sitcom called *Stories of an Editorial Office*. He gave a deadpan briefing to his new group of script writers gathered, again, in a hotel suite. "*Yearning* made the audience cry, now we'll make them laugh. The center is spending a lot of money on this—nice hotel, good food, and hot water twenty-four hours a day—so you guys will have to put your hearts into this gig. You have five days to give me an episode-by-episode synopsis, then you are free to go home." "Otherwise," Li Xiaoming threw in with a broad grin on his face, "the bill is yours." The sitcom turned out to be a hit this spring. Although it didn't generate the same degree of national heat that *Yearning* did, it is tremendously popular among urban audiences. Zheng Xiaolong has also made a business trip to New York, where BTAC plans to set up a video outlet, selling videotapes to the Chinese audience oversees.

Li Xiaoming is making a bet, too. He says BTAC is going to produce several indoor dramas this year, all following the work method of *Yearning*. He predicts that the nineties will be the decade of sentimental soap operas: "They'll flood Chinese television," he says confidently.

The day before I left Beijing, I phoned Zheng Wanlong to say good-bye. I was feeling a bit melancholy, partly because I was leaving, partly because a friend of mine, a Beijing film director, had just dropped by, quite depressed. Her movie project had just been killed—rejected by the studio officials—because it was not politically "healthy" enough—and she had turned down an offer to direct a well-paid TV show to pursue it. She described how hard it was nowadays to make the kind of movies she cared to make. "Between the official propaganda movies and the commercial blockbusters, you really don't have much leeway," she said bitterly. "Either way you have to compromise. You can't find a piece of clean soil anymore." I told Zheng about this. He, too, knew the director well. There was a pause on the other end of the line. Then he said: "Look, this is your hometown, but you don't live here anymore. You only come to visit. Let's see, how should I put it? . . . Say someone goes to Mt. Tai for a visit. He stands on the peak, and he admires the beautiful sunrise. But then he sees how poorly the villagers live at the foot of the mountain, how badly they manage their affairs. So he wants to criticize their lifestyle, even to judge. But the villagers are stuck in that lot. They live at the foot of the mountain, and they have to get on with their lives there. And that's all there is to it."

3

A City without Walls

My friend Chen Jiangong has made up his mind. A writer born in 1949—the year the communists took over China—and well-known for his graceful, nostalgic stories about Beijing, Chen is now turning his talents from fiction to television. By Chinese standards, this is a drastic move. Chen has crossed the boundary from elite to pop, and it has taken years of writer's block, soul-searching over "face-losing," and a collapsed market for serious fiction for him to take the step. But one thing remains constant for Chen: his obsession with Beijing. He has just finished a long soap opera script, named after a famous old Beijing street, which dramatizes the changes the city has seen.

When we met recently in his apartment, he looked relaxed. He said he needed to get out more, because he was getting rather flabby and weak-wristed from months of laboring by a desk, "getting the gig done." On that freezing cold February day, though, it felt just right to sip tea and swap jokes, warming up for a lamb hot-pot. Chen's hot-pot has a sort of cult reputation among Beijing's writers, because he approaches it the same way he approaches writing: meticulously and well-steeped in another era. The lamb, the sauce, the brass pot, the charcoal—*everything* has a story behind it, some historical references going back to a distant past, to another way of life—so much so that you are not just cooking some lamb in a pot of scalding water, you are practicing important rituals, reliving a different sensibility. You travel in time as you eat.

This time, he lapses into a story about bird enthusiasts in Beijing. To train larks and parrots, Chen told me, they get up very early in the morning, take their birdcages and bike to the city's outskirts. "Because nowadays the city is too noisy, filled with people shoving about and talking dirty. They don't want their birds to get a dirty mouth." And suddenly, he hits on an image that compresses all his complicated feelings about Beijing's changes. "Modern Beijing," he says, "is a city where it's impossible to find a spot to hang up one's birdcage." To understand what he means, though, one has to know about an older, more classic Beijing image: a gentleman with his tamed birds in a bamboo cage hanging on a branch in a quiet park or in a merry teahouse, or simply in his own courtyard. It is the quintessential image of leisure and a certain type of cultivation. The birdcage is a symbol whose disappearance would mean that a certain lifestyle and a whole set of values had gone with it. Despite having grown up in Mao's new China, deep down Chen is a stubborn romantic whose sympathies belong ultimately to the old culture. In real life, he is sufficiently agile to tap dance to the rhythms of the times—he lives cheerfully in a prefabricated, boxy apartment embellished with Japanese electronics, writing on a newly purchased Chinese word processor, and he even thrives at his job with the official Writers Association—but, essentially, he carves out a living by portraying in agreeably touching stories the "beauty of the sunset," or the pathos of the old culture.

Chen has tons of friends he describes as "true Beijingers." He hangs out with them and is proud he isn't one of those writers whose only friends are other writers and critics. He loves to tell stories to prove that some old Beijing customs and slang are still alive. He knows of a judge, for example, who can settle a bitter suit over housing not by invoking codes of law but by appealing to both parties' common sense of fairness—the traditional, civilized Beijing way; he also knows a fellow who can chant, authentically, over thirty varieties of old Beijing vendors' rhymes—an ingenious, charming form of street-lane hawking going back to the turn of the century. Chen is making a tape of these rhymes, hoping that the city museums will archive it; he also plans to take his authentic fellow to places like a German cultural center in Beijing, where his friend, a Sinologist named Lutz Schreiner, is the director, and such old folk art is sure to be appreciated. From time to time, Chen gets so whipped up by these activities that he starts to sound like an old-fashioned, angry cultural conservative, lamenting Beijingers' ignorance about the city's past, and complaining about "a younger generation that has lost all the civilized values and aesthetics." Somehow, writing television shows in the straitjacket of market rules and entertainment formulas hasn't squashed Chen's elitist belief in the writer's responsibility and ability to educate and to enlighten. Yes, he insists, the birdcage is still there—if only people know its value and beauty, they'll cherish and appreciate it. In moments like this, the irony eludes him that nobody in Beijing wants to hear his friend's authentic chants except the people at a *German* cultural center, and that his tape will simply end up in an unvisited folk art museum, in some obscure archive, collecting dust.

LUTZ SCHREINER is sort of a cultural crusader, too. He is a tall, dark-skinned man from Munich, with rumpled, casual, good clothes and a mop of curly brown hair in a state of constant revolt. Lutz has written a book on

China and won a prize for his translation of a Chinese novel. He is a voracious reader, who estimates that 80 percent of the books he has read are in Chinese, and 20 percent in German and other languages. Now, though, he says all the important, useful things he's learned in his life come from the 20 percent. He told me he's getting "field burnout" and is fed up with Beijing, a city he now feels stranded in. These are startling pronouncements, because I know how fiercely he had argued in 1989, after the Tiananmen massacre, that his center must stay in Beijing. Moral sanctions were not something Lutz opposed, not with his Berlin radical background and Bavarian country conscience, but he believed that keeping all possible venues of contact open was a more important, and tougher, way to go—one that involves more complicated, more intriguing negotiations, often compromises, in the effort to do good within a totalitarian system. In some ways it's like playing chess with the devil: a risky game in which one puts one's soul on the line and hopes to hoodwink him through clever maneuvers. Lutz still believes in his choice, but is no longer so certain if it was the right one for *him*, or if he has played the game the right way. His scholarly programs and literary conferences have been blocked again and again by Party officials or ignored by the public. Post-Tiananmen Beijing moved in a direction that took people like Lutz by surprise: they feel ambivalent about the clamor for economic progress, which tend to drown out the tough political and cultural issues. For Lutz, frustration and a terrible sense of isolation are daily realities. Has he been in touch with "the real China"? He tells me stories about a friend of his, a German businessman who has lived in Beijing for years and made tons of money: he is the only foreigner in Beijing who's been accepted ino the Diaoyutai Club, a social club of top Chinese leaders, and swims in the same pool with, say, Party General Secretary Jiang Zemin. That sort of intimacy with the power center provides the political lubricant for all his business deals. "A real cynic, but quite sophisticated," Lutz said with grudging admiration. "He's bored by money now, and writes brilliant short stories he never sends out to publish, just for the fun of it. Whereas I, with all my qualms and principles, get my harmless programs shot down by mistrust. Maybe I should turn the operation over to him."

Lutz and I had a drink in the café of a monstrously big joint-venture hotel in downtown Beijing. Service was sluggish, and being the only Chinese customer around—female, with a white man in all his six-four bulk—I was getting cryptic stares from the cluster of waitresses loitering by the bar. They were teenage girls dressed in glitzy, exotic hotel uniforms that made them look like something between characters in a period piece and dancers at a village fair. Outside, under a polluted gray sky, agglomerations of bicycles, buses, and cars moved slowly along Changan Avenue, Beijing's main thoroughfare. In a tone of quiet exasperation, Lutz said: "Beijing is the only city in the world I know of that has acquired all the monstrosities of a metropolis without becoming cosmopolitan." As if to prove and fight this point, Lutz has been trying to bring out a cosmopolitan book about Beijing, written both by Chinese and Westerners, funded by a German press, and intended for a European audience. He has asked various Beijing writers to contribute; so far the effort has brought nothing but frustration and disappointment. "It's like doing anything else here, you have to play politics, use connections, fight the bureaucrats, explain everything and get misunderstood by everybody, including your friends." One such friend is Chen Jiangong, who has agreed to write a piece for the book. Lutz had explained to Chen that the book should convey a sense of what it is like to live in today's Beijing, and talked about his plans: a chapter on crowded space and the absence of privacy, another on municipal politics, perhaps with a portrait of the hard-line mayor, Chen Xitong, and then maybe a report on Beijing's black market and prostitution ring. Three weeks later, Chen Jiangong handed in an outline of *his* picture of Beijing: the rough edges were gone, and it was—in Lutz's words—"dripping with nostalgic gentility." Chen extolled the elegant charms of the old Beijing lifestyle—a world that vanished long ago, in Lutz's opinion.

Did Chen and Lutz really misunderstand each other so completely? Lutz lives in an elegant, Chinese revival-style courtyard house on the west side of Beijing, on a large estate now rented by various moneyed Western institutions and firms such as the Deutsche Bank. Lutz's rent is four thousand deutsche marks a month, a figure that causes him constant embarrassment. It's not offensive by Chinese custom to ask about rent, and his Chinese visitors have never failed to ask—nor to be openly astonished—by the answer. For all this contribution of foreign currency, Lutz gets not only maid service but also maximum security. Unless Lutz personally drives them through in his silver Volkswagen, his Chinese guests have to register at the main gate, where an armed soldier stands on duty twenty-four hours a day. So Lutz sits in a lounge chair under his beautiful willow tree in his beautiful courtyard, hankering for cosmopolitanism, but he has no way of escaping the irony of his situation. On the other side of the city, Chen Jiangong lives in a cheap concrete slab, his rooms are crammed and his neighbors noisy, and traffic jams creep by right under his window. But Chen writes away at his desk, and in writing he reaches out to another way of life, unfolding calmly in elegant, shaded courtyards with languid figures and chirpy birds. The two men are peering through different lenses, but in a way they are really frowning at the same picture and out to prove a similar point.

THERE IS a sense of loss about Beijing. There are people who say the loss the city has endured in the past forty years is unspeakable. Some say that what the communists did to the city is a crime, that they should be held as *qianguzuiren*, "criminals for eternity," because they dismantled the magnificent city walls, an architectural wonder of history, and used the bricks to build useless anti–air raid tunnels, and because they let the Red Guards run wild during the Cultural Revolution, smashing and looting so many of the city's cultural monuments and treasures. The communists waged a class war, bashing "class enemies" with ideological diatribes and wiping out social distinctions. They aimed to make 95 percent of the people in Beijing equal. In reality they made them equally poor and made them get equally bad educations and lead equally dull lives. They drove blindly for modernization: factories were built all over the city, peasants swarmed in from the provinces to "expand the working class forces," electricity ran short, the air turned dirty, buildings took on a faceless, ascetic look, housing got crowded, and urban planning became a perpetually amateurish experiment subject to bad politics and poor management. For an ancient imperial city that used to set a unifying aesthetic standard for the whole nation, the new Beijing has a radically splintered image. It has taken on the appearance of a proletarian-peasant metropolis striving to get rich, a hodgepodge of clashing styles and sensibilities.

These are heavy, angry charges, and they come most of all from those who know about Beijing's past firsthand but no longer live there. I know a couple from Beijing who have made New York their home for the last forty years, gentle people from rich old Beijing families. When they went to visit their native city in 1988, the new city they found themselves in was so uncongenial, so altered from the old city of their youth, which they had romanticized from afar, that they left never wanting to return. Another man from a similar background came back from his tour shaken with anger. He said that as he walked around Beijing, he felt *lost* on many levels—geographically confused, culturally disoriented, and psychologically unsettled. "The walls!" he shouted. "They tore the city walls down!" At my questions, though, he choked up and refused to talk more about it.

To understand the cultural ethos of Beijing, of its transformation in a matter of fifty years from a great medieval capital into a contemporary city, you have to go back to the walls. Chen Jiangong, for one, likes to point out that in old Beijing there were more walls than houses. There were the city walls, which enclosed the city in two majestic rectangles with a length of about twenty-six miles. Everywhere within the city were the walls of courtyard houses, from the biggest—the royal palaces at the very center of the city— down to the humblest cottages. The social status of an inhabitant dictated the size of his house and the length of his walls. In some ways, old Beijing was a magnificently walled-in courtyard with an infinite succession of smaller walled-in courtyards. Ask directions, and you'd be guided with reference to the walls; what's more, you'd hear not about "left" or "right" but "north/south" or "east/west," because the walls and the streets were laid out arrow-straight on these axes. To the extent that a built environment was a product of the human world, the culture of old Beijing was a culture of walls. Walls had everything to do with the city's aura of mystery and grandeur, with the Beijingers' strong sense of direction, space and class, their notion of privacy, and their claustrophobic prejudices. "They tore down the city walls in the fifties," Chen said pensively, "but the walls in people's minds didn't come down for a long time."

In fact, Western modernity had encroached into old Beijing long before the communists got there. After the fall of the Qing Dynasty in 1911, the various republican governments made sporadic gestures towards modernizing Beijing: they bulldozed some palace walls and garden mansions to lay trolley tracks and to erect buildings somewhat in the Western style; they expanded a few quaint, narrow streets into wider boulevards for traffic; they even tore off two corners of the city walls so the railway could pass through. By and large, though, there had been too many wars and coups d'etat to worry about a new vision for Beijing, so the basic framework was left untouched. Thus, its last imperial splendor was already crumbling when Mao's troops entered.

Mao set out right away to modernize Beijing on a large scale. In 1949, there were only fifteen architects in the whole of Beijing, only five of whom could design so much as a five-story building. Since nobody "modern" was talking to Mao at that point except Stalin, it was natural that the Soviet advisers and experts got the royal treatment in China. They arrived in throngs with money, technology, and above all vision. A team of Soviet experts, special guests of the Beijing mayor, conducted a survey in town and proposed a blueprint for a new Beijing straight out of their thirties Moscow plan. It boiled down to two focal points: Beijing must be industrialized, and it must be consolidated into a symbol of the socialist state.

Despite the Sino-Soviet falling-out in 1960, this was the vision that set the general direction for Beijing's development over the next thirty years. With the help of the Soviets, the Chinese built hundreds of factory yards in and around Beijing, developed workers' satellite towns, and turned Beijing into a major industrial center. In order to mold Beijing into a socialist capital, the government dismantled all but two of the ancient city gates, tore down numerous temples and courtyard houses, cleaned out old teahouses and pleasure zones, and lined the main streets with official monuments, government offices, standardized state-run stores, and plain apartment buildings. The private sector was nationalized, and artists and craftsmen were absorbed into the state workforce. Folk fairs and street festivals disappeared; and in their place parades and rallies rose to become important holiday rituals. Tiananmen Square was expanded several times over and paved with granite, the better to stage parades. The most famous building project of this period was the 1958 Ten Big Projects for National Celebration, giant structures conceived primarily as symbolic monuments to the socialist state, such as the Great Hall of the People and the Museum of Revolutionary History. They tossed together ingredients of Soviet, classical Chinese, and modernist architectures. It was a heroic effort to evoke a new sense of the sublime; unfortunately, it didn't work.

By the end of the fifties, the Soviet-style modernization had changed Beijing profoundly. In comparing two photo albums of Beijing street scenes—one set of photos had been taken in the forties, and the other, in the fifties—I was struck by the sharp differences in aura. The Beijing of the fifties exuded a certain austere virtue—the clean streets, the plain, orderly buildings, the people in their uniform clothes smiling their cheerful, disciplined smiles. The old city's multi-faceted sophistication and romantic glow had been wiped out.

The first large-scale dismantling of the city walls took place toward the end of that decade, when the hotheaded Beijing party committee decided that these cumbersome, useless blocks of bricks not only blocked modern-day traffic but were a symbol of feudalism. However, before the dismantling of the massive walls could be completed, the country plunged into a series of economic and political disasters: throughout the sixties and the Cultural Revolution, various political campaigns consumed the nation, and urban planning came to a halt. Construction during this period was random, paying no attention to form, quality, or environment.

Materials needed for civil defense and for the construction of a subway line finally finished off the remainder of the city walls. By 1970, Mao had become so paranoid about Soviet invasions that he threw every Chinese city into frantic preparations for war. For a while, tunnel-digging became a national occupation. I was an elementary school student in Beijing back then, and to this day I remember vividly how my school arranged the curriculum around the digging schedule, dividing everyone into work shifts and, after the tunnel was completed, practicing air-raid evacuation. Meanwhile, all along the route of the residual city walls, the Red Guards supervised the "black elements"—persecuted professors and cadres—in hacking down the bricks with picks and shovels in order to clear the way for a future subway system. People picked bricks and stones from the rubble and used them for the air-raid tunnels. In a strange way, Mao carried on the Chinese tradition beautifully: the ancient defense system of the city walls had been rendered obsolete by modern aerial warfare; to create a more up-to-date defense—with *Chinese* characteristics—Mao replaced the old walls with winding underground walls. Some of the old bricks were put to good use!

Today, the tunnels still lie under the city, useless and forgotten. Above them, the city pulses with a peacetime energy and the subway system is heavily used (Beijing's population has soared from the 1.6 million in 1949 to over 10 million at present). Whatever ancient sites survived the shocking changes of modernization now seem dislocated, like mutilated limbs on a new body. The Forbidden City, for instance, sprawls in its dilapidated splendor behind Tiananmen like an embalmed and isolated relic of the distant past. Directly across the street lies Mao's mausoleum: the Chairman, too, is embalmed and isolated, in better trim because he is a relic of a more recent past. Both sites have become Beijing's tourist attractions. People line up to pay homage, to satisfy curiosity, to get sentimental about history, for both eras are gone forever.

GIVEN THE historical circumstances, many people consider the changes Beijing has undergone inevitable. The one man who had a grand, alternative vision for Beijing was a Chinese architect named Liang Sicheng. The scion of a legendary elite family and trained at the University of Pennsylvania in the twenties, Liang was a preeminent scholar in Chinese architecture but was also at home with Western urban planning. His 1950 plan for Beijing has become a classic, enjoying the sort of reputation in China's urban planning circles that Le Corbusier's 1925 Voisin Plan for Paris does in the West (although the two plans' ultimate concerns are diametrically opposed). Le Corbusier wanted to wipe out the historic center of Paris in order to install a rigid modernist system of tall buildings and superhighways. Liang believed that you could have your cake and eat it too: he wanted to keep all of old Beijing enclosed in its city walls, turning it into a great museum and cultural center, and to build a new, modern city next to it. He also had the brilliant idea of lining the route atop the city walls with potted plants and flowers and benches, transforming the ring of walls into an elevated park. These strategies, he believed, would allow Beijing to leapfrog through time while avoiding all the mistakes Western cities had made: a modernization that would contain the explosive effects of rapid development *and* keep an ancient masterpiece for aesthetic appreciation!

Liang was typical of his generation of elite intellectuals; his cosmopolitan erudition did nothing to weaken his patriotism. Most educated Chinese, chagrined by the World War II Japanese occupation and fearful of colonization, had supported communism and bowed to Mao out of nationalist fervor. For his part, Mao courted famous intellectuals like Liang. Liang was flattered and excited, for with the backing of a strong, concerned government, he could do great things on a grand scale. It was with a sense of empowerment and mission that he received his appointment to the Beijing Urban Planning Committee, and he couldn't have felt more acutely the gravity of drawing a new plan for Beijing. Working day and night with a young associate, Liang believed that the fate of a great city was lying at their fingertips. He was soon disappointed. The municipal government held a meeting and voted overwhelmingly against his plan. The Soviet advisers openly sneered at it as "mistaken" and "impractical."

I recently talked to Liang's son, Mr. Liang Congjie, who was still seething about his father's—and the city's—misfortune. "If his plan had been realized," he said, "Beijing would be a different city today." A few years ago, he showed up at a conference honoring his father's career, made an emotional speech, saying that if his father had returned from America in 1949 instead of 1929, there would have been no career to honor—and then left.

Mr. Chu Chuanheng, who had been the Beijing mayor's assistant on urban construction back in the fifties, doesn't share the sentiment at all: "I believe we made the right judgment about the plan. The state had no money to do what Mr. Liang proposed, and the old city would have been left to die if we had simply developed a new modern city outside it. Experts tend to split hairs, but they don't see the big picture," he says.

Back then, the mayor of Beijing, Peng Zhen, had taken Liang up to the rostrum of Tiananmen to see the big picture. Mayor Peng, a robust man from the military, belonged to the trusted clique of leaders around Mao until he was purged during the Cultural Revolution. Looking out over the city from the rostrum, Peng told Liang that Chairman Mao had stood there with him recently and said the view would be quite different in the future: "We'll see a forest of chimneys from here!" the Chairman had grandly pronounced. So Mayor Peng patted Liang on the shoulders: "Imagine that, Mr. Liang! You must have a broad mind and see the big picture." Liang almost fainted at these words.

Chu admits that, for a long time, the government lacked quality people in urban planning. "Back in the fifties, a lot of our cadres came from villages and didn't even know how to use a toilet bowl — they thought it was a garbage can and stuffed it with rubbish — how could you expect them to build modern cities? They were peasants! Beijing has had three waves of peasant takeover: 1949 was the first; then the Cultural Revolution, when army officers and rural cadres took over the city's leadership. The third wave was the eighties."

Chu had been a big shot in the eighties, serving rigorously as a vice minister of urban and rural construction, and pushing Deng's reform programs. Although he is getting ready for retirement now, he still holds several high-ranking advisory positions and is always on the run. His wife doesn't see him much at home: last year he spent over two hundred days on the road, flying in and out of the country, and whenever he's home, the phone rings off the hook and visitors knock on the door to complain or to ask for favors. The pace has slowed down, compared to the days when he was first appointed vice minister. Chu describes the first months of his job — after he was promoted from the municipal government and thrown into the viper's nest of interministerial politics at a national level — as a bureaucratic nightmare. He had no idea that everything was so entangled: "In a way, reform is about recasting power," Chu said philosophically. "We are in a transitional, restructuring period where the division of power and responsibility is blurred. Naturally everybody scrambles to get a bigger slice of the pie. Since our ministry issues land and building licences, it's viewed as a profit zone, a fat chunk everybody wants to sink his teeth into." Pressed for examples, Chu came up with the Ministry of Transportation and the Ministry of Irrigation: "Their main domain was suburbs and interprovincial zones, but they would insist on their rights in city planning because that's where they could make a buck. Then the other ministries also had their own interests in mind and they made their demands. So planning gets completely messed up. How can you have real planning when your coordination system breaks down?" The subject seems to bring back a rush of bad memories for Chu. "To tell you the truth, the situation was so messy and the problems were so endless that sometimes, when I finally got to bed, I wished I would never have to wake up again." These experiences haven't destroyed Chu's faith in communism or reform, though; he has nothing but hope for Beijing's future. "Look, the city walls are part of what's behind us now. It's useless to gnaw our insides out about loss. We are faced with a mountain of problems, but we are feeling our way step by step, and we're getting better every day. I've always believed in looking ahead."

• • •

In a way, looking ahead has been a national attitude in the post-Mao China. In Beijing, a city that has lost so much so quickly, it's remarkable how little people speak of loss. Official censorship certainly plays a part in this: forty years of endless campaigns have so saturated the society that surveillance has become a way of life. Mao is still a god—though a human god, so the Party will agree that he did make a few mistakes; but to turn the case against Mao is, by extension, to go against the system. Too dangerous. The current leadership permits sob stories about the atrocities of the Cultural Revolution as long as the victims blame it all on the previous leadership, especially the notorious Gang of Four, led by Madam Mao. As for the deeper loss—the loss of trust and faith, loss of cultural sophistication and a different way of life—public discussions on such things have been nearly nonexistent.

This silence stems from a deep-seated stoicism for which political pressure alone cannot account. It has to do with a fundamental philosophical attitude. Chinese have endured massive destruction, wars, and mismanagement for centuries, and sometimes, things have gone totally out of control. For lack of better solutions, however, people have simply grown thicker skins or eased the pain by looking the other way. George Kates, an American who lived in Beijing in the 1930s, wrote a quirky memoir called *The Years That Were Fat*. He noticed a "rubbed" quality of the Chinese, an elasticity characteristic of their social interactions, which he saw as an escapist tactic that provided their only means of avoiding unpleasant situations since they cannot change the system. He even admired this trait, seeing it as a way to retain grace and dignity under oppressive circumstances. As it turned out, the system changed quite radically soon after Kates left China, but the escapist attitude has proven to be deeper and more resilient than political systems. Over and over again, the prevailing Chinese attitude in the aftermath of disasters seems to be: after all, what's gone is gone, and one must move on by focusing on the gains, on the positive side. In other words, you rub off the rough edges of history by rubbing off the rough edges of your own skin.

The willingness to forget about past sorrows also has to do with the new opportunities Deng's reform has brought to town. Despite all the lip service Deng has paid to Mao and the Maoist vision, if one scrapes off the ideological coating, Deng's pragmatic policies have put the country on a very different course. Just compare the landmark buildings in Beijing and you will see an amusing contrast between Mao and Deng. The famous buildings of Mao's era, whether high-minded state function halls or cheap housing projects, had more to do with political symbolism and ideological purity than practical returns. During Deng's era, commercial interest and daily life have increasingly become the central motif for construction. In the past ten years, the government built more residential apartments than factory yards, and it has been more eager to court foreign businesses than to assert China's independence. Notably, it was for tourism, not nationalism, that various historical sites were renovated or rebuilt, including a section of the city walls.

For an entire decade, Beijing was turned into a construction site. Day in, day out, you could hear the hiss of the cranes and watch scaffolds going up and brown dust settling down. Local residents have been excited about the build-up. On my visits, relatives and friends were always quick to point out to me all the new buildings that had sprung up here and there. They are signs of "a very good situation," my father used to say, "the fruits of reform." Looking at these new giants wrapped in their showy glass or granite shells, I would nod, and think to myself that they clearly looked like fruits from an ailing old tree: they made the tree look even older, and they themselves seemed to have caught the disease. True, these buildings brought in some new energy; but, with the shabbiness surrounding them, they also heightened the overall feeling of disjunction. I feel tongue-tied in front of my Beijing relatives and friends, witnessing their genuine excitement, even pride, over something like the Great Wall Hotel, one of Beijing's first gigantic joint-venture hotels. Erected abruptly in the midst of a drab neighborhood with battered Cultural Revolution slogans still on some of the walls, this steel and glass high-rise was viewed as a breakthrough design at the time, and its cafés and cinema have provided sorely needed relief to local residents—that is, the ones who could afford it. Sitting there with a banana split or double espresso, serenaded by a Mozart string quartet played softly by an all-Chinese ensemble dressed in black tie, surrounded by three-piece suits, imitation jeans and fake designer jackets, Asian faces mixing with blue eyes and blond hair, how can one resist the impression, however transient, that China truly is joining the global village?

Wang Yi, author of a book on traditional Chinese Gardens and a friend, told me that his son went blank when asked what the Cultural Revolution was. The boy said nowadays nobody talked about such things at school. Wang is horrified by how fast past tragedies are being forgotten, how short the national memory is. Gulping down several pots of tea, he talks nonstop for six hours about things in the past tense: how the Red Guards ransacked his parents' house, how he himself "broke with" his parents out of a sense of political righteousness, how much people's destructive patterns were rooted in history, in ancient phenomena like witchcraft rituals and palace burnings. "The first thing a conquering army would do when it entered the capital was to set the palaces on fire. That was part of burying the evil past and getting a fresh start.

It happened all through the centuries, up to the Qing dynasty; it was exceptional for so many of the Ming palaces to survive. People became more civilized, but only to a certain degree." His book on gardens, he says, is not just some esoteric, academic study; rather, it is a commentary on the beauty as well as the dark side of Chinese culture and history.

When I bring up the issue of Beijing's vanished city walls, Wang jumps up as though he has waited for years to let loose on the subject. He's been wanting to write about it "because that was a microcosm of what happened to our culture." He plunged into a long explanation of what the walls symbolized and what it meant to have a city *without* the walls. I remind him of various European cities that destroyed their old city walls in the process of modernization. "But I'm not arguing for wholesale preservation," Wang Yi interrupts. "What I'm trying to point out is simply this: The degree of maturity and sophistication classical Chinese city design had attained was so high, it had become a completely self-referential system, a perfect expression of a codified aesthetics that had gone static. Unable to make the next leap, to revolutionize itself, it had been dwelling on ever-more minute modifications of details. It was like an elaborate structure in which every single building block was placed on a precise spot in a precise relation to the other parts and to the whole, so if you removed any single block, the entire structure would collapse in a heap."

Wang's remark reminds me of a point that Liang made about his 1950 plan for Beijing, when he observed that the masterly design of old Beijing embodied such artistic integrity that new, modernist buildings just wouldn't sit well within it. The problem is, raising consciousness about what exactly one is departing from, or emphasizing what is incompatible between two separately evolved systems, doesn't quite answer the question of how one should proceed from there. Back in 1950, Liang suggested moderate reform: adopting new materials on occasion (replacing wood and brick with metal and concrete) but sticking to Chinese structural methods and styles; unfortunately, his ideas on this remained highly sketchy.

In the current milieu of global postmodern nostalgia for historic artifacts and critiques of the failures of modernist city planning, how can we mediate the tensions and links between past and present, between yearnings for continuity and desires for change, between increasingly entangled cultural spheres and conflicting sensibilities? You want heritage, yet you also want to enjoy technological efficiency. The question takes on a peculiar poignancy and complexity in a setting such as Beijing, one of the great symbols of Eastern antiquity, as it approaches modernity with the ethos of a third world economy, a totalitarian polity, and powerful memories and habits of its past imperial glories and humiliations. Questions of this magnitude overwhelm Wang Yi, who is otherwise an ambitious hard-hitter given to grandiose critical projects.

And then there are the practical constraints. When I asked Wang what was holding him back from writing about the city walls, he said, sighing, "It would have no chance of getting published here." Why? "Well," he shrugged despondently, "most people don't give a damn, and some people care about it too much."

EDUCATED CHINESE have learned a great deal from the follies of history in the past forty years. Most of all they have learned about fear: not merely fear of power and persecution, but also fear of responsibility, fear of questioning, fear of thinking independently.

In the reform climate of the eighties, Chinese intellectual discourse has seen some quite dynamic moments. Architectural circles, partly because of their exposure to foreign journals, have led the way in the debate over "culture" and, more than many others, have sought to rethink tradition and modernity. Postmodernism was introduced as early as 1980. A group of architects and scholars formed an unofficial organization in Beijing, the Salon of Contemporary Chinese Architectural Culture, which held discussions and printed books in order to promote a more liberal dialogue. It soon became fashionable to talk about the cultural factor in architecture and urban planning. People brandished phrases like "environmental consciousness," "creative fusion," and "polyphonic structures" as frequently as they used to brandish party jargons like "antibourgeois struggle" and "proletarian virtues." Then came the Tiananmen massacre, and things tightened down again. The Salon was suspended, and many people shrank back to their old cautiousness and private pessimism.

Not Professor Lao Nu, one of Liang Sicheng's foremost disciples and an eminent scholar of architecture in Beijing, who seems not to have grown gingerly or have mellowed much with his advanced age and wisdom. In fact, during our conversations about Beijing's planning and architecture, sparks of passion and wrath threatened to melt the room's walls. "It's hopeless," professor Lao said, throwing up his hands and moving restlessly in the creaky old chair on which he was sitting. "The old city has vanished forever, destroyed, broken. Whatever is left is rotting away, deteriorating, or worse, restored with appalling vulgarity. And the new buildings are ugly, always compromised, curtailed to suit politics, not style or function." Lao detests compromise. He is the kind of man who would go all out for an ideal, and an ideal for him has a purity of its own. The classics, he believes, should be left alone, preserved as pure classics, whereas new architecture should take on a clear-cut new image, embracing modernity completely. Though in his student days he was closely identified with Liang Sicheng, nowadays people hear Lao talk more about Le Corbusier than about his Chinese mentor. In fact, he has become rather reticent, even critical, toward Liang.

Liang died a heartbroken man during the Cultural Revolution. Having written earnest self-criticisms and pledged "eternal loyalty" to the party, he survived a 1955 campaign against his "pro-ancient" ideas and managed to retain his post at the Beijing Urban Planning Committee. Later, he even joined the Party, but during the Cultural Revolution the old dirt was dug up again, and Liang suffered a new round of attacks and humiliations. Up until his final days, he tried earnestly, pathetically, to understand why he was wrong and the Party right. He didn't live to see rehabilitation or to hear the flood of praise about his career, which only came in the eighties.

Despite all the miseries he suffered, there are people now who question the role Liang played in those years. To some, Liang was not merely a victim but also a collaborator: political naïveté and bookish character aside, hadn't Liang consciously used his powerful position to promote only his classicist approach in the name of "nationalism" while snuffing out other trends of a more modernist bent? According to some peoples' accounts, in the fifties, when he was acting as vice chairman of the Beijing Urban Planning Committee, Liang turned down any building proposal that didn't use traditional Chinese pavilion roofs. Indeed, his name became almost synonymous with the big roof. To this day, the style is holding strong as the symbol of "Chineseness," and officials often force it onto projects. There is a well-known joke among Beijing architects: How do you get your plan approved? Simply put a few pavilion roofs in your pocket when you go to see the mayor. The joke is no exaggeration if you take a walk around town: there are plenty of pavilion rooftops squatting over new modernist buildings, like an odd afterthought in children's drawings. Folklore has dubbed this style "wearing the Western suit with melon-skin hat," the small hat traditional gentlemen used to wear with a Chinese gown.

Further, some feel that Liang's desire to keep up with the party policies went too far. At the beginning of the Cultural Revolution, in response to Mao's call for educational reform, he was among the first to suggest that universities should abolish architecture departments and let them be absorbed by departments of civil engineering. Although such efforts didn't prevent his personal misfortune, they did help to wreck many scholarly careers and to set the field back for many years.

No one I encountered has a personal vendetta against Liang, least of all his students. In a way, forgiving Liang's actions is as necessary and important as forgiving one's own, since his story is merely one in a thousand among a whole generation of educated Chinese who bought the party's ideology and willingly reformed themselves. Even in death, Liang's shadow haunts the battle scene. People such as Professor Lao are upset with Liang's high traditionalism primarily because officials and conservative architects use it even today to further their own politics while suppressing others. It often seems to be the same old battle fought with slightly different rhetorics and warriors. The terms of debate have a banal, tiresome sound — tradition or modernity? Chinese or Western? Communism or capitalism? Pavilion roofs or square boxes? Courtyard houses or apartment rows? Everything is too clear-cut, everything gets reduced to ideological stereotypes.

Professor Lao's position is clear: "Times have changed," he said firmly. "Modern life demands modern architecture. Let's face it: China had a grand, beautiful architectural tradition, but it's dead. For centuries it reproduced itself and made little progress. Why pretend we can revive it now or fit it into a new era? We are not fooling anyone but ourselves." His unequivocal radicalism upsets many. Party apparatchiks as well as traditionalists insist on a Chinese core, the former for reasons of political nationalism, the latter for "aesthetic supremacy."

Even some young liberals feel uneasy about Lao's views, finding them too essentialist and absolute. "I like and respect Mr. Lao as a person," a young architectural scholar, Shen Kening, said to me after much musing. "He has a basic integrity, and has done a great service to the field by introducing Western modernism. But I'm afraid I cannot agree with his general position. It's not a matter of going West or East, right or left; tradition has deep, entangled roots in our national consciousness, it seeps through our present problems. Until we really understand our own heritage, there is no way we could even diagnose our problems, let alone propose any solutions." Here he paused again, his voice growing more ponderous, almost melancholy. "It may take another generation to sort things out, and several generations down the road to produce something truly worthy." Shen himself is sorting things out by tracing them back to the very beginning. At present, he works for an American architecture firm in Wisconsin, though he still writes specialized, academic articles — with titles like "Residential Patterns in a Pre-historic Chinese Village Settlement" — for Beijing journals.

Despite their differences, both Shen and Professor Lao belong to the pessimist camp. Everyone in the field knows about an article written by a

Western architect after an extensive survey of Chinese architecture in the mid-eighties. The article's title became famous: "Contemporary Chinese Architecture: Nothing Worth Learning." Lao and Shen would probably agree with the verdict. Given present circumstances—official control, poor education, and lack of vision—they don't see much hope for the future, either. Lao once said to me: "China's old equilibrium was lost in the Opium War, in 1840. It's never been regained. The country has been staggering to catch up with the West. The harder it tries, the worse it staggers. It zigzags ahead a bit, but the West is moving along too, and faster. The gap will only get bigger."

NOT EVERYONE is so down on the situation. The two founders of the architecture salon, Wang Mingxian and Gu Mengchao, talked confidently about the future. Gu's optimism was buoyed by a recent visit to Shanghai, although he had grave reservations about what he saw as the "officialization of Shanghai." "With all the new big hotels and big plazas, it's becoming more and more like Beijing—large, intimidating, and inconvenient," he complained. There is a strong humanist streak in his assessment of urban development. Although he hasn't read Jane Jacobs's classic thesis on urban neighborhood culture, his ideas are very much about building a city around neighborhoods for the ordinary residents, rather than building it around official culture or for high, abstract ideas. Gu feels that Chinese architects can do a lot in this direction. Citing a recent controversy over a project of "neocourt-yard buildings," he emphasized that interesting experiments had not been stopped by the post-Tiananmen repression.

Wang Mingxian, younger and with a college degree in literature, is given over to a more embellished optimism. Pacing his cramped, gloomy office full of stacked cabinets spilling dusty papers and files, he went on for hours about all things positive. As an editor for the official magazine *Chinese Architecture*, he has earned the reputation of being a tireless activist to open up and promote new architecture. Before the salon was suspended, he and Gu often pitched in money from their own pockets to fund the salon's activities. They remain proud that their efforts broke significant ground. "There is a new consciousness among our scholars and architects," Wang said. "Before, people never treated architecture as something cultural—it was either political, or practical. A scholar watched which way the political wind was blowing. An architect looked strictly under his nose and drew a building plan the way a village carpenter uses a ruler to make a chest. But now, we have creative people at work, and the general level of the field has gone up."

What about the loss? Some people feel that Beijing is ruined already, that the space is so messed up it's hard to plan anything. Wang frowned. "That's a matter of perspective—I think the space is fine. Beijing is not like Shanghai or Canton, it's not that cramped and built up. There are a lot of spaces for expansion, for improvement. And things are moving along. It's easy to criticize, to complain about some new disastrous decisions, some coarse buildings. But if you look around, there is also beautiful work being done, under incredibly difficult circumstances." To prove this, he pulled out a half-page newspaper review he wrote about five such works. I glanced at the title: "Five Constellations in the Sky of Contemporary Chinese Architecture."

Wang's favorite "constellation" is the Olympic Center, a complex of auditoriums, shops and activity centers constructed in 1990 for the Asian Games. It's located on the north side, a good distance from downtown Beijing. Wang urged me to see it: "Trust me, it's worth a trip. The pity is," he sighed, a genuine look of regret creeping onto his face, "winter is not the best season to appreciate its beauty."

The next morning, I was on the site. It was very cold, and a howling wind froze everything into stiff silhouettes. The only event scheduled on the grounds that day was an ice sculpture show in one of the exhibition halls. I bought a tour ticket and wandered the grounds. The site was chosen and developed with care to geography: it balanced off the north side of Beijing's central north-south axis, and its internal road system was designed to correspond exactly with Beijing's road system. Two auditoriums loom against an open horizon, each with huge silver roofs sloping down in gracious arcs like bird's wings, supported by pillars rising up. It's not hard to detect a playful borrowing from the traditional pavilion roof, but the use of new structuring methods and materials like colored metal boards give the roofs a slick new look. The interior is slick too, especially the building housing a ten-lane swimming pool and six thousand seats, covered by a dome done up in exposed, intricately knotted telphers. This auditorium alone cost about $23 million. Surrounding the outdoor race tracks, there are the ring-shaped driveways and terraces for walking, all neatly divided by elevated tiers and platforms. There are other grace notes, too, like a sinuous artificial lake, sculptures, and flower planters scattered around. Even the roadside lamps have nice touches of detail. I was impressed—they may not be the "cutting-edge works of international architecture up to 2050," as a billboard at the entrance boasts, but they certainly show character and style. These are definitely not the mediocre, slapdash affairs one sees everywhere in Beijing.

Across the lot are rows of creamy pink apartment buildings, the residential part of the "Asian Games Village." Built in haste to house the foreign athletes, they are now rented out as apartments. A friend of mine, a scrawny, bespectacled young magazine editor, has moved into one of them. He said the interior finish was so lousy that things are already crumbling: indeed, I saw little of him on this trip, as he spent a full month's leave repainting and fixing things up in his new home. Finally he himself crumbled, lying in bed with a high fever and gastric spasms. Five weeks after he and his family moved in the gas pipes still had not been opened, so they had to cook on a little coal stove. Still, they are the envy of all their friends: the Asian Games Village is considered chic, high living, and my friend has turned an extra room into a study. In his old two-room apartment, the bedroom doubled as the living room *and* dining room. I myself had many meals with him and his wife right by their double bed, while their small son practiced the violin in the next room or played ping-pong against the wall. "I'm very content," my friend sighed. "Now I have a room I can shut myself up in." And how much luckier can you get in Beijing? The average living space in 1986 was just under eight square yards per person, but that was the official account, which is as unreliable as a Chinese toilet—it fluctuates freely: the official population count is always too low, the production ratio always too high. So, square yardage notwithstanding, in reality you feel you have no privacy at all, very often not even space to breathe.

I phoned Wang Mingxian to tell him how much I appreciated the Olympic Center, even in winter. He was pleased. "You should try to meet Ma Guoxin, Olympic's chief designer. He's one of our best architects working today, and a cultivated person. Trust me," Wang said. "It's worth a trip."

I MADE phone calls. Two days later, I showed up in Ma's office—thirty minutes late because my cab got stuck in traffic and I had to climb twelve floors, since there was a power cut in his building. I was relieved to find him still waiting there. "Sorry," he said. "*I'm* sorry," I muttered, a bit out of breath.

For an architect of prominence and fame, Ma and his office struck me as oddly plain. He was wearing a drab gray Mao suit, with two blue sleeve-guards pinned over the elbows and an old knit wool hat to keep warm. Covered in dust and paint stains, he could have been a model worker who had stepped out of a propaganda movie. The office looked like a chaotic warehouse: large wooden panels, drawing boards, rolls of papers, and buckets of brushes were everywhere. There were only two small stools, and the room was so cluttered I had to squeeze awkwardly to sit on one. Just as I was wondering if this was really his office, Ma apologized again: he had thought this room would be quieter, "more convenient." I knew then he must share his main office with other people and didn't want to be interviewed there.

Once we started talking, Ma changed into a different person. With ease and a good deal of charm, he glided over a wide range of subjects during our long, discursive chat. He compared the ethos of preindustrial cities with the aesthetics of postmodernism. He discussed Daniel Bell and Karl Marx. To illustrate how absurd and misplaced a certain argument about the architect Philip Johnson and neoclassicism was, he cited eleventh-century Song Dynasty architectural works. And to give me a sense of exactly how important money is in architecture, he told with great verve a story about I. M. Pei, the Chinese-American master, building the Fragrant Hill Hotel in Beijing. I mentioned some of Professor Lao's scathing remarks: "In China," Lao had said, "you have rocket satellites shooting off on the one hand, and a lot of people without pants to wear on the other—but everybody jumps up and down about the satellites, because the country needs so desperately to be proud." Ma broke into a laugh, shaking his head softly. "Mr. Lao has a temperament like Lu Xun's"—Lu Xun was the most celebrated twentieth-century Chinese writer, well-known for his vitriolic attacks on the Chinese character. And this set Ma off on literature: he ruminated over images of Beijing in fiction, quoting works by Chen Jiangong and Liu Xinwu along the way.

What about the image of his Olympic Center? Launched in the wake of the Tiananmen massacre, the Asian Games project had been a noisy part of the official campaign to win back the international community. The Chinese populace had been divided over it. For the chief architect, the pressure to create the "correct image" at such a tense moment must have been extraordinary. How did Ma handle the situation so that his work won praise from everyone—the officials, the architectural community, and the local people?

"If you want to get things done within the system," Ma told me, smiling charmingly, "the key word is *double code*"—he says "double code" twice, first in Chinese, then in English. Then he told me a story. After designing the main auditorium, he ran an introductory session for the officials who could pass it or kill it on the spot depending on, say, what they had had for lunch. Ma showed them his blueprint together with slides of the Forbidden City, and went into fantastic elaborations about their resemblances. By the end of the session, everybody was happily convinced that Ma's new auditorium, like the Temple of Great Harmony, the main palace inside the Forbidden City, would be a symbol of the national spirit, a modern expression of the Chinese heritage. "It's nothing like it, of course," Ma shrugged. "But that was the acceptable code language for them—so why not?"

This brought to mind another story I had heard. As construction on the Olympic Center was about to get started, some municipal officials surveying the site began to have doubts about Ma's political correctness: signs of Western bourgeois influence abounded; where was the Chinese spirit? Rumors soon flew about that the hard-liners were planning a campaign against Ma, that the Olympic project would be suspended for investigation. The night the rumors reached Ma, he went straight to the site and ordered the work team to drive the first piles into the ground. A fait accompli. Once the work had started, it was that much harder to call it off. And somehow, Ma got away with it: construction proceeded, partly thanks to time pressures. Throughout the construction, though, Ma had to live with the dubious prospect that he was simply being used for the last time, squeezed dry; once the work was done, he would be finished off and turned into a political target. In the end, he lucked out again—but this time it took the emperor himself to save Ma. The day construction was completed, Deng Xiaoping dropped by to look around. "Very good," Deng said simply before leaving: "Shows them the Chinese moon is round, too!" That closed the book. From there on, praises showered over Ma and his "masterpiece of the Chinese spirit."

Well, is this a true story? Ma smiled, shaking his head. "I'm sorry," he answered, deadpan now. "I have no comment." I smiled, too, and dropped the question. I realized that Ma was a good poker player and foxy in ways Professor Lao was not. Ma was a perfect product of the system: his college degree was from Qinghua University, the best architecture department in the country, and from a very young age he was involved in all sorts of major government projects, from the International Club to Mao's mausoleum. From 1981 to 1983, he was sent to Japan to study with the world-renowned architect Kenzo Tange. And when I. M. Pei came to Beijing, Ma was his host. He has been through a lot and gone to a lot of places, so he knows quite well the gap, often a gulf, that lies between China and the rest of the world; he knows, too, the trapdoors and loopholes within the system at home. What do you do if you grew up in one world, have a solid career and are rooted in it, and then acquired sensibilities from other worlds? What does it mean when you talk about artistic and intellectual integrity in a situation like today's China? Ma, like a lot of Chinese architects, must know what happened to the heady Soviet art movement of the early twenties, to people like Vladimir Tatlin and Melnikov. For a short while in 1925, young Melnikov was the toast of Paris and raved about by such Western greats as Hoffmann, Le Corbusier, and Perret, but that sort of celebrity did him in back home: his career as an architect after that was limited to building a great house for himself. The house is one of the twentieth century's architectural wonders, but he was never allowed to build anything else. In light of all that, I feel I understand Ma's strategy. Some people might call it moral subterfuge or outright compromise, others might call it "working the system creatively."

Returning from Japan, from Kenzo Tange, Ma went back to Qinghua University for a Ph.D., taking courses on history and theory, and working, on and off, on his dissertation about Japanese architecture, which he eventually turned in after finishing the Olympic Center. He said it was his way of coping with the realization that architects need to be more "cultured": "You must absorb a great deal from other cultures before your imagination can spring off to create something original," Ma said. On the other hand, I read a speech he gave not long ago on Chinese urban planning; it was so full of official jargon and obfuscation I couldn't bear to finish it.

There was, then, the giant plaster panda squatting on the Olympic site. The panda, coquettishly named *Panpan* ("waiting with longing"), was the Asian Games' official emblem. Intellectuals saw it as sinister kitsch. Rumor spread that the double ring sign with a red torch that Panpan held up in her paws had a double meaning; it should really be read as "6.4—a drop of blood." June 4 is how the Chinese refer to the Tiananmen massacre. Originally, Ma had planned abstract sculptures for the site, but the officials objected that they were too Westernized and insisted on the panda. Ma's assistants were dismayed, but he cheered them up with his own interpretation: "It's not so bad," Ma told them. "In the West, designers sometimes set pop icons on a modernist site, too. With a sense of humor, you'll see a kind of postmodernist play here, because the panda creates an interesting tension with the rest of the buildings." I couldn't help chuckling over Ma's shrewd maneuver. "Take Chicago," Ma said to me. "You have Mickey Mouse and the Bulls squatting over some of the downtown buildings, don't you?" I nodded, amazed by his ready worldly knowledge.

Before leaving, I told Ma if he ever gets a chance to visit Chicago, I'd be glad to show him around town. Ma said his upcoming trip was to Barcelona. Ma in springtime Barcelona? Not in this gray Mao suit with the sleeve-guards, surely. "It'll be just beautiful!" he said dreamily, and here his thoughts skimmed again. "You know," he gazed toward the window, his voice ever so casual, "if we had cleared up the space around the Forbidden City and wrapped a two-hundred-meter-wide green belt around it, it would be quite nice. But sure," he swung right back to me, "I'll probably go to the States later this year, and I'll see if I can drop by Chicago. For modernist architecture, it's a must, isn't it?"

TWO DAYS before leaving Beijing, I had lunch with an old friend who, though his profession is researcher at a folk art institute, has embarked on a thriving career of writing stand-up comedy. As we met in front of his institute, it dawned on me that it was housed in one of the greatest Qing Dynasty mansions in Beijing—Prince Gong's Mansion. Seeing my curiosity, my friend took me in for a stroll. The estate was surprisingly well preserved: an intricate maze of courtyards, stone paths, old houses, and squat pines stood in perfect arrangements. So did the winding corridors, ornate roofs, and window lattices, their faded colors adding a quickening melancholy to their grace. This was the creation of the mandarin aristocracy in its ripest stage, its aura of majestic elegance at once grand and forbidding. But I peeked into a few rooms. A standard Chinese office scene jumped into view: cheap, cumbersome desks and chairs, heavy, Soviet-style sofas with dust covers and laced doilies, walls with brown water stains, calendars showing trite landscapes or gaudy movie stars, and—of course—those sedate figures in dour clothes sipping tea or huddling over a newspaper. The contrast between the old mansion and its inhabitants made me think of fictional occupations in a time warp, yet I knew this was an authentic mélange of cultural contradictions that are now abundant in Beijing.

As though to culminate this sense of contradiction, in the back garden we bumped into a dense mob of People's Liberation Army soldiers! Against an old temple painted in dull ochre, the dazzling mass of their bright green uniforms made me jump—and I caught a quick glimps of a movie camera! Were they shooting a movie? A commercial? Military home video?

At lunch I got sentimental and told my friend that I was going to climb up the Drum Tower for a last view of Beijing. He shook his head, but said he would come along. No need to go back to the institute anyway, since he is only required there one day a week, and half of that day is spent in "political studies." "My salary is so low it's barely enough for my four cab rides to work. I go by cab anyway because buses are so exhausting, and I've got to save the energy for my real work at home." He earns a good living by writing for television or composing ads for, say, herb pills.

Built during the thirteenth century Yuan Dynasty, the Drum Tower is the oldest major public structure surviving in Beijing. It, too, has become tourist property. There is an entrance fee, but no other visitors were in sight. The old woman behind the ticket window was dozing off. We climbed up the dank stone steps inside a dark tunnel; they were so steep I became dizzy looking over my shoulders. At the top, the stairs led into an oblong pavilion. A giant bronze drum stood in a dark corner, emanating a dull, solitary sheen. To our surprise, the rest of the pavilion was refurbished with an exhibit of old Beijing shop signs. They came in a charming variety: brilliant silk banners with embroidered names, painted boards with gold inscriptions, quaint picture signs—scissors, hats, a sesame oil bottle, a kite—each breathing a life of its own. My friend and I walked around mesmerized; it felt like walking down a memory lane in a dream.

Finally, we stepped out to the observation deck. It was not a clear day: a thin fog stitched the air like an invisible net, and Beijing lay under our eyes, a blurry mass of grayish shapes of different heights and sizes. Cars and crowds crawled slowly. Tiny figures popped in and out of crabbed lanes. At the edges of vision, clumps of tall buildings were strewn jaggedly across the horizon. Maybe when there are more of them, the city will look less naked and open; maybe the skyline will be tomorrow's city wall. The deck surrounding the pavilion is broad, and we walked slowly around it, taking in the whole city, the entire broken vista under the pale sun. Once again, there was nobody else up there. After a while, my friend turned to me and said: "You know, this is weird: this tower used to be the center of Beijing—so for a Chinese, this point under our feet used to be the center of the universe. And the drum beat at night gave people a sense of time. But now, of all the ten million people in Beijing, nobody thinks of coming up here, not even for a five-minute view." I said if it weren't for me, he himself wouldn't have come. He said: "That's just what I'm saying—and you come here because you no longer live here." It's like visiting a dead symbol, he says, and knowing it's got nothing to do with the vibrant life, which is elsewhere. "Beijing has moved on," he said. "Young people would rather go sit in those new revolving cafés or go disco dancing. Old people wouldn't come here either; the steps are too much for them and, anyway, they'd rather go to the parks to exercise. This place makes you feel old and cut off. It's just not a good feeling."

4

SHADOWS ON THE SCREEN

CHEN KAIGE'S film *Farewell My Concubine* may be Chinese cinema's greatest success, in the West, at least. It opened in the United States in the fall of 1993 to showers of critical accolades and entranced, steady audiences. The *New York Times* found it "one of those very rare film spectacles that deliver just about everything," and the *Washington Post* called it "lavish, splendorous, ornate"; the *Los Angeles Times* called it "gorgeous and intoxicating," and *Newsweek* hailed it as "a cinematic grand slam" with "the lushness of Bertolucci and the sweeping narrative confidence of an old Hollywood epic." The *San Francisco Chronicle* described it as a "breakthrough," an "intricately beautiful film" in the school of *Gone With the Wind* and *Doctor Zhivago*. In New York, Madonna stopped by a party for Chen to tell him how much she liked it.

Amid all these hosannas from the West, Chinese officialdom has been gritting its teeth, more perturbed than pleased by the situation. Like many apparently inward cultures, China has an almost paradoxical craving for the laurels of external validation. Yet Chen's movie has been banned there, albeit temporarily, and it is even held partially responsible for a chill in Chinese media circles. After Chen was called to the minister of propaganda for a long chat, he dropped two politically sensitive projects he was considering for his next film—including one about the harrowing experiences of a prisoner during the Cultural Revolution—and settled for a love story safely set in precommunist China. Meanwhile, his producers and distributors in Hong Kong and United States are hoping to get *Farewell* into the Oscar competition as a Hong Kong entry.

"I'm disturbed by the way Chinese cinema is growing fashionable in the West," a French woman active in the film industry recently told me. She has long been an enthusiastic promoter of new Chinese cinema, but she now worries about its cooptation by Hollywood and the Western mainstream. To her and many others in China, the uneven fortunes of *Farewell* are emblematic of Chinese cinema's dilemmas as it approaches maturity. And at the center of all this ferment, buffeted between Western approbation and Chinese disapproval, is Chen Kaige himself, the tortured, brilliant, and charismatic creator of *Farewell*.

For Chen, the turning point really came at Cannes. On May 24, 1993, after days of rumors, whispers, and hand-wringing suspense, the official announcement was made: *Farewell My Concubine*, his three-hour epic about love and death at the Beijing Opera, had been awarded the top prize at the festival, the Palme d'Or. Since Jane Campion, director of *The Piano*, the co-winner, was seven months pregnant and had returned to Australia the previous Friday, the glory and glamour of the moment fell upon Chen Kaige alone. It was an evening of paparazzi, floral bouquets, and a black-tie champagne party. The next day, the *New York Times* showed a beaming Chen in a dinner jacket, one hand clutching his trophy, the other flashing a V sign.

It was a most uncharacteristic pose for those who knew him, but Chen had every reason in the world to relish the moment. He had earned a place in the history books alongside other film luminaries; and the honor would undoubtedly help at the boxoffice inside and outside China. He was *minglishuangshou*, as Chinese would say, "reaping fame and fortune." And something else, too—vindication.

Given his public tact and reserve, Chen was hardly inclined to allude to professional rivalry, but anybody who knew anything about Chinese cinema would know two things: that the celebrated filmmaker Zhang Yimou had started out as Chen's cinematographer, and that ever since they split up, Zhang had been on a winning streak and Chen on a losing one.

It was Chen who left the starting gate first, Chen whose *Yellow Earth* heralded the arrival in 1984 of China's acclaimed Fifth Generation, those filmmakers who came of age after Mao. Yet, for several years now, Zhang was the Chinese name that appeared at every international film festival and on every awards list—Zhang who had received two Oscar nominations (for *Ju Dou* and *Raise the Red Lantern*) and a glittering assortment of other international prizes.

Indeed, virtually every one of Zhang's works has collected some notable award or other. And when he accepted a leading role in Wu Tianming's *Old Well*—his first acting gig—the Tokyo Film Festival gave him the Best Actor award too. There seemed to be nothing the man couldn't do; the Chinese popular press was mesmerized by his accomplishments. He was regularly depicted as an elemental force of Chinese creativity: a genius, maestro, wizard, demiurge . . . a meteor blazing its way across our skies. Later, he was humorously given the nickname *dejiangzhuanyehu*, or "the awards expert"—a pun on a Chinese expression for the peasant entrepreneur who gets rich by a single trade, as in "the rabbit-raising expert." Adding to his mystique, his relationship with the beautiful Gong Li, the star of all his movies, has long been a hot item in China's gossipy tabloids—which have also been serializing a sordidly detailed account of the affair written by Zhang's estranged wife. There was no avoiding the glamorous pair on magazine covers: Gong Li, pale and delicate, standing beside Zhang Yimou, tense, scrubby, brooding. The public couldn't get enough of them.

Meanwhile, Chen Kaige, once hailed as a leader of a renaissance in Chinese filmmaking in the eighties, was making flop after flop, earning the rather dubious title of *zhelidaoyan*, "the philosophical director"—in other words, the sort of director whose highbrow films no one wants much to see. Naturally, Chen's attitude toward his former colleague's brilliant career was a subject of intense interest and speculation. A much-discussed profile of Zhang in Shanghai's equivalent of *Esquire* reported that Chen once went to the toilet with a newspaper article announcing a major prize Zhang Yimou had just won, and emerged almost an hour later, cursing, "He's a fucking cameraman, *my* cameraman!"

But hadn't everything now been set right? After all, it would be hard to overstate the cachet of the Palme d'Or among Chinese filmmakers, for whom the award is the ultimate symbol of international recognition. (That no Chinese writer has ever been judged worthy of the Nobel Prize is seen, by China's litterateurs and apparatchiks alike, as a standing reproach.) What made Chen's eventual triumph all the sweeter was the fact that Cannes had been the site of his previous humiliation. Before *Farewell*, Chen had two of his movies shown here. The first visit, in 1988, ended in disaster. Chen brought *King of Children*, a ponderous if beautifully shot film about a young teacher in a small village, which he then considered his best work. He had his eyes on the Golden Palm, but he got the "Golden Alarm Clock" instead—for "the most boring picture of the year." Although for the tired critics and reporters the award was just a silly joke, it was no fun for Chen, who was already facing trouble back home for making strenuously experimental movies that were losing both money and audiences.

In 1991, after two years of tough fund-raising in America and grueling production circumstances in China, Chen returned to Cannes with *Life on a String*, a movie about a saintly, blind musician. Once again, the audience response was lukewarm and the reviews terrible. To make things worse, for obscure reasons the movie failed to pass the Chinese censors and was never released in China. One supportive film critic from Beijing had been following Chen's experiences in Cannes with growing apprehension. After the Golden Alarm Clock episode, the critic shook his head: "Chen's got one more movie to go." After *Life on a String*, the critic sighed softly: "It doesn't look good. I hope they'll give him another chance, just one more." He knew Chen's career was hanging on a thread. And it wasn't just Chen's career either, since film-making wasn't just his livelihood—it was his life. Chen's hair soon began to turn white.

CHEN'S UPBRINGING may have steeled him for defeat, but it hadn't led him to expect it. Long before he took his place at the head of the Fifth Generation, long before *Farewell* struck gold at Cannes, Chen had struck people as a golden boy. He was born in 1952 in Beijing to artistic parents, his father a well-known film director, his mother an actress and film editor. Since his father, whom he would later describe as the classically sober, aloof Chinese patriarch, was often away on film locations, Chen and his sister were left in the care of two loving women: Chen's mother and a Manchu nanny who lived with the family. In the relative tranquillity of pre–Cultural Revolution Beijing, Chen recalls a childhood spent wandering through charming, old neighborhoods, lolling by flower and goldfish vendors' carts, and playing games by the local swimming pool with kindergarten friends. The family lived in an elegant, walled-in compound, once the mansion of a Manchu prince in the early Qing Dynasty, where Chen's mother, dressed in silk pajamas, would settle into a bamboo lounge chair in the courtyard and teach her young son to recite classical poems selected to complement the changing seasons. "Beijing was then like the reflection of the turrets in the city moat," he would write in his memoirs, "a serene dream in a breeze, swaying yet unbroken."

The nanny had come from a noble Manchu family that used to be in charge of supplying flowers for ceremonial use in the Qing court, though she herself had spent her adulthood in the republican era earning a living by hand. Chen was fascinated by her past; the dignity and decency with which she had risen above her family misfortune left a deep impression on him. At thirteen, Chen went to the finest boys' middle school in Beijing, where the classrooms were filled with the sons of top Party leaders, before whom the future of the country seemed to lie.

With such a background, Chen seemed destined to shine in the worlds of the arts. Certainly, there was an air about the young man: he had thick, jet-black hair, which he always brushed back neatly, and would fix his companions with an intense stare as if he were studying the inner workings of their minds. In a crowd, he maintained his natural reserve; but in more intimate settings, he often impressed friends with the Tang Dynasty poems that tripped off his tongue. He was a trim six feet tall, wore good clothes, smoked expensive cigarettes with flair, and spoke with an elegant Beijing accent sprinkled with well-chosen classical phrases—all of which set him apart from the multitude.

Still, perhaps his features were almost too clean, too neatly chiseled to be associated with a head full of deep thoughts. Perhaps there was too much of a matinee-idol look about Chen, whose face suggested a manicured young Toshiro Mifune. In the mid-eighties, Chen decided to sport a beard, complete with mustache and sideburns. The shrubbery made him look more bohemian, but also lent him a certain regal dignity. Indeed, some commented that on the set Chen both looked and acted like an emperor. Nor did it escape notice when the bearded look spread among young Beijing film types, especially young directors, who would bound around town in faded jeans and baseball caps, turning people on and off like electric switches. Of course, none could quite carry it off as well as Chen—without the height and sleek good looks, the beards tended to look slovenly, accentuating any incipient pudginess.

Zhang Yimou, too, would become an icon, but he would never be a style-maker in the same sort of way. In some obvious respects, Zhang and Chen made a classic odd couple, yin and yang: whatever Chen was, Zhang was not. Raised in a provincial town far north of the capital, Zhang, with his crew cut and short, stocky build, looks like an average village farm boy. In fact, his mother was a dermatologist, but his father was largely unemployed because he had been an officer in the Kuomintang Nationalist army, fighting on the "wrong side"; and Zhang grew up in the shadow of his father's political stigma. Years of tough labor on a farm and in a cotton mill have left marks both on his countenance and his character. He has the sort of face that can startle you when you begin to look at it closely. When he shuts his mouth, his cheeks cave in so abruptly, so deeply, it evokes the old Chinese expression *tiantadixian*, "the heaven collapses and the earth caves in." There's something resolutely somber, even saturnine, about him. He doesn't talk to people unless he has to, and then he seldom enjoys talking unless it's about movies or the film industry.

In his student days, he used to drag his schoolmates into serving as models for his photography; it was his only hobby, and, of course, the one he would turn into his profession. People often see him as a sort of countrified savant: it's as if he might have devoted his genius to producing big, beautiful tomatoes, but he just happens to make big, beautiful movies instead. Even after his phenomenal success, he still knocks around in plain jeans and plain, unstylish shirts. He insists—either with pride or modesty, it's hard to tell—that he doesn't know a word of English. With peasant robustness, he doesn't mind eating noodles all the time. And by now it's a well-known story in China that he sold his blood to buy his first camera.

Conflicting reports abound about Zhang. Of those who have worked for him, some describe a genuine man of the people, a director who never throws a fit, who does everything together with his crew, including roughing it in backwater locations and digging ditches for a set; others describe a slave driver. Everybody agrees that he's a workaholic, but that's because he's got too many *jins* of creative oil to burn. Once I was sitting with a boisterous roomful of Zhang's crew members. They were puffing on cigarettes, enjoying the videotapes they shot of three potential movie locations, and joking about how one of them had gone off to chase a big-bottomed country belle into the haystack with his camera. Zhang walked in, his eyes lowered in a pensive moment: the room went absolutely silent. What he has isn't charisma, exactly, but gravitas. The next minute, everyone was deep into a debate about some technical problem. Zhang was very precise, very thorough; he encourages discussion but is always in control. Then came time to choose locations. Two minutes into viewing, long before the haystack scene, Zhang killed the tape: "OK, next one. I don't think this place looks right." The cameraman looked relieved: he knew Zhang wouldn't have been amused when the videocam left the gorgeous location to set off after the gorgeous girl.

IF ZHANG has the gravity of a dark, collapsed star, then the suave, articulate Chen Kaige is commanding in another way. Born a Mandarin and schooled for command, Chen is one of those whose specialness has never been in doubt, who gains authority simply by taking it for granted. He takes seriously, maybe too seriously, the responsibilities that come with power and privilege, since he takes his achievements to be the achievements of his culture. Even back at the film school, Chen had a reputation for erudition and eloquence, someone given to reading hard books and discussing large issues. On the basketball court, he played the lead, getting all the attention while Zhang Yimou, as a backup, shuffled along the sidelines, waiting silently for his turn.

For all their differences in personality and family background, however, the two classmates shared something important: the Cultural Revolution. More than anything else, this was what prevented Chen from becoming a spoiled urban dandy forever sheltered from real hardship and pain. Those were formative years for him, so much so that in 1989 he wrote a soul-searching memoir entitled, rather self-consciously, *The Young Kaige*. (Since Kaige in Chinese means "song of victory," the title can also be read as "Victory Songs of Youth.") In its way, it's a gem: sensitive, lyrical, bristling with insights.

Chen's characteristic grand gestures are there ("To know myself is to know the world," Chen announces in the preface), but it transcends the platitudes through its intensely felt descriptions of his harrowing experiences.

The Cultural Revolution meant that, in adolescence, Chen would witness his parents' political downfall, a reversal of fortune that culminated in a mass "denunciation rally" where Chen shoved and yelled at his father. It meant watching his Red Guard classmates ransack his house and burn the family books. Chen's memoirs render both incidents in meticulous detail, with a deep sense of guilt and sorrow. Equally moving is Chen's description of the moment of his Manchu nanny's departure. When she strokes Chen's hand and tells him that she has been through it all before, that this is not the first time something like this had happened—for even emperors had burned books—the passage displays the laconic beauty of Chen's prose at its best and most poignant.

Although Chen has never made a autobiographical film in the manner of, say, François Truffaut or Louis Malle, shadows of his experiences in the Cultural Revolution do fall upon his oeuvre. Certainly, this is the case with *King of Children*, an allegory of the cultural confinements of the Maoist epoch. A more trenchant example, though, is his *Big Parade*, the only film Chen himself openly admits to be a failure ("not perfect," in his own words). The film tells of how the ruthless training for an honor-bound National Day military parade threatens to turn a platoon of People's Liberation Army soldiers into brutal automatons. It's a powerful but by no means original vision, certainly not after Stanley Kubrick's *Full Metal Jacket,* for instance. But for those who know him, the film is inescapably bound up with Chen's own experience as an infantryman.

Another consequence of the Cultural Revolution for Chen was that, after middle school, he was sent to a forest range in the remote south. There he was inducted into the regional army on the merit of his height and basketball skills, and served five years before returning to Beijing. Sometime in the seventies, he told me, his unit was sent to clamp down on a minority uprising in the south, where a whole town of armed rebels had taken to underground tunnels. In the midst of bloody fighting, a soldier from Chen's brigade disappeared. On the final day of the operation, just when his comrades had given him up for dead, the missing soldier suddenly emerged with his bayonet. His eyes were glazed, his face gaunt. Before the comrades could embrace him, he began to empty out all the pockets of his tattered, blood-stained uniform . . . leaving a small pile on the ground of severed human ears.

The soldier then told his comrades of how he got lost in the tunnels, and how, during the ensuing days, he butchered one after another of the rebels he encountered in the dark, making sure to save their ears for the body count. "The young man fairly gloated at the prospect of having his chest covered with medals and military honors," Chen told me with a shudder. His lingering sense of horror seemed to find cinematic expression in *The Big Parade*.

IN A larger sense, the very mission of the Fifth Generation was an act of rebellion against the artistic strictures of Maoism. Indeed, whatever their individual merits, all the films made by these directors would have been unthinkable just a few years earlier. Under the four decades of communist rule, Chinese cinema often seemed to be one long reel of propaganda. My generation of Chinese grew up with about two dozen revolutionary war movies: half of them local products, the other half imported from brother socialist countries—the Soviet Union, North Korea, Albania. As a teenager, I saw *Lenin in October* about ten times, and could recite half the lines from *Heroic Sons and Daughters*, a Chinese movie about the Korean War. Not until 1978, in my freshman year at Beijing University, did I see a film that offered no socialist uplift: it was an Indian movie, a romantic tearjerker that, for the first time, had us all crying profusely over something other than a revolution.

That was the year when the cultural thaw had begun. The Cultural Revolution officially ended in 1976, the year Mao died and a coup d'etat led to the arrest of the Gang of Four. Just two years later—with the return to power of Deng Xiaoping and the watershed Third Plenum of the Eleventh Party Conference, which called for "emancipating the mind"—political and cultural liberalization was underway. The ensuing years of the late seventies and early eighties were dubbed by some the "Beijing spring": outside of official control, poetry magazines and art exhibits flourished—there was even a new genre of fiction known as "scar literature," which dealt with the atrocities of the Cultural Revolution. By the mid-eighties, China's artists and intellectuals were caught up in something called the "culture craze," in which the concept of culture, rather than ideology or politics, became the focus of talk about China's distinctive history and heritage.

Surveying the successive classes of students who graduated from the Beijing Film Academy since it was founded in 1956, scholars have listed a total of four generations of Chinese filmmakers up to 1980. The Fourth Generation included middle-aged directors emerging around 1980, whose works began to move away from the constraints of ideology. But the real departure in cinematic style came when Chen and his classmates from the academy burst onto the scene. The rise of this Fifth Generation coincided with the culture craze and reflected its general preoccupation with the true meaning of Chinese history and culture.

This preference for the grand gesture and concern with the big picture was also the result of the course of study they had gone through. Back then, in 1978–82, they had mostly watched and admired Western European films. (Chen himself has confessed that he didn't care much for Hollywood movies.) So, from the dusty back alley of China's post–Cultural Revolution wasteland, they had peered into the glorious days of the high modernist European masters: François Truffaut, Jean-Luc Godard, Ingmar Bergman, Michelangelo Antonioni, Bernardo Bertolucci. Sergei Eisenstein and Akira Kurosawa were up there too, though less central, as were a few Chinese efforts from the thirties and forties. It wasn't a broad vision of twentieth-century cinema, and there was no such thing as a well-rounded education in contemporary China; but in those hopeful years when China had just reopened to the world, these students were the country's best and brightest. Armed with new equipment and heads full of the innovative techniques, they shared a fervent desire to reinvent Chinese cinema.

As soon as Chen landed his first project, he hired Zhang, who had majored in cinematography, as his director of photography. Chen, with his effortless sense of entitlement, was the natural leader of the pack, but he had early recognized the extraordinary abilities of his darker, more tightly wound classmate; for all their differences in temperament, talent would bond with talent. Fusing their ambitions, the two worked closely together on *Yellow Earth,* gripped with the excitement felt by people doing something that simply hasn't been done before.

Besides, it was almost a dare. In the rigid Chinese studio system, they were considered far too young to be entering the game at this advanced level, which meant they were playing every moment to win. "It was like first love," Chen later remarked. "We were all so passionate." Zhang would recall that Chen talked incessantly over their long journey to northern Shanxxi, where the film was shot. Chen was fired up with ideas, thoughts, reflections, all quite grand and philosophical. "I just listened," Zhang later told one of his crew members, grinning. "Frankly, half the time I didn't understand a thing."

The film had a minimal story line: a communist "art worker" goes to a poor village to collect folk songs. What made the film a breakthrough was its captivating visual imagination, the way it made the natural landscape— earth, mountains, river—look alive, even sensual. (Dwarfed by the vast scale, the human subjects sometimes seem little more than stage props.) The film inspired enthusiastic reviews in Europe and fervent debates at home. It was a work that made many in the West sit up and take notice: reviewers were amazed that this level of cinematic sophistication existed in China. Back home, most people didn't know quite what to make of it: the old guard saw something like a *monstre sacre* in its formative stage; the intellectual elite saw a monument of contemporary art. In its way, *Yellow Earth* became an instant classic, collecting prizes in London and Hawaii—and even one for cinematography in Beijing. It was to be the curtain raiser for China's new cinema.

A string of Fifth Generation films followed, and new luminaries of filmmaking were heralded: Tian Zhuangzhuang, Zhang Junzhao, Zhang Yimou . . . all from the same school, indeed, the same class, with Chen Kaige leading the glittering parade. To follow their work was to watch a group of eager, audacious young men playing with lenses, lights, film stocks, and filters, and discovering the cinematic pleasures of spectacle. If some of their films betrayed a hint of amateurishness, if many of them lacked absorbing drama, all of them *looked* gorgeous: such vibrant colors, such artful composition! And the youthful passion and seriousness of purpose with which they approached their weighty themes were quite touching, even when not entirely engaging. Even their detractors had to admit that they were a refreshing change from the drab vistas and stale formulas of "revolutionary" cinema.

Meanwhile the artistic elite, basking in an increasingly open political environment, was growing impatient for outside recognition. "Go to the world!" was the slogan of the day, which generally meant also that the world should come to China and embrace its best—to wit, those artists and intellectuals who were promoting the slogan. In those days in China, when hundreds of thousands of people had taken to reading underground poetry, serious fiction, *qianwei* (a literal rendering of "avant-garde") represented not just arthouse fare restricted to a small elite but a counterculture with cachet: vangardism, yes, but with something of a popular following. This was when the buzz had grown to such a point that some Europeans were predicting a sort of cinematic yellow peril. By 1988, the Rotterdam Film Festival had included Chen Kaige on a list of "twenty directors of the future." As one rapturous Beijing film critic pointed out, the great Godard was on the same list, and his name came *after* Chen's.

CHEN'S RELATIONSHIP with Zhang Yimou changed irrevocably when Zhang made his debut as a director in 1987 with the film *Red Sorghum*. Few in China realized its implications at the time. Only much later did critics come to see that *Red Sorghum* was the film that, in a way, sounded the death knell of the Fifth Generation. It was still an art film, but it left the back door open a crack, and a star crept in: Gong Li. Her bold gait and her barely contained sexuality set her apart: she didn't swallow her sobs, she screamed and sang at the top of her lungs as she tumbled into the fire island of a sorghum field and made it with a man she hardly knew. Sex had finally come to "serious" Chinese cinema.

Next to Zhang's own debut work, the pallid suggestion of erotic tension in *Yellow Earth* seemed almost effete. From that point on, Zhang applied his ravishing cinematography to his favorite set of themes: sex, lies, and violence. And power, of course, power always, at the center of everything: the male hierarchy, the old men squatting in shadowy corners, certain that the last laugh will be theirs. Zhang painted his splendid colors across the screen and brought his camera to exotic locales, lingering on silky and supple figures. Moreover, being a good, conventional dramatist, Zhang never let his story line slacken. In China, Chen's *Yellow Earth* had inspired critical accolades and admiration; Zhang's *Red Sorghum* was filling theaters.

Nor had Chen, now working without Zhang, been able to follow up on his early success: *King of Children* sank like a stone. Despite the uncertainties of his directorial career, though, Chen managed to retain his prestige as a symbol and spokesman in the heyday of the culture craze. So it was, with his well-groomed beard, black tie, and white shirt starched stiff, that Chen contemplated the world from the cover of *Eastern Chronicle,* a swanky magazine for the Beijing elite. The portrait, framed in a border of deep black, suggested an old edition of *GQ*—until you read the caption inside, which came from Chen's notebook: "If culture can be seen as a rolling snowball, before you find out what this snowball really is, you say: 'Look! How big is our snowball!' That kind of pride is very blind. Only when you know clearly what the culture you carry on your back is and what you want to do with it, do you have the right to say that you are truly a man of culture."

Chen's lofty sentiments were heartfelt, and entirely in keeping with the mood of the moment. This was early 1989. The culture craze was now in full swing, and the oft-repeated imperative to "think big" was giving many people headaches. Everyone who considered him- or herself an intellectual—which in China basically comes down to everyone with a college diploma—was darkly introspective or trying to be, asking the big questions of the day: What is culture, what is our duty to civilization, and what must we do about this great sinking, rotting ship of ours called the Chinese nation? By then, Chen Kaige had left for America, but because of his ambitious films and his international reputation as the maker of *Yellow Earth,* the media still considered him to have an iconic stature equal to the sacred mission China's elite had taken upon itself.

A few months later, that mission collapsed at Tiananmen Square.

By the time I saw Chen again in the autumn of 1989, in Manhattan, he had lost his beard, and some of his aura of command. Then in his second year as a visiting fellow at New York University's film school, he had taken to wearing polo shirts and dark jackets; while he retained that touch of fastidiousness, almost primness, on the whole he looked like just another well-dressed foreigner in town. I'd last seen him a year earlier, and we had talked about his future projects and a screenplay I was asked to adapt from one of my novellas, which Zhang Nuanxin, a director and one of Chen's teachers at the Beijing Film Academy, was trying to make into a movie. Things had looked endlessly promising, for Chen and for the larger arts scene in China. Yet, one year later, as we sat eating jerk chicken and a vaguely exotic island salad in a Jamaican restaurant decorated like a giant jukebox, there was a feeling of life having come full circle. For our generation of writers and artists, the past few years had been a time of pressure and hectic glamour, of ferment and enormous possibility; it was a time to smash forms and formulas, to be at the center of something larger than ourselves. Now the feeling had passed.

When the bill came and Chen hastened to pull out his American Express card, all seemed—at least to me—to dwindle into comfortable ordinariness. We were just another pair of expats with plastic.

BUT CHEN was taking in America. Ensconced in a cozy Upper West Side apartment overlooking Central Park, Chen and his wife Hong Huang, who worked for a German company in New York, appeared to have found, or created, a mini yuppie heaven. Elegant art books, copies of *Vogue*, various upscale mail-order fashion catalogues were strewn about their living room. Guests of different colors, nationalities, and accents flocked in and out; long rows of elegant shoes lined their doorway—Hong Huang joked that Chen was developing a shoe fetish. Chen spoke half-apologetically about his own fascination with television commercials: "So many interesting shots." He was doing some work, too, shooting a rock video for the rock group Duran Duran as well as a short film called *A Maoist in New York*. His English was improving quickly, and he'd even gotten his immigration papers more or less in order.

He and Hong Huang hosted small parties late into the night: there was always music and wine, sometimes dancing by candlelight, the flames flickering through red glass, long shadows twisting ghostlike on the walls. The atmosphere was heavy with the resinous fragrance of smoke and a vague awareness of a new sensibility being tried out, a new phase being experienced. On summer nights, the windows would be opened to let in fresh air as hosts and guests would sit or lie on the carpeted floor in hushed silence, gazing at the moon over Central Park. There were times when the air shimmered with a certain self-conscious sensuality, and when the unreality of it all, the novelty, brought its own sense of transport.

Film seldom entered conversations. Only much later did I hear of the money problems: fund-raising in Europe and America for an avant-garde Chinese director was no easy task. What I remember most, though, was Chen's emerging obsession with royalty and aristocracy. The only time I heard filmmaking mentioned was after he told his favorite story about the fall of the last emperor of the Ming Dynasty, Chongzhin, and his futile effort to fend off the peasant rebels and the Manchu invaders. Chen is a gifted story-teller, with an eye for quirky details and tragic grandeur: "His majesty was galloping on a white horse, alone, back and forth across the besieged capital, trying desperately to mobilize his subjects to fight with him against the barbarous invaders . . . only to find white flags going up from the court behind him, and smoke billowing everywhere."

Chen's hand occasionally slashed the air, as if he were cracking a whip at a horse he was riding. "You see, the ministers had betrayed him, petty thieves had broken into the palaces and set up fires and pots to melt down the gold from the national treasures they had stolen." Oh, the treachery, the cowardice, the greed of the commoners! This was just the sort of epic tragedy that Chen Kaige was born to paint across the big screen. "Emperor Chongzhin was a cultivated man, a wise ruler, but in the end he had to hang himself on a tree over Coal Hill." Chen shook his head at the injustice of it all. In time, of course, the peasant rebels would cede the power to the Manchu invaders, who would civilize themselves, establish themselves as another aristocracy, and their rule—that of the Qing Dynasty—would survive until the 1911 republican revolution. "One day, when I have a lot of money," he said in a dreamy voice, "I will make it all into a big picture."

Chen came alive at these moments. On the other side of the world from Beijing, he told his fabulous tales about dead emperors, showed me the fat books he was poring over, on European and Chinese monarchies, and talked a good deal about the noble Manchu blood in his own veins. The first time he met my husband, who also happens to have some Manchu ancestry, Chen managed to spend half the dinner conversation on the question of Manchu nobility. This invited merciless ribbing from his wife, who had a sly, funky sense of humor: "Being from the gutter," said Hong—granddaughter of an eminent Mandarin scholar whom Mao held in high esteem, and daughter of Mao's translator—"I guess I married up." But Chen pressed on with childlike oblivion: the subject was simply too important, too delicious for him to be derailed by her wry asides. That dinner was the last time I saw Chen Kaige before he returned to China to shoot *Life on a String.*

F O R A film that opened in only a few theaters, *Life on a String* received an inordinate amount of badmouthing among Chinese intellectuals around the world; this signified, among other things, Chen's stature in their eyes. Everybody who had seen it—and some who had only heard it described—wanted to testify to how unbearable it all was. There was held to be something ridiculous about Chen's attempt to turn his central character, a blind folk musician, into a savior of the universe by seating him on a mountain peak and having him sing to fighting clans. The idea was that the saint's style of singing (which someone memorably described as a cross between Cat Stevens and Beethoven) so moved the Chinese peasants that they lay down their spades and petty squabbles. The audiences, on the other hand, were not so moved: the consensus was that Chen's grandiose romanticism and lecture-mongering had gotten so out of hand here that he would become a butt of universal mockery. The standard joke about the film was a pun on its Chinese title, which meant "sing as you walk"; it was now rhymed with "snooze as you watch." Even Chen's admirers among the critical elite covered their eyes.

Soon, though, most intellectuals would contend with far weightier matters concerning the sweeping changes taking place in Chinese society. Three years after Tiananmen, the atmosphere in Beijing had gone from quiet gloom to resigned normalcy and then, by 1992, to a din of activity. Under the cloud of political dishonor, the Chinese gross national product had continued its rapid climb; the economy, as if pulled by a runaway train, was accelerating toward private sector prosperity. Nor was the cultural realm unaffected by these changes: ideological education was out, elite sentiments ignored, and ordinary people were clamoring for cultural goods long overdue—soft rock, kung fu videos, sitcoms and variety shows, tabloid newspapers, and karaoke bars. The government was pleased to acquiesce: if political liberties were still sharply curtailed, and if many in the educated classes were hopelessly disaffected, why not placate the masses with nightlife and other harmless diversions? Most of the trends and many of the goods had been imported from Pacific rim neighbors—principally Hong Kong and Taiwan, where the market was mature, the packaging slicker. Still, local pop artists were quickly getting the hang of it all—and they'd better, for in the hurried pursuit of money and merrier lifestyles, Deng's subjects were losing the stoic patience Mao's subjects once displayed.

This was also the time in which the state film industry crumpled like the proverbial paper tiger. When Chen and his colleagues started their careers, money was not something to be worried about. Their films, made with extravagant sets, often in remote locations, were solidly backed by the official studios, however unsuccessful they were financially. The situation could not last. Trapped in a vicious cycle of bad films, bad politics, and bad management, the big studios were going bankrupt in all but name. By the time the state monopoly started to loosen its grip over film markets, the audience for local movies had dropped off. The question "Who is your favorite movie star?" was most likely to elicit names like Sylvester Stallone or Nastassia Kinski. True, *Rambo* had been a national hit as early as the mid-eighties, but because new Western blockbusters were too costly to import, Hong Kong horror flicks and martial art schlock dominated moviegoers' fantasies, with cops and bandits zooming across wide screens, leaving trails of carnage and destruction — buildings demolished, corpses piled high, audiences in a stupor of excitement, and local filmmakers in a daze. Responding to an apparently insatiable appetite for such fare, local theaters expanded their offerings: many now opened video projection rooms, cafés with cable TV, special all-night shows with box seats for lovers — all in-house designs featuring the latest releases from Hong Kong. On those occasions when only mainland-made movies were available, some exhibitors took to shutting down the theater completely, since they could only expect to lose money.

Caught in a state of institutional disarray, mainland filmmakers scrambled to cope on their own, reeling in coproductions in which foreign donors or production companies typically provided most of the budget and assumed de facto control of the production and of distribution outside China. Worst hit was the generation of filmmakers who came after Chen and Zhang. By that time the state bank was depleted, but whereas the big names of the Fifth Generation had earned enough of a reputation to secure foreign funds, the new crop of upstarts were left to struggle in their shadow with little state support. Even for established names, the situation added new pressures to win international prizes: on top of what they did for the national psyche, they provided calculable marketing advantages, a seal of commercial viability.

Chen Kaige didn't like what he saw. Later, he denounced it openly as an era of hopeless cultural decline, when idealism was mocked, refinement and elegance shoved aside, and vulgarity reigned supreme. Feeling cut off, he made it clear that it was an era to which he himself did not care to belong. The three years in New York had robbed him of his earlier self-assurance, along with some of the old camaraderie. "I'm in a pretty difficult position," he admitted at the time, in a dejected voice. "Sometimes I feel pretty helpless . . . I don't know who I could talk to in China." Approaching forty, Chen felt like an old soul. It must have been a hard time for him, his friends murmured: while nursing his wounds over yet another flop, and while dealing with larger disappointments about China's shifting cultural compass, he had to watch Zhang Yimou's skyrocketing ascent to international fame, accompanied by the boisterous touting of the popular Chinese media. With official censorship (*Ju Do* and *Raise the Red Lantern* were initially banned in China, though both have since become available) and sexual scandal only providing an extra frisson, Zhang was emerging as one of China's first superstars on the international scene. And Chen, some feared, was slowly disappearing into the man's deepening shadow.

It was in this fraught cultural moment that fierce debates broke out, mostly within Chinese intellectual circles in and outside the mainland, over the meaning of Zhang's popular success. Did he owe his popularity to the shrewd marketing of Oriental exotica to the West? His films seemed so far removed from the lived experiences of contemporary China, yet were adorned with so many foreign prizes, that some suspected they were made precisely with that aim in mind. Thus the prominent dissident journalist Dai Qing, in a seething article on *Raise the Red Lantern*, cited one by one the movie's "grating inauthenticities" in its depiction of ritual customs, and concluded that "this kind of film is really shot for the casual pleasures of foreigners." She called on the Chinese audiences not to "close their eyes" to Zhang's artistic dishonesty "just because they dislike the hard-liners in Beijing."

It was a drastic turnabout: soon the entire cinematic avant-garde was under attack. All these years the Fifth Generation had been sent out to conquer the world, to plant Chinese flags all over the cinematic map—and now, suddenly, they were getting hit from behind. To make matters worse, it came mostly from their old cheerleaders, the very critics who had once defended them from their enemies at home. *Today*, the Chinese exile magazine that had been the most famous underground avant-garde magazine in Beijing a decade before, launched the offensive in 1992 with a special volume on the new Chinese cinema filled with scathing essays on its aesthetic and moral failures. Others in the critical elite soon followed suit. The Fifth Generation, once heralded as brilliant enfants terribles, were now to be unmasked as a group of overrated, callow, and pretentious self-promoters.

The charge of inauthenticity was just for openers. Chen Kaige, whose name was identified with the rise of the Fifth Generation, was a prime target. His films, it was determined, portrayed the peasantry in a way that was both overly romanticized and essentially exploitative; his movies were sexist, narcissistic, and sentimental; they exhibited a bad case of academic symbol-saturation; they were ponderous, heavy-handed, overly intellectualized, and laden with the ideas of a half-baked philosopher. Chen himself, they agreed, had lost his head over a few condescending compliments from the Great White World.

Indeed, while Zhang Yimou took his share of blows, it was Chen Kaige who, after seven lean years, somehow made the better punching bag. Some now recalled that what was so very impressive about Chen's first two features, *Yellow Earth* and *The Big Parade*, was Zhang's camera work; take away Zhang's contribution, they argued, and you'd be mostly impressed by their flaws. Wasn't that indeed the case with Chen's movies since Zhang's departure?

It was an accusation that could not but draw blood. In truth, the two filmmakers had always been linked more by circumstances than by shared style or sensibility. Zhang has always been outcome-oriented, and he makes no apologies for being mindful of his audience. Chen has been more self-involved, charting thematic diagrams of his own metaphysical angst. When Western film people ask Zhang which Western master has influenced him the most, he likes to talk to them about Fei Mu, one of the few great Chinese filmmakers from the thirties and a total unknown to the rest of the world. Chen, on the other hand, never hesitated to speak of his admiration for the cinema of European modernism. Both Zhang and Chen have a penchant for allegory, but within that mode, Chen was a romantic, Zhang a realist. Chen liked to ponder ideas; Zhang was a craftsman with little patience for philosophizing. Zhang kept his distance, at least on the surface, from present-day China; Chen insisted on contemporary settings for his films. Even aside from the obvious contrasts in temperament and background, it was hard to imagine two more distinct approaches to filmmaking.

Until, in a curious way, Chen and Zhang traded places. Certainly, Zhang surprised his audience this year with *The Story of Qiu Ju*. Using concealed cameras and documentary techniques, *The Story of Qiu Ju* is the first of Zhang's films to be set in contemporary China, its rural setting rendered with exacting verisimilitude. "Pageantry," as a disappointed American reviewer pointed out, "has dwindled into rote." But most other reviewers admired Zhang's brave stylistic departure and were taken with the film's attempt to tackle the intricate issue of justice in today's China. With this decidedly unexotic portrait of China, Zhang has even regained a measure of respect from China's elite, who applauded the appearance of the "genuine" Zhang. (Of course, the average Chinese moviegoer found all this business of noodle-slurping and dialect-mumbling a genuine nuisance. What's the point of keeping Gong Li wrapped up in all those drab layers, they wondered? And before the point became clear, they'd lost patience and sauntered out of the theater.)

AT THE same time, Chen was heading off in the opposite direction, back into the glorious past of the Beijing Opera. *Farewell My Concubine* starts in the twenties, detailing life in a Beijing Opera training school. It progresses through the next two decades at a leisurely pace, and races through the Cultural Revolution in the final episodes. Nobody knew exactly how Chen negotiated financing with the powerful Hong Kong producer Hsu Feng. A former movie star herself, Madame Hsu is married to a businessman who owns concerns in both Taiwan and Hong Kong. They are just the kind of high-profile investors that the mainland government, with its policy of economic pragmatism, is currently eager to court. Madame Hsu made it quite clear that she was banking on Chen, "a major mainland director," with the intention of securing a major international prize, as well as major boxoffice success. After Hsu approached Chen about adapting *Farewell My Concubine*, a not-so-major novel by the Hong Kong author Lilian Lee, he remained undecided about the project for a long time. (According to one report, Zhang had also been offered the property and passed on it.)

When Chen finally said yes, the one thing he made publicly clear was that he wanted to add a section about the Cultural Revolution, without which he found the narrative lacking in weight. From that point on, the project rolled into high gear: Lee handed in a first draft, and Chen set about rewriting it with Lu Wei, a script writer from the Xian Film Studio (who has since helped adapt a novel for Zhang's new movie). Weight was again found lacking in the role of the leading female, a saucy prostitute who stirs up trouble and teases out the sexual ambiguities between the two leading men; this was duly beefed up. By then, everybody knew the lead female role had gone to Gong Li. None other than John Lone, Bertolucci's last emperor of China, was slated to play the male lead, but the deal fell through when Lone demanded what Madame Hsu viewed as too much money up front. The part finally went to Leslie Cheung, a Hong Kong singer and movie icon — one of those versatile superstars in the East Asia pop scene. Cheung had taken up residence in Canada at the time, in a sort of semiretirement, but he wanted the part so badly — he saw it as the definitive role of his career — that he didn't mind modest pay.

By Hollywood standards, a budget of twenty million Hong Kong dollars (less than $3 million U.S.) means a cheap production and a cheap cast — but if you're spending it on a Chinese set with a mostly Chinese crew, it's enough to make you feel like an emperor. Poor financing has already reduced many major Chinese studios today to little more than bargain rental outfits. "When it comes to film making, money is the bottom line," Chen said to me after shooting. "It's the lubricant that allows your ideas to flow." But money also meant recognizable faces. Using established stars was something that Chen, as a matter of principle, had avoided up to *Farewell;* indeed, it had been part of the Fifth Generation's ethic to insist on picking actors from an unknown, unspoiled talent pool, and letting them blossom together with a young film-maker. Zhang Yimou had broken the rule with his first feature: *Red Sorghum* starred Jiang Wen, the most famous male actor in China; and Zhang has continued to feature Gong Li in all his films. Still, whatever has been said about Zhang's commercial instinct, he and Gong Li did indeed blossom together. For Chen, who had adhered to the Fifth Generation's anticelebrity ethic for so long, this departure from previous practice looked a little like selling out. Some even took it as a sign of how far Chen's fortunes had fallen: his position was so weak he had to ask Zhang's leading lady for help.

Other controversies attended the production. For a while, rumors circulated in Beijing that *Farewell* would not get through the censors because it dealt with the taboo subject of homosexuality. This was a natural assumption in China, where homosexuality has long been considered perverse or criminal. At least until 1991, government clinics offered treatments such as "hate therapy" and "electric therapy" to "cure" homosexuals. (In "hate therapy," the patient would be asked to think of flies or the skeletons of those who had died of AIDS whenever he experienced homosexual arousal. In "electric therapy," the doctor would show a video of men having sex and then apply an electrified probe to the patient's erect penis, so that he would associate gay sex with painful shocks.) Any form of "kinky" sexuality seemed enough to make the members of China's officialdom cringe—a fact that became apparent with the banning of Zhang Yimou's two Oscar-nominated films. What dismayed the officials was not only their "unhealthy politics" but also their "unhealthy sex." These two stories about the oppressive rule of old men were politically obnoxious, but what tipped the balance was the suggestion of incest and the decadent foreplay ritual of foot massage.

Later on, it seemed as if Chen himself had tiptoed around his taboo subject. After the film was shown in Hong Kong and was due to enter competition at Cannes, *China Daily,* a Beijing-based English language newspaper, reported that he had cut the original novel's "hints of homosexuality and stressed the descriptions of human feelings and frailties." Chen himself told the Hong Kong media that although he achieved a new understanding of homosexual love from his years in New York, it was not his movie's central subject—betrayal was. Evidently, others agreed: to his great relief, Chen had by then gotten the long-awaited "yes" from the Chinese censors.

THE PALME d'Or should have laid to rest any uncertainty hanging over the fate of the three-hour film. Chinese television announced the Cannes award for *Farewell My Concubine* without delay. This time, it looked like the sense of national honor might overcome all obstacles. And Chen's handling of the taboo subject, for better or worse, has a quality of exquisite gentility rare in melodrama. It's a bit like watching an oriental masquerade ball. After seeing the film, a leading Chinese film critic turned to me with a look of perplexity: "What does this tell us about homosexuality, really?" I thought of Yukio Mishima's novel *Confessions of a Mask* and wondered whether Chen's film had less to do with confessions than masks. Wasn't that the point about masks: the possibility that behind one, you might just see another, and another—that maybe there isn't one true face? Maybe by muting the homosexual theme, Chen wasn't simply skirting the real issue at hand; maybe he was trying to limn a fluid psychological reality.

"And what about the Cultural Revolution?" the film critic pressed on. "We all went through it—does that part of the movie feel real to you?" A film director I met in Beijing was even more blunt: "The movie is totally false." He looked at me truculently, anticipating a challenge. Then he threw up his hands: "I'm happy for Chen Kaige, but if candyfloss is the current vogue in Europe, where are the rest of us going to go?" He happens to be one of the young Chinese directors making offbeat, low-budget films in a style best described as gritty urban realism: mean streets, cramped rooms, trapped, small characters, all of it worlds away from the gloss, the exotica, the spectacle of Chen's latest. To an even younger generation of filmmakers, the bold vision of the Fifth Generation, once so fresh and startling, is already being dismissed as so much cinematic fustian.

Perhaps the most revealing commentary on the film, however, comes from Chen himself: "To a great extent, I identify with Cheng Dieyi: he's a great master of Beijing Opera, but an idiot in life. He often confuses the real world with the world on stage. Someone like him is very lonely as he goes on the stage. But everything about him, including his jealousy, has the effect of a spectacle: it's very beautiful [to watch him]." I mentioned that some saw the film as a grandiose epic. "It's not an epic," Chen said emphatically. "It's a personal story about a few individuals."

And perhaps, for Chen, this *is* a personal story, one that has little to do with sexuality or the political history of the Cultural Revolution. At the center of this picture is an unfolding duel between two men. Cheng Dieyi is portrayed as a consummate artist who endures almost inhuman pain and discipline, a man who suffers from confused identities and perpetual loneliness. Driven by jealousy, he ends up betraying the one he loves—and then, for the ideal of high art, he slays himself with his lover's sword, in the grand finale of a stage performance. Duan Xiaolou, his stage partner and a great artist as well, is at first his close friend, and then betrays him by falling in love with a prostitute. The greater betrayal lies ahead though: as a performer, Duan conforms to the vulgarities of a coarsened age, betraying Cheng and their shared art in order to be accepted by the masses.

Of course, the story has many more twists and turns—as a good, long melodrama should—but if one must pick out a central theme, then betrayal it is: an artist's betrayal of another, one man's betrayal of art. All directors leave their own shadow and light on the screen, and Chen is no exception. Watching the film, I couldn't help noticing how Chen's camera caresses Cheng Dieyi, imbues every scene of the Beijing Opera's heyday with the glow of nostalgia; the film is suffused with longing and admiration for a form of art so pure, so high it could only end in the highest form of tragedy. Perhaps, then, the film itself can be seen as an allegory of the partnership and rivalry of Chen and Zhang. Perhaps, too, it represents the tensions within Chen himself.

WHEN CHINESE film people ask Zhang Yimou what he thinks of his other less popular Fifth Generation colleagues, if the competition isn't becoming an ugly strain among old pals, Zhang usually cuts them short. "Our cinema is still at a difficult phase of emergence," he says. "We should be generous to each other, instead of trashing people." For all the mystique of the Fifth Generation, he insists that his generation has no big talent; he shakes his head, smiling at himself, at his own tendency toward solemnity. In his interviews, Zhang tends to come across as someone with a rough, simple grace—a kind of heavyweight champion who can poke fun at his own cumbersome bulk.

One breezy April evening this year, I went to a crew meeting that Zhang was holding about the film he was working on. Gong Li was in Hong Kong, and everyone in the hotel suite was male except for me, an observer. The Hotel Xiyuan is a plush establishment in Beijing, filled with elegant boutiques, cafés, restaurants, and hotel guests dressed in cosmopolitan styles, though of a recognizably Asian cut. Zhang was living there at the time, and I imagined it must be a good place for a famous workaholic like him to hide out: he really didn't have to step out for anything or worry about being mobbed here. "My works up to now are all stylized art films," Zhang said, discussing his plans.

"This time it's going to be a mainstream movie." Around midnight, with Zhang reminding everyone that they must set out early next morning on a field trip outside Beijing, someone brought up *Farewell My Concubine*, noting drily that it's easier to watch than Chen's other films. Zhang listened for a moment, then took over the subject. "Usually, Kaige's pictures are made of many pauses," he said, deadpan, "so you can get a clear view and think. This time with *Farewell* it's like this"—now Zhang stepped sideways across the room like a monkey, his hands crossing in rhythm, his face coming alive with a succession of startling expressions—"*step, step, stop; step, step, stop*: the pauses are still there, but it does move ahead a bit in between." Then just as abruptly, he was back in his seat, anchored and still, his face blank, mind locked into some unknown thoughts, while the room convulsed with laughter. The mimicry *was* funny—and a marvelously concise illustration of film narrative.

Perhaps at last, Chen, the *zhelidaoyan*, the philosophical director, had told a story in a way that would engage a larger audience. However, in China as elsewhere, popular success often comes at the expense of critical approval. A famous Chinese critic sympathetic to Chen once told me, "Zhang is a well-packaged cultural star, whereas Chen is a more serious filmmaker. Chen's got a broader range of knowledge and interests to work with, but it's up to him to blend them together smoothly." After seeing their new films this year, the critic pronounced his verdict succinctly: "Now, Zhang is a fake peasant, Chen is a fake Mandarin."

MANY CHINESE critics and filmmakers prefer nowadays to discuss Hou Hsiao Hsien, the prominent Taiwan director whose *City of Sadness* won the top prize at Venice in 1989. In *Today*'s special film volume, authors were as reverent about Hou as they were hostile toward the Fifth Generation: they loved his long shots, his deceptively simple characters, and thought his films captured the spirit of classical Chinese poetry. Hou was, in short, the *real* Chinese master, doing something the Fifth Generation tried to simulate with style. Curiously, Hou's new film, *The Puppet Master*, received the same kind of response from American reviewers like Vincent Canby and Dave Kehr, both of whom found it brilliantly innovative. Yet there are plenty of people, both in Taiwan and in the West, who find Hou's films a bit too rambling. Competing with *Farewell* at Cannes, *The Puppet Master* won the Special Jury's Award.

In a conversation with Chen before Cannes, I asked him what he thought of the accusation of "catering to Western tastes." For a split second his face froze; then, using a set Chinese phrase, he replied simply, "You know, when you talk standing up, it doesn't hurt your back"—in other words, it's easy for someone to talk who isn't in his position. After a while, he came to the sort of concessions he feels are necessary: "You cannot dig too deeply into Chinese issues, or foreigners won't understand. Even in Hong Kong and Taiwan they won't get it." He says he has high esteem for Zhang Daqian, a great Chinese painter famous for his chameleon changes in styles. "A true master, I think, should be a master of change." I mention Hou Hsiao Hsien. In glacial tones, Chen says: "He won't change, of course. He's a national treasure in Taiwan."

That balmy spring afternoon, in my mother's apartment on the east side of Beijing, we rambled on about many things. We talked about *Basic Instinct* and *The Crying Game*, new Chinese novels, and good restaurants in the city. I asked Chen if he had planned to settle back in Beijing permanently when he left New York; he shook his head gently. I know that he and his wife had been living in a hotel for the past few years, but now are separated. The hotel is one of those "modern," almost posh hotels in Beijing, a sprawling gray compound occupied largely by foreigners. How does it feel to live in a hotel in your own hometown? I ask. Chen shakes his head again: he doesn't recommend it.

Chen's beeper sounds many times over the course of the afternoon. The calls come mostly from his lawyer: Chen is embroiled in a libel suit against a Beijing reporter, which has been the talk at a lot of dinner parties in town. Much of it, people say, has to do with the fact that the reporter felt slighted by him. In a profile, the reporter described Chen as condescending to the Chinese and eager to please the foreigners. At one point he called Chen "a tired dog running between East and West without a master" (an allusion to a famous comment made by a farmer about Confucius, who had frequently traveled between the ancient warring states trying to sell his philosophy to a master); at another, he insulted Chen's father. The case is symptomatic of the present media atmosphere in China: it's hard to tell fact from fiction—fact-checking is minimal in reporting—and in the pursuit of lively, confrontational journalism, reporters have taken to launching sensationalized attacks on a chosen celebrity. There are many things that China has never had before but are now present in overabundance: the celebrity libel suit is one of them. This year, it seems every star is suing some reporter.

By dinnertime, an out-of-court settlement has been reached, Chen tells me. We decide not to go out. What with business booming, constant construction, and a sudden flood of new cars, the city's traffic jams have run amok just in the past six months. At this rate, some experts predict, it will be as awful as Bangkok or Taipei in five years. Beijing might emerge as yet another densely populated, badly polluted, cheerfully prosperous Asian metropolis. That afternoon, Chen called me on his cellular phone from a cab: he was stuck in midtown traffic, late by nearly an hour. So now we sit down to a simple dinner my mother prepared.

"I'm turning into a royalist," Chen tells me. "China could not have been a great unified nation but for the imperial powers and Confucius. It's been passed down through generations: Chinese people always need an object of worship, an emperor sitting at the top. Without it, chaos is bound to break out." I think back to many previous conversations, but even more, to Bertolucci's film *The Last Emperor*. When the Italian master was weaving his grand oriental fantasy inside the Forbidden City in 1987, Chen had been on the set, transfixed by the recreated scenes of pomp and grandeur of China's royal past. Eventually, he too would appear on the screen as the chief of the royal palace guards. When the deposed emperor is feeling isolated and restless in the Forbidden City and wants to venture out into the republican world, it is Chen, dressed in full Manchu colors and sword in hand, who rushes to have the palace gate blocked. It is Chen who kneels down before the young emperor, silently entreating His Majesty to abide by the rules of the monarchy. The emperor, pale with fury, submits.

The intervening years, it is clear, have only heightened Chen's sense that China's redemption will lie in its ancestral traditions. He quotes the words of a Taiwanese friend: "I hope one day Chinese will be both wealthy and in love with *li*." *Li*, the concept central to Confucianism, refers to a whole set of civil codes, rituals, and social hierarchy. "It's going to take time," he assures me, "but I'm convinced China will formulate a Confucian type of culture." The sentiment makes me uneasy; I think of my many radical-turned-neoconservative Chinese friends, of the fiercely nationalist sentiments that have been warming up alongside a heated economy. Yet the days and nights of red terror and hooligan anarchy during the Cultural Revolution are burned into my memory, as they are in the memory of a whole generation. Many of us were once fervent Red Guards ourselves, joyfully destroying everything we were taught to consider remnants of a feudal culture, programmed to "make revolution." And so I can understand how my friends feel today—I can even feel the quiet despair beneath the heady optimism. Chen's talk of neo-Confucianism unsettles me, but I find it hard to reproach him. His nostalgia seems to stem from a terrible need, an elegiac yearning for an identity that an entire nation, he fears, may have lost.

I look him over: black polo shirt, soft gray sports jacket, black leather shoes. It's all there, the cosmopolitan style, the casual, understated elegance; yet there remains an unspoken tension. It's like the English words that leap out occasionally from Chen's conversational flow: they're meant to emphasize shades of meaning, but they also suggest the other side of Chen's anxious cosmopolitanism, a measure of alienation from the culture that both nurtured and rebuffed him.

In a sense, his dilemmas, his longings, are those of the Chinese elite. Once he had believed that it could all come together: an avant-garde cinema, an enlightened audience, his intellectual mission accomplished, and the world offering a standing ovation. Instead, he had found himself abandoned by his intellectual supporters and dependent on the largesse of a public he saw as coarse, fickle, undeterred in their materialism, and uncomprehending of art. And the insecure, vacillating officialdom only confirmed his worst suspicions. Bad news came in August: one week after *Farewell My Concubine* opened in Shanghai, the authorities abruptly banned it. Was it because of the homosexual theme, the Cultural Revolution, or the film's tragic ending? As usual, the politburo, which was rumored to have screened the film, didn't think it owed anybody an explanation. Miramax, which would soon release the film in Europe and America, expressed its disappointment. Chen told Western reporters that he felt "hurt" when this kind of thing happened in his country. But weeks later, after some minor editing, without any explanation, the ban was lifted just as abruptly as it was imposed. Although tickets were expensive, audiences generally enjoyed the film. Chinese officials even went out of their way to organize some screenings. It was a "face issue," the cynics say, because in the same month China was trying to create the appearance of openness in order to court the Olympics.

IN SEPTEMBER, though, the Olympic honor went to Sydney. And in October, when the Tokyo Film Festival showed two nonofficially produced Chinese films, both containing "negative" portrayals of contemporary Chinese life, it proved to be one embarrassment too many. The Chinese delegation stormed out of the festival to protest, and the film bureau back home moved to tighten censorship on independent productions and taboo political subjects. Given the erratic character of Chinese cultural policy, some people are predicting that in the next ten years or so, the best of Chinese cinema is likely to lead a glamorous exile life, finding its real home not in China but in the West.

"It's just a commercial film," Chen Kaige told me preemptively when, a few months earlier, I first mentioned that I had seen *Farewell*. Was he worried that this film about artistic betrayal was itself a betrayal, or was he merely worried that I would think so? Certainly, it isn't the kind of pure avant-garde cinema that he hoped would be his enduring legacy. Even so, he is pleased at its success, and inclined to speak of it less defensively now. I looked at the gray streaks in his hair, the small wrinkles spreading around his eyes. He'd grown older, his laughter shorter and less easy than I had remembered; but he also seemed more composed, more confident, than he had for a long time. In a few days, a gold-plated trophy would restore him to his pride of place in Chinese cinema. Even before the award, though, as he headed back into the night streets of Beijing, he had the air of the man who knows whatever sacrifices and concessions he has made will have been worth it.

5

THE WHOPPER

Tier 1: Communism Lite

ON JANUARY 1, 1993, *China Culture Gazette* (*CCG*), the official organ of China's Ministry of Culture, was transformed. For years *CCG* had been an infamous stronghold of the hard-line apparatchiks, choking with dull, harsh tirades of Communist Party propaganda. With a new issue of its weekend edition — the *Cultural Weekend* — the paper changed color overnight: from red to yellow.

Nude pictures did the trick. The four-page *Cultural Weekend* on that day displayed so many photographs of nude and seminude women (most of whom were busty Westerners) that it instantly became known as "the coolest paper in Beijing." It also ran a front-page interview on the subject of nudity with Liu Xiaoqing, China's brash movie queen. The issue sold like hotcakes.

The Ministry of Propaganda was furious. The Ministry of Culture wasn't happy about it, either. Rumor had it that Communist Party General Secretary Jiang Zemin, who has a propensity for showing off his "high-culture taste," happened to pick up a copy of *CCG* at a subway station. The general secretary couldn't believe what he saw, and afterwards expressed grave concerns about the moral health of society.

Graver concerns these days center around economics. Considered to be on the front line of ideological battles, Chinese print media have always been both financially dependent on the party and under its tight control. For the past four decades, the basic axiom taught in all Chinese journalism departments was "news is the Party's throat and tongue." Every newspaper had — and still has — a Party secretary, who would often take the post of the chief editor as well, and who would report not so much to his readers but directly to his Party boss.

However, with the economic reform, and with new papers and journals springing up to compete with the old ones, the situation had changed significantly. *CCG* had been in the red politically and financially — in fact, the paper was so deep in debt that it was on the brink of folding, and everyone on the staff knew that the Party wouldn't bail them out. As inflation had continued and the price of paper had climbed, the government had ladled out only the same meager subsidy.

Fortunately, just around this time, Deng Xiaoping, China's de facto emperor, issued his call for wider and deeper marketization. Following Deng's orders, the General Press and Publishing Administration announced new guidelines. Publishers were given more power to decide matters such as printing adult erotic materials and kung fu novels; the previous ban on printing pictures of girls in bikinis, foreign movie stars, and pop singers on Chinese calendars was lifted, and publishers in specialized fields could now cross over to general subjects in order to boost sales.

So, when Zhang Zuomin, a short, urchinlike former Red Guard, took charge of *Cultural Weekend,* he was given a free hand to make it profitable — and he knew exactly what direction to go in and how far to go. What was remarkable was that *CCG*'s hard-line chief editor stood firmly behind Zhang when the nudity scandal broke. The wily old apparachnik even snapped at his grumbling superiors at the ministries. "Are we no longer 'marching toward the market'?" he demanded, employing a Party slogan currently in fashion. "If not, I quit."

Such a rationale could not be questioned for the moment, so the muttering stopped. *Cultural Weekend*'s circulation soared to 260,000 — not as high as some of China's most popular papers and magazines, with circulations of a half million or more, but breaking *CCG*'s old record by far. Thanks to a steady outpouring of front-page reports on women, sex, and the pop culture scene, written by Zhang Zuomin himself, *Cultural Weekend* soon became one of "the four little dragons of the Beijing press," and Zhang the newspaper man everyone loves to hate. While some dismiss him as a disgrace to the profession, others acknowledge grudgingly that he may be a journalist for his times.

Zhang himself seems to delight in his notoriety, and he takes pride in all the irreverent pranks he has gotten away with over the years. "I'm making a name now, so I need to shake things up a bit, to send some shock waves to the market," he told me. "In any event, I believe we must smash open Chinese culture, and apply 'the great fearless spirit' to our newspaper work." He was lapsing into Red Guard jargon! Indeed, it was during the lawless period of the Cultural Revolution that it dawned on Zhang that a newspaper could be a profitable venture. He and some young comrades had once printed a small propaganda sheet with a stolen mimeograph machine, and Zhang had pocketed the profit they made from selling the first batch. Another "fearless" act Zhang proudly recounted to me was that in 1987 he had worn plastic sandals while covering a high-level state function. "The chairman of China was present!" Zhang bragged. "I'm sure I was the one and only person who did *that.*" All the same, Zhang knows what lines he cannot cross: "I will not run anything antiparty in my paper," he said emphatically, "and I will not run pornography." He went into an absurdly meticulous explanation about how the degree of bodily exposure in the nude photos he prints falls well within the prescribed rules of decorum. This seems to be a particularly Chinese technique among the professional orders: the art of creatively interpreting Party policies to protect and advance your own interests, while in the course of it portraying yourself as engaged in a nobly subversive cause.

IN THEIR pursuit of the average reader, many papers are testing the new boundaries the government has staked out. The average reader is apparently tired of "hard news"—the kind of stories found in the official print media that go on and on about Party congresses, production rates, and ideological education but remain silent about political oppression and abuses of power. How much more inviting is gossip about movie stars and millionaires! Look at those colorful photos, sensational titles, lurid tales! Readers are sure to gulp it down. With the new formula, the papers have begun to support themselves, attract advertisements, and relieve the government of its financial burden, but only at the expense of the official papers. Once-dominant organs—such as *People's Daily* and *Guangming Daily*—still arrive in the offices of all state enterprises nationwide; but few look to them for interesting coverage of popular events. They can't compete with what's on the newsstands.

Some frown at the vulgarity of it all, some criticize the degrading fact that most Chinese journalists now take fees or bribes from the people they report on, and some think that all this "soft news" is the new opium for the masses, intended to distract them from harsh realities. "I'm deeply disappointed by our reporters," said the prominent dissident journalist Dai Qing. "They are totally corrupted by commercialization." Another noted magazine editor hissed, "All these noises they've made, and you can't find even one paper of a quality and weight that's comparable to *World Economic Herald*"—referring to a Shanghai-based reformist paper that the government shut down around the time of Tiananmen Square. (A good number of dissident journals that had been quietly building up semiautonomous bases within or on the margin of the official press were also either suspended or purged, destroying almost overnight the scattered yet lively pre-Tiananmen growth of a Chinese version of "civil society" structures. Dai Qing herself was jailed for a year, and her reporting is still banned in China.)

Chen Xilin, the young director of the weekend edition of the sober and serious *China Business Times*, is impatient with such criticism. "Don't talk to me about Tiananmen; it gives me a headache. Those elites have done a good job of enlightening us. They taught us a lesson. But their time is over. Tragic, yes, but that's history. The new elite is a lot smarter, and one thing is certain about the future of China: it belongs to smart people."

With his reputation for having created the first Chinese paper for white-collar professionals, Chen is typical of China's post-Tiananmen elite; he works hard and plays hard. He edits by day, frequents expensive restaurants and karaoke bars in the evening with visiting Hong Kong and Taiwan colleagues (who pay the bill), and stays up late with pots of coffee to draw editorial cartoons for his paper and to dash out short essays that bring him extra income. By shunning harsh political propaganda and focusing on the economy and lifestyles, his paper embodies a brand of journalism that is smart, slick, and politically moderate.

Chen's contempt for papers like *Cultural Weekend* is thinly veiled: "It's OK—but I wouldn't call it journalism." On the whole, though, he is optimistic about Chinese media: "After a while, some of these small, gossipy papers will fold, some will remain. The society always needs this sort of reading, but not so much of it. They play an important role in the eventual freeing of the press: they've broken up the official news language, shifted the concerns from the government and state affairs to ordinary people and social lives. They are already affecting the big papers, forcing them to loosen up a bit, to compete, to be more attractive to readers. Isn't this a victory in itself?"

A lot of people in the profession echo this sentiment. Many people I meet in Beijing these days have changed their minds about Tiananmen. They see direct confrontation with the state as hopeless and politically immature, and see Western democracy as unfit for Chinese circumstances. Four years ago, Deng Xiaoping was widely cursed as the butcher of his own people; today many talk about him as the wise patriarch who knows the only right way to handle the messy transitions China is going through. "It's like getting a hard punch in the face from your father," said a media reporter who had been deeply involved with the Tiananmen protests, "very hard to get over. Only by and by, do you realize he's your father after all. And there is nothing you can do but slowly chip away at that hard socialist wall." Heroism is dropped; pragmatism is embraced. This surge of what the Chinese call "new conservatism" recalls the ancient Taoist wisdom: water is the strongest thing in the world.

Can the soft really hit hard? Or is this all a matter of self-delusion, an easy rhetoric to absolve people of moral responsibility in treacherous circumstances? The answers to these questions aren't clear; what *is* clear is that ponderous questions of this sort are out of keeping with the tenor of the times. Today, the national mood favors News Lite. Culture Lite. Communism Lite.

Old taboos are being broken and new frontiers crossed, but the transgressors often wear a sly grin, ready to duck or backtrack at the first sign of danger. Gone is the kind of romantic uplift with which the Chinese cultural scene was imbued in the eighties.

Tiananmen was a turning point, though the direction the country has taken up in the wake of the tanks and blood caught many by surprise. As the engine of economic reform has shifted into overdrive, the largest population on earth has set off on a frantic race for material wealth. Popular culture is shifting gears too.

"Serve the people" was once Mao's famous slogan; now it is seeing a second, speedier life in which even the Chairman himself is repackaged and served up. One of the best-selling cassettes in China in 1992 is *Red Sun*, an adaptation of famous old hymns praising Mao to soft rock rhythms with electronic synthesizers. The vogue spread quickly: all sorts of revolutionary songs are dug up and set to the beat of the new time. Mao meets Muzak and MTV.

The scene has changed so quickly, and quite often so absurdly, that for those who labor in the culture industry, adaptability has become a quality both valuable and suspect. There is a generational split too. Those who stick to the good old socialist habit of taking the long view and sitting things out, watch with growing apprehension. These tend to be people over 45. Those who seize the moment with entrepreneurial flair—often people in their twenties and thirties—see a different vista and have different stories to tell. "It's like watching a bunch of monkeys throwing somersaults," a Beijing movie director coolly remarked to me. "Energetic, fun, agile, but oh the dust! So much dust is kicked up."

THE KING of these agile monkeys is Wang Shuo, the thirty-five-year-old Beijing "hooligan writer" with a knack for turning culture into a commodity. A colorful character with a roguish sense of humor, Wang started out as a fiction writer, then moved on to writing scripts for movies and television, all as a free-lancer and all with sweeping success. He has helped to create three of the most talked-about television series in recent years. The last one, a soap opera called *No Choice in Loving You*, set a precedent: instead of producing the series in house, CCTV (Central Chinese Television), China's most official television network, had to pay a handsome price to buy it. Wang has a publicist's knack for attracting media attention, and a politician's shrewdness for sidestepping sensitive issues. He advertises himself the way celebrities do and talks about fame and money with open bravado. The tabloids love him, and he never fails to supply them with a punchy line or two. He certainly has what Beijingers call "an oily mouth and a slippery tongue," but when it comes to political dissent, he is definitely not a loose cannon: if you ask him a question about human rights, you are likely to be treated with a joke that makes the question seem ridiculous. Wang is the first writer since Mao to publish a four-volume *Selected Works*.

Wang admits that his commercial instincts were honed from his early days hustling as a small businessman: "I learned to watch what my customers need." Posing as a writer for common folks, he uses his homegrown, sardonic wit to mock both the communist ideologues and the elite intellectuals. While he pokes fun at the former carefully, the latter are really his favorite target. One of Wang's famous epigrams goes: "Before you die, have your high!" And one of Wang's highs is to let his cynical, smartass hooligan antiheroes poke fun at everything holy and serious. "I can't stand people with a sense of mission," he declares.

Wang remains a controversial figure in spite of (or because of) his immense popularity in the pop culture scene. People are passionately divided over what "the Wang Shuo phenomenon" means. For some, it is an alarming sign of the nihilism among the young generation. One of the famous lines in *No Choice in Loving You*, for instance, has a young man tell his girlfriend, "Although my feelings for you don't add up to love, they are more than enough for marriage." Citing this, the noted young Shanghai literary critic Wang Xiaoming wrote:

> Here is the currently trendy Beijing youth culture, and Wang Shuo's works are its artistic expression: to be cool is to mock everything. It results from disillusionment and a sense of powerlessness; it's a logical spasm of a withering Chinese spirit that has been under oppression for half a century. It mocks a dated official ideology which has long lost its grip over the public; more deadly, it dissolves all that might form the foundation of any new spiritual belief, including reason, passion for rebellion, and even certain basic values such as sincerity, steadfastness, respect for others. In fact, it has already been acquiesced to by the authorities, becoming a part of the new ruling ideology. What's amusing is that the trend thinks of itself as having something in common with postmodernism in the West. There is nothing more laughable than this.

Wang's fans, however, defend him ardently. China's educated elite has long been alienated from the ordinary people, they argue, and there was always something hypocritical and hollow about their timid idealism and oppositional posturing, since they themselves were politically and economically dependent on the state. Wang, on the other hand, is a true independent spirit: he earns a living on his own and refuses to participate in any political game.

He cares about ordinary readers and is refreshingly candid about matters like money and success. Some contend his cynicism is long overdue.

One of Wang's avid readers is Fang Lijun, a young Beijing painter known for his large portraits of merry, dopey-looking urban hoodlums, which he has successfully marketed to foreign patrons. Fang echoes Wang Shuo this way: "We prefer to be called the lost, bored, crisis-ridden, bewildered hoodlums, but we will not be cheated again. Don't think about educating us with old methods, for we shall put ten thousand question marks across all dogmas, then negate them and toss them on the trash heap." Fang's combination of defiance, disillusionment, and determination is a sentiment increasingly common in today's China. As he concludes cheerfully, "Only a jackass would fall into a trap after having fallen into it a hundred times."

Tier 2: McArt, with Small Fries

IN LATE April, two months into my stay in Beijing, news came through the grapevines that a big art exhibit was to open at a prime location—the McDonald's in downtown Beijing. An art show at McDonald's? It struck me as doubly odd. First, McDonald's in Beijing has the distinction of being the only McDonald's in the world with a Communist Party secretary. However, this seems not to have barred its management from taking the universal corporate view: sponsoring art is good publicity for business. Second, there was the list of the artists in the show: some had the distinction of being members of China's avant-garde who, only a few years ago, had displayed experimental works in major Chinese museums. But that obviously has not made them hesitate to move their works to a McDonald's. In fact, it was precisely the point: now they want to sell art to ordinary consumers.

This effort required some ingenuity. Among the many pieces shown were denim outfits covered with Jasper Johns–style designs, recorded cassettes of pop songs taken from famous advertising lines, and greeting cards with Ninja Turtles and Superman emblazoned on reproductions of antique Chinese vases. One greeting card showed a bizarre creature—with the body of a dragon, the head of Donald Duck, a foot in a Nike sneaker, and claws clutching a stack of dollar bills—against a Ming vase pattern. The artists gave the show a trendy, sales-oriented title: "New History: 1993 Mass Consumption." They issued beguiling, earnestly lowbrow statements such as: "We want to change our elitist attitude. We'd like to get our art into commercial circulation." Some might call this kitsch, but doing so would undercut the radical nature of staging such a show at McDonald's—for what other place could better highlight the idea of "art as fast food, ready to serve the people"? Push things to an extreme, and, with a bit of luck, you may end up at the cutting-edge all over again. Indeed, the local intellectual grapevine was of the view (in other words, was hoping secretly) that this would be another ground-breaking action in the Chinese art scene. In later accounts, it might come to be tagged as, say, the "Whopperfication of Chinese Art," or, to be more site-specific, the "McDonaldization."

By April 28 it was all set: the artists had arrived by train, their "products"— "Not *works*, just *products*!" they kept correcting me—had arrived by truck and foreign reporters were notified, as were friends and a long list of con-cerned, important citizens. A friend of mine, a long-haired rock musician, phoned up just an hour before the opening, informing me in great haste: "Want to see an event? Go to McDonald's now!" He was rushing to finish his final round of calls.

To everyone's disappointment, though, the show organizers had forgotten to notify the Beijing police, who detained the artists the night before the opening and canceled the show in the morning. The People's Congress has just ended, and the fourth Tiananmen massacre anniversary was drawing close: it was a sensitive time of the year in Beijing. The long-haired rock musician hissed afterward, "Bunch of dopes, coming in from the provinces with their eyes closed. Or were they just hoping not to get caught?" He was more annoyed with the bumbling artists than with the merciless police. Already, his voice was lapsing back to boredom: there was to be no event after all.

So it was business as usual when I arrived at McDonald's that day: potential art buyers stood in long, orderly lines to get their Big Macs and fries, ignorant of the better goods they could have purchased instead. On the stairs I ran into Ren Jian, the leading artist in the canceled show. Wearing plain jeans without his Jasper Johns design, he looked rather artless—and clearly sleep-less—but otherwise cool. Greeting me casually without slowing down his brisk pace, he squeezed two words between his teeth: "Be careful." Suddenly I noticed the clusters of idle individuals around: the place was filled with plain-clothes policemen.

The irony, of course, is that these artists really meant no harm. They'd like to make a stir, but only the sort of stir that would help get their "products" sold. They were ready to cooperate with the police, but they were wrong to assume that the police would give them a chance to cooperate. In the past four years, the cultural scene in China has changed a great deal, but certain things won't change for a long time to come.

• • •

RE N J I A N showed work in the First Chinese Modernist Art Exhibit in 1989, which opened in the National Fine Art Museum, and opened with a bang: a young woman artist took out a revolver and fired two shots at her own installation, and riot police in full gear rushed in to make arrests and close the exhibition down for inspection. When the show resumed, publicity was maximum: for two weeks it was the talk of the town. The public was so shocked and excited by various behaviors of the "action artists" (distributing condoms, selling shrimps, washing feet in a basin with Ronald Reagan's head painted all over it, and so on) that the show had to shut down once more when the museum, the public security bureau and *Beijing Daily* all received bomb threats. It was a hard act to follow. That was the heyday of the avant-garde, when the government was more tolerant, the artists bolder, and the public more responsive. Today, the same kind of show probably wouldn't cause a ripple, and the police would make sure to shut it down for good. People are too busy getting rich or making ends meet, and those with time and money to spend are not likely to spend it on the avant-garde. The mixing of economic openness with tight political control is proving to be a poisonous potion for counterculture artists, who lose out on every front: most have lost their domestic audience and their economic advantage, some have lost their defiant idealism, but none have lost the police.

Already, intellectuals talk about the pre-Tiananmen period with incredible nostalgia: that was the golden age for arts and ideas, but now we are in the age of the gold rush, a paradise for hustlers and the tasteless masses. When there are so many real scandals out in the open, who has the patience for the art of fake scandals? When you can get so many quick and easy thrills through the tabloids and best-sellers, who cares about slower-paced books and difficult readings just because some call it "writing" or "literature"? These may be simplistic distinctions, but who has the time for complications in an overly complicated world?

Such is the pathos of the avant-garde in a fermenting transcommunist third world milieu: in a country where "marching toward the market" is described as an advance, and commercialization is viewed as the inevitable route for guarding national interests, the avant-garde lags feebly behind; they have, in a way, become the rear guard. Standing at the crossroad between aristocratic patronage and the bourgeois marketplace, the nineteenth-century Parisian Bohemian artists at least knew what lay behind them and what lay ahead. But what values and heritage are the Chinese avant-garde trying to uphold and defend? And for whom? The Party had been too much for them:

in the eighties it was both their patron and their target, their blessing and their curse. They had built a career out of biting the hand that fed them, because that hand had robbed them of the riches of history and culture. Today, the artistic rebels have been dumped, crippled orphans with chains around their ankles, in a curious place called "the socialist market," which may be the coldest place on earth in spite of the deafening clamor for prosperity. Just what right do they have here to consider themselves trendy and ahead of the society? Many of them can't even afford to buy a pair of decent shoes! And the shine on their erstwhile prestige is growing dull, rather like the scruffy, old shoes they drag about: they used to set a trend, now they aren't even good enough to stop the cold.

Some kind of change is necessary.

MCDONALD'S CANNOT be their destination. The trick, though, involves proving their artistic worth to the consumers of Big Macs. The "normalization" of Chinese art is under way: those who are moving out of their paralyzing depression but have not abandoned their profession must now compete for places in their respective fields.

Aesthetic norms, for the time being, are largely set in Hong Kong and Taiwan, where most of Asia's wealthy are concentrated. The judges are often from there too. These smart, professional art dealers can create wonders on the market, and they are a species not yet born on mainland China. In the past few years, they have opened in Hong Kong an almost unthinkable market for Chinese oil paintings, turning an essentially Western form of art into an expensive local fad. Today, some dealers are trying their luck with promoting the mainland avant-garde, envisioning huge dollar signs down the road.

These dealers know how to use political sympathy to spark market interest, as was made clear in both the title and the media coverage of this year's "Post-Tiananmen Chinese Art Exhibit" in Hong Kong. The Hong Kong curatorial team coined classifications like "Political Pop" or "Cynical Realism," knowing the full impact of Tiananmen in the minds of potential collectors. Yet they also pride themselves as true connoisseurs of good art—and, as such, they were able to arrange deals in which some Chinese dissident art pieces fetched thirty thousand dollars and more. Four Political Pop painters, moreover, became the first mainland Chinese artists shown at the Venice Biennale. Handled by their Hong Kong, Taiwan and European brokers, the mainland avant-garde may have a real shot at a new life on the international scene. Some Chinese artists may feel uneasy about the jaded Western sympathy, or about being patted on the shoulder as a suffering, exotic third world darling, but after all, it's a more friendly and sophisticated place than the "socialist market" at home. And haven't the Chinese avant-garde been craving international recognition all these years?

The happy ending, of course, can only be reserved for a select few.

I RODE my bike with two friends, an art critic and a painter-turned-businessman, to the "painters' village" at Yuan Ming Yuan, a sort of a peasant version of SoHo on the outskirts of Beijing. A few dozens painters, mostly struggling young men without a Beijing residence permit, have rented small, pristine cottages here in order to live and paint.

The art critic knew several residents here, but since most of them have no telephone, we couldn't contact them in advance — so when we arrived, we knocked at a couple of doors. Nobody answered in the first place, a one-room cottage. A neighbor, an old peasant woman, came out and told us that there had been an all-night drinking party, and everyone had left that morning. Nobody was at the second place either, but it was a courtyard house, and the yard door was left open. Ignoring the warning — "Mad dog inside, please ring bell" — written on the door, the art critic stepped right in to leave a note. I looked around the yard: no sign of a dog, only artworks on display. All abstract installations, each with a title written out in Chinese and English next to it on the wall. The art critic informed me that a lot of foreign diplomats and some foreign tourists have been dropping by, since the village had recently received some coverage in the news. I stared at one installation entitled "Life Trembled to Recover": a few tiny white skeletons, two electric bulbs and a dirty basketball, all wired together and hanging from a rotten tree trunk. The artist, the art critic told me, is an older man of some distant fame who now volunteers as a liaison person for the villagers.

Then we visited Ding Cong, one of the success stories in the village. A Taipei gallery signed a longterm contract with him: he must produce at least five paintings per year, and in return the gallery offers him a good living. So Ding moved out of his small cottage and got himself a spacious courtyard house about a mile away from the village. He has a telephone, and was expecting us that afternoon. Dressed in denim from head to toe, Ding had quietly intense manners. He wore thick, black-rimmed glasses, and his face was very pale and serious. His courtyard is quaintly Bohemian, with a stone water tank. The rooms he showed us are all spartan and unadorned with domestic trinkets. In one of his two studio rooms, a small single bed is placed by the window, with blankets neatly folded military-style. Everything seemed piously austere. The house sits in the middle of farmland, and a warm breeze carried the smell of hay and dung. In the middle of the night, Ding can stand in his courtyard and look at the wide expanse of a starry sky. Here it is not so absurd to talk about communicating with the divine spirits, which is what Ding claims to do in his art. After we had looked at rows of large and small canvases covered with thick, violent oil splashes of brown mountains, earth, and enormously elongated human figures crouching in anguished postures, the air seemed to grow heavy and stuffy in his studio. Ding offered us cans of Sprite. My two friends fell into a rather heated discussion over a new magazine, *The Art Market,* what the trends were that year, whether money is a good thing or not for Chinese artists, who's making it and who isn't. "Let's not talk about money," Ding suddenly interrupted. "*Meijin* (it's not uplifting). It doesn't make you feel good."

Unfortunately, the feel-good subjects (art itself) didn't last very long either. I was sure that Ding was disappointed by the whole conversation. Everybody jumped up at my first suggestion to leave.

On the way out of the village, the art critic remembered someone else he knew, whom he wanted to say hello to. We all ended up in yet another cottage: this time, after some serious pounding, the artist-in-residence emerged with disheveled hair and bare feet. A diminutive young man with an open, friendly grin, he had been to the all-night party and was still sleeping it off. He grabbed the art critic's arm and wanted us all to have a good drink with him. There's no water in the house, he apologized, but don't you people want a drink? He pointed at the small cluster of liquor bottles on the table.

He had three small rooms and shared a narrow courtyard with another family, which made him a member of the upper middle class in the village. It was a good life there, he said. I was told that he has a girlfriend who has a job in the city, waitressing or some such thing. One of his rooms was stacked up wall to wall with paintings; some of the rolled up, dusty canvases were clearly his own unsold works. There was a cluttered hominess to the bedroom and the studio-cum-sitting room. Judging from what was on the walls, he was an abstract installation artist: nothing terrible, but nothing that caught my eye. He had been living from hand to mouth, and maybe always would. Maybe one day his girlfriend will leave him—that happens often in the village—or maybe he will give it all up and become, say, a good carpenter and a happy father. Nobody stays in such a painter's village forever—it would be very sad. But for the time being, with a sprightly expression on his face, this young man spoke of the good fortunes of some of his avant-garde buddies. The selected few. So-and-so had been poor for years, and didn't care, just painted and painted, and then one day was discovered, justly, and became rich and famous. Now he lives in the city, got himself a foreign mistress, tours Europe, and only comes by once in a while to his old cottage when he needs some quiet to paint. It's all fair and just, the young man said, because So-and-so is really good, and whoever is good deserves it.

Tier 3: Paper Money

CORRUPTION IN China's newsrooms has gotten so out of hand it's beginning to make news itself. While Americans are fretting about "checkbook journalism," China's problem is exactly the opposite: too many journalists get paid by those they report on. The result is that most of what the Chinese read in the paper or see on television as "news" these days is little more than paid advertising.

The transactions aren't always in cash. Some journalists take stock and bonds from companies they write about, others take cameras, television sets, computers, automobiles, furniture, or even apartments. The mainstay of the system, though, is the "red bag" phenomenon—which refers to the traditional custom of offering a gift of money wrapped in red paper. Nowadays, a plain white envelope replaces the emblematic red paper—after all, one mustn't go about it *too* ostentatiously. When a journalist goes to a press conference, he or she nonchalantly picks up the cash-stuffed envelope at the door, along with other materials, such as the "report" to be filed on the person or company supplying the envelope. A press conference without red bags could count on the early departure of half of the reporters in attendance, and word of mouth would travel swiftly, ensuring that the cheapskate host organization will suffer a collective press boycott.

The fact that advertising is still a novelty to the Chinese press may be one reason the public confuses it with news. It was only since the "spring wind of marketization" in the late eighties, as the government subventions dwindled, that Chinese papers and television stations began to seek advertising money in earnest. However, with survival at issue, media managers played hardball. Some papers give their journalists an obligatory annual quota for obtaining advertisements; some journalists even use the threat of negative publicity to blackmail companies into placing ads in their papers. A well-known scandal of this type involved the Tianjin-based company that produces Huaqi Fruit Tea. When it refused to pay the modest eight thousand yuan "service fee" requested by a magazine, the angry magazine editor used his press connections to spread reports that the quality of Huaqi Fruit Tea was not up to standard. Orders for the product dropped rapidly after the report, resulting in an overstock worth eighty million yuan. Other companies learned the lesson: don't mess with journalists.

As advertising prices rise steadily, some advertisers have begun to make deals with journalists: instead of paying, say, eighty thousand yuan for a proper advertisement, they pay a journalist ten thousand yuan under the table to write up a full-page favorable report on the manufacturer. "News" is more effective advertising—and the journalist can make three years' salary in one shot. And as the business of "paid news" has become lucrative, agents have emerged to professionalize it. Whoever wants friendly media exposure can sign up with such an agent, who then procures a willing reporter or a news editor to print or broadcast the desired news report for a price. Both parties are spared awkward negotiations; the reporter or editor can make all the arrangements without leaving the office.

Somehow, though, word of "bad reporters" has started to spread. A popular ditty sums it up this way:

> The first-rate reporter plays with the stocks,
> The second-rate reporter gets advertisements,
> The third-rate reporter takes bribes,
> The fourth-rate reporter writes for other papers,
> The fifth-rate reporter writes for his own paper.

A Beijing television program director told me that aside from the international news and top-level state news, everything else in the news section of the television has money behind it. Money is paid not only to the network but is also slipped under the table to reporters and staff editors. She gave me an example. "You know the popular central television program *Half Hour on the Economy*? Well, all the reporters and editors on it are loaded, because the whole business sector in the country lines up to get in there." I asked if she could help me get an interview with one of the program staff. She stared at me in disbelief. "What for? You think they'd be eager to confess how much graft they all took in?"

Another young journalist told me stories about his corrupt boss. The chief editor at his paper, a married man, used public funds to set up three different places for his three mistresses, he claimed. "He had the nerve to bring one of them to a dance party at the paper! I danced with her just to sound her out about the old man's virility, so I could spread rumors around afterward." I shook my head, but couldn't help laughing. "He deserves it!" he insisted. "Everybody at the paper knows about his embezzlement, and my friends at the paper and I even wrote an anonymous letter about it to the municipal investigation committee. But nothing ever comes of it. He's still the big boss. And when you have a corrupt boss like that, how can you expect the rest of us to be clean?" He himself has just become an agent for a private advertising company where cheating is, he said, workaday business. "After being a journalist," he bragged, "your skin is so thick you can do anything or succeed in any other rotten profession."

This spring in Beijing, a local reporter offered me an extra invitation card to an expensive press junket. The occasion was the release of a series of paperback romances by a Hong Kong novelist; the publisher, Joint Literature Press, was one of China's most prestigious houses. The affair was held at a swanky, four-star hotel decorated with the usual chandeliers and waterfalls, and served by a stiffly outfitted staff.

As we lined up to enter the conference room, my friend signed in first and was given a green bag the size of a standard shopping bag. "Just give the name of a local paper," he whispered to me. But when my turn came, my mind drew a blank, so I signed in with the name of my research center in Chicago. Abruptly, a young bespectacled woman behind the long table leaped up and hurriedly consulted with the two other staff members. I heard a few murmured words and received a few glances before their huddle broke up. Then the young woman, with an ever so friendly smile, handed me a red bag.

Inside the conference room, my friend shook his head at me. "Why didn't you do as I said? I bet you got only 'spiritual food.'" He was right, of course. As beers and various refreshments were being served, we opened our bags: his contained a set of the paperback romance novels, promotional literature on the Hong Kong novelist (including one written in the format of a press report), and a white envelope with a one-hundred-yuan bill. Mine contained nothing but the set of paperbacks, which seemed to be the sort of books that stock the wire racks of American supermarkets. I looked around the roomful of guests and reporters. The reporters all had green bags, others had blue bags; I seemed to be the only one honored with a red bag. The blue-bag constituency, I soon found out, were members of Beijing's literati: veteran literary officials and critics who might be called upon to give congratulatory speeches. Their press kits plainly contained gifts of a different order.

Naturally, all speakers were quite complimentary of the Hong Kong novelist. There was something comic about the high seriousness with which each speaker lauded the literary merits of the new publication: the language, the characterization, the plot structures, and so on. The list of eulogists included some genuine luminaries, including the head of the Literature Institute from the Chinese Academy of Social Sciences. The real host of this expensive reception, I was told, was the Hong Kong novelist herself, who had flown in with her rich businessman husband. A fiftyish woman in heavy makeup and a white miniskirt, she demurely told the reporters about her pious Christian beliefs and the solitary pains of the writer's life.

Afterward, I asked my reporter friend how he would evaluate this press conference. He shrugged: "Pretty standard stuff. The red bag wasn't much, but it came on top of a pretty decent reception with beverages and stuff." I asked him if he was now going to write a report about it. He said he actually had to write two: one would be a brief piece for his own paper, but the other would take a bit of work, because it was a well-paid commission from a friend of his. Did the friend happen to be a friend of the Hong Kong novelist? He hesitated, but finally told me: "Well, it's a sort of business arrangement. My friend's company is interested in doing business with the novelist's husband."

Journalists tend to blame the epidemic of graft on the meager salaries they receive. If they don't take a red bag or two, how can they pay their bills these days? Then too, the kind of professional education Chinese journalists receive at schools and at work doesn't help. Proper political conduct has always been emphasized over proper professional conduct. The typical Chinese editor does not mind his reporters looking after their own welfare, but he *does* mind infractions of the political rules: one "incorrect" investigative report may cost him his own job.

Many Chinese believe that the arrival of capitalism makes all this inevitable, at least until a more developed legal and professional framework emerges. Some economists even have a term for this state of affairs, "inclusive corruption." They point to a trickle-down effect: if so many people participate in it and benefit from it, isn't it just another mode of redistributing wealth?

The real problem is that this sort of pervasive corruption breeds equally pervasive cynicism. Whatever advantages such arrangements have for cash-starved newspapers, the cost in public trust has been immeasurable. A young Beijing technician I know bought a pair of sneakers that had been recommended by a local newspaper report; two weeks later, the soles fell off. "All our lives we lived a political lie, and now we are living an economic lie," he told me, shaking his head at his credulousness. "The one sure thing you learn from this life is, an honest person is always at a disadvantage."

But even more worrisome was the reaction of one young man who appeared on Beijing Television Network when they questioned people in the street about what they considered the "most enviable profession today." His answer was immediate: "Reporter." Why? "Because reporters are practical-minded . . . just think of all the material benefits you can get."

Tier 4: Food Is Heaven

> I want to eat!
> Anything that flies in the sky but kites,
> Anything that has four legs on the earth but stools.
> *—Pledges of a Chinese gourmet*

HERE ARE the menus for two banquets held in honor of visiting dignitaries; they were printed in a Chinese newspaper for the reader's amusement:

MENU 1:
Boiled eggs with asparagus
Chicken livers
Fried rice
Carrots, spinach
Egg pudding
Strawberries
Cheese

Host: Queen of England
Guests: top Chinese statesmen

MENU 2:
Seafood platter
Young chicken
Baked tomatoes
Green peas
Lemon ice

Host: George Schultz, Secretary of State, USA
Guests: top Chinese statesmen

To a Chinese reader, this is the kind of joke that has a certain national proportion, and the newspaper commentator knew it. "By Chinese standards," he wrote, "these menus are at the level of a snack shop. In China, any banquet at any restaurant of any star rank would be far superior in sumptuousness to this."

When the South Korean President Kim Jungsam treated his guests to a simple bowl of noodles at his inauguration luncheon, it made headlines across many Chinese newspapers. What—is this a *joke*? A bowl of noodles, and nothing else? No lobster sashimi, no shark-fin soup? OK, Mr. Kim might be trying to make a point about his good intentions of running a self-restrained, virtuous government—but this was trying too hard.

For most Chinese today, when it comes to eating, qualities like simplicity, restraint, and virtue are not merely irrelevant; they are precisely what you cast off so long as you can afford to. The popular, admired, and inspiring attitude is to eat with abandon, to eat sinfully, to eat with style and flair and extravagance and ecstasy, as if there is no tomorrow.

This is probably the most savored aspect of the current Chinese economic prosperity: suddenly, there is so much to eat! You see edible things everywhere: the store shelves stuffed and stacked high with groceries of all sorts, the restaurant menus getting more and more lavish and dazzling, the street food fairs emerging in every city and town, the dinner party tables laden with dish upon dish, the long lanes of farmer's markets full of the freshest produce at affordable prices—fish jumping in buckets of water, turtles crawling in bamboo cages, chickens noisily talking to ducks, snakes slithering silently . . . and all are sure to be gulped down, with pleasure.

Austerity is gone, hedonism is in. The annual expense of functional banquets on mainland China these days is reportedly 100 billion yuan (about $19 billion). And that's only *official* feasts. As for the ordinary folks, Mencius, the number-two sage after Confucius, had this to say about them: "For the ordinary folks, food is heaven."

This is a China both ancient and new. Whatever businesses may have brought you to our land, ladies and gentlemen, you are cordially invited to share our table.

Have food, will do.

FOR ANY Chinese over thirty-five, memories of the great famine of 1960–63 must still linger on.

The famine was preceded by Mao's famous "Great Leap Forward," which, in retrospect, was really the beginning of a nationwide great leap into irrationality. How could people actually believe such lunatic reporting as wheat growing so densely in the field that it won't even bend with a baby rolling on top of it? But they did. In those days, the Chinese Communist Party had an incorruptible image; it held fantastic powers over people's imagination. It made people believe that the human will could create miracles, that economically China could surpass England and catch up with America in a matter of a few years, that a communist paradise was within reach. But famine came instead, and exercised *its* power relentlessly.

Born in late 1959, I was a baby delivered right into the famine. By the time I turned three, the famine had taken thirty million hungry souls and left the country devastated. It is said that in those years, even Chairman Mao and Premier Zhou Enlai had no meat on their plates. Even in big cities such as Beijing, people could get no more than a small bowl of rice in their stomachs each day. Bodily resistances ran so low that hepatitis and all sorts of epidemics raged out of control. People went to bed at eight every evening because they had no energy left to do anything else. And they would gloat over some tiny radish purchased at ten times the normal price from a peasant vendor; after making it into a clear soup seasoned with nothing but salt, they'd consider it an excellent dinner.

Yet, amazingly, the irrationality went on. All sorts of magical solutions were invented and earnestly taken up. Rice, for example, was said to rise twice as much if you just doubled the cooking time and added water to it after the first half of the steaming; scholars wrote articles about how much more nutritious this "double-steamed rice" was than normal steamed rice, and the government called on people to adopt the method widely. An even more puffed-up thing was "black tea fungus," a kind of duckweed one could grow at home in a water tank or a vat and eat as food; scholars wrote about the exceptional amount of protein this fungus contained, and claimed that it could even cure cancer. For a while, one could find a vat of black tea fungus brewing in almost every household: somehow the famine hadn't made people any less gullible. Their faith in the system remained virtually unbroken.

Still, the famine raged on. Due to food shortages and malnutrition, dropsy became widespread. My parents had to run all over Beijing in order to scrape up some milk powder or soybean milk for me. Even though their own stomachs were often empty, or half stuffed with chaff and wild herbs, they made desperate attempts to feed me properly. Still, I grew up with slightly bowed legs; like most people of my generation—nicknamed "the beansprouts generation"—I have a stringy figure.

By the time of my earliest memories, the famine had receded. Many things were still rationed: grain, meat, cooking oil, in fact almost all the essential food items—but at least we could once again eat three meals a day. The government relaxed economic policies; the commune system returned, partially, to conditional private ownership, and it worked. Agricultural output rose, the country was slowly recovering. In my memory, the only thing reminiscent of the famine years was a children's game: in springtime, we would go around the neighborhood, beat the branches of tall Chinese scholar trees with long bamboo poles, and collect the small white flowers that fell to the ground, and, carefully blowing the dust off, we would eat them. The flowers had a faint fragrance, the taste was not particularly unpleasant, but after you chewed several mouthfuls, a puckery, almost bitter flavor would linger on your tongue for a long while, bringing to mind the shabby taste of hunger, shortages, and poverty.

MY HUSBAND, Benjamin Lee, nutty anthropologist and organizer of international conferences, after countless work meals and banquets he had been pleased or pressed to attend over the years in Hong Kong, Taiwan, and mainland China, observed: "China has, it seems to me, as many public spheres as there are banquet tables." He was traveling in China, working on an academic exchange program involving debates about Jürgen Habermas's theory of the public sphere. "If you want to get a sense of what's going on in China, you've got to sniff around at the banquet tables."

"*Corruption*! Corruption is what's going on at the banquet tables," says Wang, a young Beijing reporter friend of mine. When a great flood broke out in the mostly rural central area of China in 1991, nobody at his paper wanted to go there. Parts of the flooded areas were poor, parts well-off since the reform of the eighties; but under the circumstances, they couldn't possibly promise a good field trip—the kind in which reporters from a major Beijing paper are plied with banquets and gifts from local officials wanting favorable press coverage. However, Wang, being an upright young reporter hungry for experience, volunteered to go. Once there, he was shocked, he tells me—not so much by the ravaged landscape as by the banquet scenes. "I went down and under to get stories about suffering and hardship, but everywhere I saw people eating and drinking up a storm, surrounded by the debris of catastrophe!" Where did the money come from? Mostly from the aid the central government allocated to the flooded regions. Everyone in Beijing had been required to donate something. My mother, for instance, had packed off a bundle of blankets and clothes; Wang himself had given away his winter cotton coat. International aid poured in, too. The bulk of it came from Hong Kong, a total of about $80 million U.S. The official media kept on talking about the solidarity of the Chinese as a nation, and how only in a socialist society is such generous mutual aid among the ordinary citizens possible. Even though a lot of ordinary citizens in Beijing were grumbling about being forced to help, Wang had not thought what the government said was completely false—until he saw how the aid money was being squandered, gulped down. At every bureaucratic level, officials in charge of flood funds found excuses to spend it generously on "work banquets."

Soon enough, Wang found himself being coopted for just such an end.

The strangest event of his trip, though, involved a small group of Christian volunteers from Hong Kong. The group had brought from their constituency a handy donation, which was to be used to rebuild a local school in a poor village. The group of young believers arrived there to supervise and help with the construction. Before stopping by their temporary tents, a local Party cadre had invited Wang to a banquet and gave him some advice: "Be careful, Little Wang," the older cadre patted his shoulders after a couple of drinks of good liquor, "those people from Hong Kong, we don't know what their real intentions are. We've got orders from above to keep folks away from them." The banquet table was covered with dishes, but the cadre apologized: "You'd have tasted some first-rate soft-shell turtles if you had come at a better time." His wrinkled face turned red, his eyes watery from liquor and food, and he told Wang: "When you reach my age, you'll appreciate the old wisdom more: the meaning of life lies in two words—eat, and drink."

The Hong Kong group was eating their dinner inside the tent when Wang called. In one glance, Wang could tell it was no banquet—just some steamed rice and soup. A young man rose and greeted Wang rather coldly, without inviting him into the tent. They stood outside and talked for a while. Before parting, the young man from Hong Kong suddenly smiled at Wang: "I thought you reporters weren't supposed to approach us." "Frankly," Wang says as he recounts this to me, "I felt like getting it all off my chest right there and then, telling him what I really thought—but I couldn't. Part of it was embarrassment. That Hong Kong guy looked so young and so innocent, sort of bookish with his glasses and a straight manner. In those surroundings, their frugality and generosity seemed almost jarring." The last words Wang heard in that poor village were from an old peasant woman. She held Wang's hands and said: "Young man, you must tell everybody it's true: the Communist Party is good! We all got our blankets here, and we have food on the table."

"THE WIND of eating and drinking with public money," as the Chinese media normally put it, has blown stronger in the recent years—so much so that whenever there is an official rectification or anticorruption campaign, the restaurateurs suffer severely. Since fancy business banquets are nearly always paid with public money, restaurant business fluctuates a good deal by the official thermometer. However, as economic reform erodes central control more and more, these campaigns no longer carry the force they once did: as soon as a campaign peters out, the winds of eating and drinking return, with a vengeance, sweeping across the country like a storm. Smiles return to the restaurateurs' faces as they watch waiters and waitresses busily zipping around the packed floors and partitioned banquet suites. It is indeed a warm, happy scene: bustling, noisy, filled with sounds of clinking glasses, lively talk, hearty laughter, and, from time to time, blissfully contented burps and the smacking of lips.

Food softens people. A good, satisfying meal often has a way of making someone a bit warmer, a bit more easygoing, to bring out his or her humanity. With a sated tongue and a full stomach, people are somehow more inclined to be generous and loose about the world and its inhabitants. The Chinese come alive at such an occasion: it's time to relax and enjoy, to appreciate food and friends, to spin tall tales, swap jokes and exchange opinions, to show character and bravado, to gossip, and to impress.

At the other extreme, though, faith in an iron will and abstract virtue, rather than acceptance of gluttony and generally flawed human nature, can be a truly scary thing. I often find the formal, incorrigible Chinese men at banquet tables more threatening: they may be incorruptible, but in their unswerving, rigid goodness they may also be more willing to kill and destroy others without blinking an eye.

Chinese culture, it is often said, is an oral one: eating and talking are two essential things the Chinese love to indulge in, and the two are best when they go together. Dinner parties and banquets are thus a central form of Chinese social communication. It's hard to think of anything else comparable to communal dining: not singing, dancing, drinking, sports, movie- or theater-going, temple- or church-visiting—none is nearly as important or as widespread. A banquet, on the other hand, is an age-old social form, well tested, well practiced, shot through with layers of complicated etiquette on scales both high and low.

All sorts of things go on around a Chinese meal table. Business and political intrigues are two of them, though usually one doesn't bring up business topics at a banquet. Rather, here one is expected to socialize, to bond, to display one's worldliness and prowess at banquet rituals, such as toasting respected elders before the younger ones, helping certain guests with certain dishes, paying compliments in the right way, and so on. In short, one should above all create a good impression—and a good impression goes a long way in business or politics.

Conversations at a banquet or a dinner party have a special thickness and style. The shape of a typical Chinese meal table is suggestive: it is a perfect round. One rarely sees rows of long banquet tables as in the West, which force guests to carry their entire conversation with one or a few other people nearby. The Chinese banquet table creates a different atmosphere and a different experience. It is almost like a show, a theater, in which a central theme or a couple of stars usually dominate at a given moment, though all have the freedom to jump in and take a turn in the performance. Surrounding the eminences, the rest can choose to watch or applaud, making wry asides or chorus noises as they like. The psychology behind this style is distinctively Chinese. At the core of it, I think, lie the roots of a deeply collective, hierarchical culture. Chinese attitudes toward gender, age, and social status all come into play at a banquet. The social hierarchy is reflected clearly here: more often than not, the older, male, powerful, and well-off ones dominate the conversation, receive the first toasting, and pay the bill. In both Hong Kong and mainland China, wealthy senior men are usually expected to pay the restaurant bills. If a woman has more money than any man at the table, in the more commercialized south, where men tend to be pragmatic, she pays; but in the more traditional north, such as in Beijing, men still find it disconcerting to let a woman pay. I have often encountered such situations in Beijing: to save my male friend's face, we end up going to small, cheap restaurants, pretending to look for "authentic local flavor," so the men can pay in the end.

TO SOME extent, a Chinese meal table is a prototypical Chinese public space, a paradigm of the Chinese society and its conventions. Maybe that's why, at least until now, it is anything but romantic. A Chinese restaurant is by definition too public a place for romance: the bright lights, the noise, the openness, the closeness of others, the smells and the jovial laughter . . . the ambience is altogether too earthy, and the idea of a romance begun in such surroundings almost turns your stomach. Afterward, maybe; but here, the most you can do with a date isn't much more than filling up for later.

Yet when it comes to showing off wealth and flair, Chinese restaurants are known above all others to go all the way. I can't think of anywhere else I've seen restaurants presenting for the super rich such astonishingly extravagant meals with such guiltless, and some might say tasteless, flair. To pay one thousand yuan per person for a Qing court-style banquet of over a hundred dishes? That's like tossing away five months of an average Chinese man's salary just for one seat. But think of the exquisite splendor of an imperial banquet room, the culinary masterpieces, the rare delicacies, the showmanship of both the chefs and the hosts . . . People are fascinated by such fare. In recent years, as the economic boom has produced more and more local millionaires, banquets like this have caught on. Sensing the public's curiosity, the local media never fail to cover them with enthusiasm. Especially in the prosperous Cantonese south, many are willing to pay extra to taste rare delicacies—again, to satisfy not only gourmet proclivities but also to show off. A man who pays a half month's salary just for a small portion of a roasted pangolin or some monkey brains is not likely to miss the opportunity of bragging to his friends the next day; "My, you don't know how delicious pangolin meat is. It's heavenly!" It is this attitude that has induced a local essayist to comment upon the pledges of the Chinese gourmet I quoted at the beginning. "Let's eat!" the essayist wrote. "After finishing off all but kites and stools, we'll just have to eat kites stir-fried with stools."

I myself haven't met any extremist gourmets in Canton. During my last few visits there, my hosts, a Cantonese couple who repeatedly took me out to sumptuous meals, loved to eat, but the meals were in no way extraordinary. They are in their late thirties and have become quite rich in the past few years through private business, but they are neither pretentious nor extravagant. The husband wore the same sports jacket every time I saw him: "I don't care about clothes at all, as long as I have something to wear," he told me. "But food is everything." To reciprocate his hospitality, I proposed several times to take them out to a nice restaurant. They would readily agree and show up promptly—but when time came to pay, the husband would quickly put his shining Great Wall credit card on the bill plate and insist firmly: "No! No! It's my treat, of course. It will always be my treat no matter where it is: here in Canton, or in Beijing, or even in America if I were to visit you there in the future. You must indulge me in this, because honestly, besides doing business, food is my only passion."

6

YELLOW PERIL

THE BEST-SELLING author in China after the great Chairman Mao may be a slight little man named Jia Pingwa. Instead of the Little Red Book, Jia has written a big yellow book—yellow being the color that signifies sex and pornography in China. In *The Abandoned Capital (Feidu)*, Jia's thick, juicy new novel about contemporary life in an old Chinese city, the red fire of revolution has long since faded. What burns in its place in the hearts and minds of today's Chinese men and women is a flame much more ancient and enduring: sex. And what does life mean besides a good fuck? Well, for the citizens of the abandoned capital, it means eating, bribing, scheming, and generally gypping each other off.

The novel and its author, though they've taken as much beating as touting, have taken China by storm. Described by the media as "the event that caused a great literary and publishing earthquake in 1993," *The Abandoned Capital* sold a half million copies within the first few months of its publication and, with more than ten pirated versions available, countless more later on. Wild accolades, from both critical and popular sources, have showered on it. The novel has been hailed, for instance, as "an epic work of the Chinese intellectual soul" and "an extraordinary monument of contemporary Chinese literature." A lot of intellectuals and Chinese literati, on the other hand, have condemned the novel, outraged by its "unbearably vulgar sex scenes" and "despicable male sexual psychology." If Jia must write nakedly about sex, they demand, why couldn't he at least write about it with some beauty and depth, as D. H. Lawrence had done? All decent, educated Chinese readers admired *Lady Chatterley's Lover*, which had only been released in China a few years earlier. Why couldn't our novelist elevate sexuality and render in it some spiritual meaning? In place of a world of emotion and romance, Jia had us toss and tumble in an arena of flesh! A Beijing graduate student drew the distinction between Lawrence and Jia this way: while reading both of them may cause a young man to masturbate, with Lawrence he may feel a bit ashamed of himself afterward, but never with Jia!

Government officials at the antipornography office weren't happy about the situation, either. For years now, they have been fighting hard the swelling "yellow trade" with arrests, bans, confiscations, even an occasional execution. This time, though, they were caught in a strange bind: *The Abandoned Capital* is penned by a famous, serious novelist who has not only a stainless political and moral record but also a reputation for having produced in the past only "pure literature." Is it possible for someone like that to have written a yellow book, or a filthy novel showing moral turpitude, as some people have claimed it to be?

Meanwhile, many elite critics openly or privately deplored yet another case of a gifted, serious writer "selling out" under commercial pressures and "degenerating" into the low ranks of pornography and *ditan wenxue*, "literature for the sidewalk stalls." The Chinese writers' imagination is withering rapidly, they lamented, and now they must resort to catering to the sex-hungry soul of the average Chinese in order to gain fame and profit. What a sad example of the vulgarization of literature!

All the same, the novel kept on selling, and people kept on talking about it. For every verdict of condemnation, there would be a matching comment of admiration and encouragement. As a matter of fact, it's been so long since a work of fiction stirred such passionate debate that some people began to wonder if this wasn't a sign of the public's renewed interest in literature. Some even hoped that the success of this one novel would help raise the market value of literature in general and enable it to "walk out from the bottom of the valley." Maybe television soaps and pop singers and karaoke bars are not going to dominate all—maybe the demand for good writing is still there.

Zhang Yiwu, a young Beijing critic noted for his essays on postmodernism, is not given to such wistful thinking. He says that *The Abandoned Capital* is a watershed event only in the sense that China, for the first time, has a commercially hyped-up major best-seller written by a serious novelist as a serious artistic work: from now on, he says, "the division between the high and the low in Chinese literature has vanished." Jia's novel, Zhang further points out, suggests that the trend of "quality writing for leisurely reading" is making a comeback. The trend had had a lively play in the Chinese literary scene back in the twenties and thirties but later was overridden by the political ideology that ushered in a literature for the proletariat. In any event, by the end of 1993, *The Abandoned Capital* had withstood (and thrived under) all the skepticism and mudslinging from the cultural elite, and became a household name in China.

Jia Pingwa is a forty-one-year-old novelist living in Xian, the capital of Shaanxi province in northeastern China. Xian is an ancient city known for its rich historical sights and, more recently, for having produced Zhang Yimou, the celebrated film director. Jia isn't riding on anyone's coattails, though: a literary prodigy with a smooth-sailing career, he is a prodigious natural writer blessed by early critical plaudits. He is also one of those serious literary postulants who has enjoyed something of a popular following. He writes both fiction and *sanwen*, a popular Chinese genre best described as a form of meditative prose essays with literary overtones, and his works have been published everywhere in China, some of them in Taiwan and Hong Kong. He is admired as a beautiful stylist, and his fluid, beguilingly simple prose seems able to charm readers across varied classes and regions. In the Xian literary scene, he has been, of course, larger than life.

Still, nobody expected *The Abandoned Capital*. Widely taken to be more or less autobiographical, it surprised many of Jia's fans like a sudden, bizarre revelation. Set in the ancient capital city of Xijing (which is easily recognizable as Xian), the novel centers around the story of Zhuang Zhidie, a middle-aged, frustrated writer whose enormous literary fame helps to pave way for both his sexual adventures and his eventual destruction. The main plot line can be summed up simply: small-town hustling writer Zhou Min comes to Xijing and tries to make a name by publishing a gossipy profile of the famous Zhuang. In it, he freely exaggerates Zhuang's past romantic liaison with a now powerful woman colleague; the woman files a libel suit that ends up involving everyone in the city's literary circles. Meanwhile, Zhuang embarks on an affair with Zhou's sexy mistress, and later begins affairs with various other women. Zhuang's wife and friends try to use all their connections and influences to settle the libel suit, to no avail; in the end, misfortune falls on most of the main characters. Zhuang loses everything—the suits, his wife, his mistresses. He gives up writing and flees the city.

This summary, though, hardly conveys the sense of this dark, dank novel that literally oozes slimy, sinister scenes and characters. Dwelling on the details of everyday events in a meticulously realist fashion, the novel unfolds gradually, almost blithely—a picture of life in an old capital city that is rotten and perverse in every way: its pervasive greed, corruption, and hypocrisy, its superstitious beliefs, its prurient repressiveness, and its stagnant powers. The author gives no specific time reference, but the story's contemporaneity is beyond question. For one thing, popular ditties about eighties corruption and the new social hierarchy are frequently cited in the novel by a prophetic old man, a sort of town freak who collects and sells garbage—any Chinese reader will instantly recognize these satirical rhymes. With its large cast of characters, the novel seems to have rounded up the usual suspects who have been running rampant and looming large under the dark Chinese sky in the wake of Mao: a phony, corrupt mayor and his corrupt, sycophantic underlings, small-time hustlers, hooligans, creeps, shameless mandarins, sham artists, entrepreneurs who make fake products, scheming family servants, a manipulative and wanton nun, a hooker who spreads veneral disease, and even an opium addict. Nobody in sight is innocent or very likable, not even the hero. With all his existential suffering and self-piteous whining about his own weakness, when the moment comes, Zhuang is quite capable of licking the asses of powerful officials, or marrying off, for his own interest, one of his mistresses to the mayor's crippled son. Through treacherous sleight of hand, he helps to kill one of his best friends in order to get his collection of rare art. The way every character in the book cheats and grabs in his or her own self-interest while paying lip service to the status quo displays a brand of ancient cynicism that, revived, is pervading Chinese society in recent years.

Central to this fin-de-siècle scenery are Zhuang Zhidie's sexual exploits. The traditional bugaboos of a well-established fortysomething male are all there to prepare us for his wild tripping-out: Zhuang is emotionally inhibited, growing skeptical about his celebrity status, fearful that his creative juices have dried up, and ashamed of the impotence he experiences with his good-hearted, thick-headed wife, who is a cold fish in bed. So when Zhou's mistress, a coquettish small-town beauty named Tang Waner, appears on the scene, this timid, repressed man of slight physique and homely looks is tranformed into a Chinese Don Juan—and he certainly finds his match in Tang. Having liberated herself from a boorish husband by eloping with Zhou to Xijing, Tang is already getting bored and restless with her new life. The moment she and Zhuang set eyes on each other at a dinner party, Tang turns hot-cheeked and Zhuang hurries to the restroom to relieve his erection. Tang and Zhuang soon take to secret rendezvous and lustful fornication—which opens the floodgates for sex with a vengeance. Between frequent sexual feats with Tang, Zhuang quickly adds his pretty housemaid and a worker's good-looking wife to his list of conquests. He never really needs to seduce these beautiful women though: they more or less drop to their knees, craving or begging for his sexual favor as soon as they learn who he is—the famous literary celebrity whom the entire city worships. His appeal is such that even a whore offers him free sex after exchanging but a few words with him. The only woman Zhuang does try to seduce is the demure wife of one of his best friends, but he fails in this: being a prudish sort, she pushes him out of her bed even as she tearfully confesses her eternal love for him. The only woman in the novel who has an education, a career, and a somewhat urban character is the well-connected colleague who files the libel suit against him. In the old days, when Zhuang was still a young man fresh from the countryside, struggling to make a name for himself in the city, he had held her in awe and had merely dared to romanticize her in his head. But during their long, bitter lawsuit, he keeps wondering if she is sour about him because he didn't make it with her back then. After losing the case, he plunges into a drunken fantasy of marrying and then humiliating her:

> [H]e has their wedding announcement printed in all newspapers, and has the ceremony take place in a luxurious hotel. After an evening of noisy celebration, he asks the guests not to leave. First he shuts the bedroom door. Then, imitating the ancient Chinese as well as the modern Westerners, he invites her to bed, reads parts of *The Golden Lotus* to her, and plays Western porno videos for her. He arouses her desire, strips her, caresses her with his hands, with some feathers, with his mouth and tongue. She gets excited, out of control, but he still rubs her, overwhelms her senses, laughingly presses against that most sensitive spot. Finally, amid her hot breathing and trembling words, he sees a stream of frothy juice welling up from the cluster of her brilliant hair. So he rubs clean his finger on her belly, picks up a piece of broken tile which he had earlier placed underneath the bed and covers her with it. Then he puts on his clothes and walks out. Solemnly he announces to the guests still gathered in the living room: from this moment on, I renounce my marriage with Jing Xueyin! Right away the news gets televised. The guests stand in astonishment, as though asking: Didn't you just marry her? Why divorce her now? He bursts out laughing: I have now fulfilled my duty!

This is by no means the most lascivious passage in the book. Filled with vengeful hatred, this is probably the tamest of all the book's sex scenes — which total over sixty, by one reviewer's count. Despite a certain archaic quality in his prose style, the author usually depicts sex graphically and in minute detail; in the fashion of hard-core porno-erotic novels. He turns up the heat, too and provides a good variety: masturbation, wet dreams aplenty, a dash of voyeurism, and even a ménage-à-trois. In a peculiar twist, though, Jia always omits the last juicy details of sexual intercourse, marking it with six conspicuous blank blocks followed by a note in parentheses: "(here the author deleted xxx words)." This self-censorship has become notorious since the novel's publication, viewed by many critics as a coy trick, a deliberate way to highlight the sex scenes and play hide-and-seek with the readers' sexual imagination. As for the scenes that have been written out fully, the author sometimes reveals a kinky taste that would easily shock a prudish reader — such as Zhuang fondly licking Tang's scabs, or Tang pasting her pubic hair onto a love letter and having it sent to Zhuang by pigeon. In a sort of *Fatal Attraction* déjà vu in reverse, the pigeon eventually ends up in a steampot: after Zhuang's wife finds out about the affair, she boils the bird into a soup and forces it down the two adulterers' throats. One may also imagine the genteel reader's reaction to another unconventional scene in which Zhuang and Tang make love soon after her abortion, leaving a big splotch of blood on the pillow; afterward, Tang embroiders it into a maple leaf design and displays the pillow as an artwork in a gallery show.

This is a radical departure for a novelist who has been famous for his peasant roots, pure spirits, and warm, colorful portraits of Chinese rural life. In fact, *The Abandoned Capital* is Jia's first novel about "the city"; some say it's his first mature novel or "middle-age" novel. Clearly, the image of Chinese urbanity in his eyes is far from pleasing. If anything, the city seems to be the gathering place for all manner of human venality, a place where things can only go from bad to worse. The city runs in a vicious cycle: its social and political system appear to be hopelessly rotten yet self-sustaining and enduring, and its citizens hopelessly cynical and cowardly yet complacent in their own petty games and vanity. In explaining the title of his novel, Jia sounded a metaphysical note. The city of Xian, he said, has been the capital of twelve dynasties in Chinese history. Although it has long declined and has by now become a backward place, pride and smugness about the past have not faded in people's minds: the result is a kind of inferior-superior mindset, a cynical wisdom arising from helplessness, an anguish from embarrassment. This cultural mindset of the Xian people is extremely typical. In a sense, Xian is the abandoned capital of China, China the abandoned capital of the world, and our earth the abandoned capital of the universe. Writing about the Xian mentality is writing about the Chinese mentality in general.

This could be deadly. Such a fatalistic, apocalyptic vision of China as an abandoned, spiritless, and decadent civilization, going nowhere at the end of the century, could be the sort of political dynamite that, before anything else, blows up the novel itself. Certainly it clashes with China's prevalent mood of prosperity and optimism, which the government promotes and a good portion of the population gladly indulge in. In keeping with its newly gained commercial instinct, the media hype surrounding the novel has predictably chosen to focus on issues of money and sex. So, fortunately—or perhaps unfortunately—another clamor has drowned out Jia's dark, pessimistic voice, for the time being at least.

Interestingly, however, the first buzz about the novel grew from an outrageous claim to high literature: "*The Abandoned Capital* is the *Dream of the Red Chamber* of our time," a newspaper article quoted someone who had read the manuscript as saying—invoking an eighteenth century Qing Dynasty masterpiece by Cao Xueqin about the fortunes and tragedies of four decadent high families, which for the Chinese is the greatest fiction classic. Evidence of *The Abandoned Capital*'s superficial resemblances is easy to find: like *Dream of the Red Chamber*, Jia also opens his novel with a long narrative introduction about four decadent, prominent men, though he eventually fleshes out only one man and his family while the other three remain sketchy. Like Cao, Jia also chronicles domestic life in a prominent house—meals, banquets, family finance, parental and marital relations, outings and parties—with almost no mention of any great historical events at the time. And like Cao, whose famous hero has become a literary archetype of *qingzhong*, a born lover, Jia also portrays his modern-day hero this way and uses his involvement with many women as a central plot line. Finally, all ends tragically just as it does in Cao's great novel: the big families collapse, the women either die or fall into disgrace, and the disillusioned hero flees the scene.

Word of *The Abandoned Capital* spread fast among publishers, precipitating a frantic bidding war for Jia's manuscript: telegrams, phone calls, letters, editors and publishers themselves, all descended on Jia for his predetermined masterpiece. He was mobbed in his hotel room when he came to Beijing in March to attend a meeting of the Political Council Congress. According to the reporters who seemed to be on the scene to cover every step of the bidding transaction, the right to publish Jia's novel even attracted bids from three non-publishing corporations and two bookstores. Eventually, Jia decided to give the rights to Beijing Press, a major state-owned publishing house that would not only publish the novel in book form but would devote an entire issue of its own literary magazine, *October*, to printing the novel. According to some reports, Jia made the decision for sentimental reasons, for the *October* editor, a fiftyish woman originally from Jia's own province, had read the manuscript nine times in a row and showed a deep understanding of it.

Meanwhile, a local paper reported that he had received payment of a million yuan, and a dozen other papers instantly picked the story up. Suddenly, the entire Chinese literary community had something to sleep on: one million for a novel not yet in print? The going rate these days is but a few thousand—and one should thank one's lucky stars for getting printed at all, for the joke of the day is that there are more people writing novels than reading novels. The new image of a Chinese man of letters is someone with thick spectacles on a big head and thin legs over old shoes—quite a pathetic creature. But a millionaire novelist! How thrilling! Even though the one million yuan payment turned out to be misinformation from an overly excited reporter (she misread 150 yuan per 1000 words as a 1,000,150 total), its sensational effect lingered on. The press speculated endlessly about the exact sum Jia received from his editors; it has never been publicly confirmed, and the press likes to keep it that way.

While still at the printer, the novel received yet another crowning from unspecified publicity sources. This time it was something that made all the book dealers, salesmen, and future readers perk their ears: "*The Abandoned Capital* is *The Golden Lotus* of our time!" *The Golden Lotus* (Jin Ping Mei), the novel with which Jia's hero arouses his female colleague in his wedding fantasy, is *the* Chinese classic of sexual debauchery of *all* time. This notoriously earthy late Ming Dynasty novel describes the life of a wealthy, dandyish merchant, Ximen Qing—in particular his tireless, randy sexual relations with his concubines, housemaids, and boys. The novel is highly valued for its literary merits as well, and it greatly influenced the author of *The Dream of the Red Chamber*, though scholars usually praise the later work for its more romantic, spiritual tone, its aristocratic refinements, and perfect literary delivery. *The Golden Lotus* has never been able to shake off its coarser image because of its excessive delight in the flesh and its lack of spiritual transcendence. To this day in China, it is nearly impossible to get an unabridged copy. The government allowed an "internal circulation" of it in the fifties; ironically, only ministers and heads of provinces were permitted copies. In the early eighties, the Qilu Press of Shandong Province obtained permission to reprint a small quantity for literary historian, but it is still inaccessible to a lot of scholars. Taking advantage of the ban, some private book vendors have surreptitiously peddled pirate copies of the complete version; worse yet, some have simply collected all the censored bits and pieces in a special juicy text, which sold for a very high price. All of this has further contributed to the myth of *The Golden Lotus* as the ultimate sex bomb in print. And now, here comes *The Abandoned Capital, The Golden Lotus* of our time! How can you beat a sales pitch like that!

Book dealers everywhere scrambled for orders. "I just leafed through some pages," one private distributor told a reporter. "Right away, I knew it would sell." According to one report, the demand for the novel at some regional book-ordering conferences climbed to hundreds of thousands of copies. To prevent pirate printing, Beijing Press even paid one hundred thousand yuan to have a protective seal put around copies of the novel. This, of course, soon proved to be useless.

Finally, in late July, the novel arrived in the book stores. On the first day, over a thousand copies were sold at a downtown Beijing bookstore, and Jia, who was there signing books, had to be carried off by the police from the crowd of fans. By September, the entire first print run of 480,000 copies was sold out. The summer issue of *October* that carried the novel sold out, too.

Hong Kong publishers began to release their elegant printing of the novel. By the time Beijing Press rushed out a second printing of about 170,000 copies, the inevitable pirate versions had already appeared on the bookstalls across the nation. Given the chaotic situation of the current Chinese book market, accurate figures of total sales are impossible to compute—but it does not seem out of line to estimate that by the end of 1993, *The Abandoned Capital* had sold well over a million copies. Some put the figure as high as several million.

All through the summer and fall of 1993, rumors of a pending ban or of official orders to criticize *The Abandoned Capital* were circulating. Browsing at a bookstall on a busy Beijing street in November, I was urged by a brisk book vendor to buy the novel "before it's banned." "It's the hottest book this year," he informed me, just in case I hadn't heard. "I still sell dozens of it every day." At a new book market on the east side of Beijing, a salesman worked on me with another line: "They say it's going to be officially criticized!" This made me smile, because right there at the marketplace several bookstores had hung posters on their doors attacking the novel. LEARN THE TRUTH ABOUT THE DESPICABLE NOVEL, one poster railed, AND TEAR AWAY THE MASK OF A SHAME-LESS WRITER! The poster was there to entice customers to buy several rushed-out books of criticisms of the novel. Skimming through a couple of them, I wondered if any official attack could be more devastating than the words of these literary critics. And surely, whoever designed these sales posters would not lose a shouting match with a propaganda officer.

After so many efforts at censorship have backfired, the government may have finally caught on, because it has grown more wary of announcing a ban. Now it's the commercial sector that knows how to exploit the Party tradition—a trend that the Party probably didn't foresee when it first commercialized Chinese publishing years ago. Chinese entrepreneurs promptly took the ball and ran with it. Using the more flexible guidelines as well as loopholes and weaknesses in the old system, they've laid out a tremendous new network of private and semiprivate book distribution channels, linking both state and private publishers with book vendors across the country. Today, this "second channel," as it is commonly known in the publishing trade, exists like a parallel structure alongside the old state-run distribution system.

Unlike its outmoded, inefficient official sibling, however, it operates primarily by profit motive and market laws. Given the transitional, poorly regulated nature of the Chinese publishing market, the second-channel entrepreneurs have a collective reputation for running their businesses in a crass, wild-west style. Many stories circulate in the state publishing circles about how untrustworthy the second channel is, how as often as not a private distributor will take your books and disappear, without paying a cent in return. Although I've heard many Chinese editors describing the second channel as a semi-underground mafia dominated by a bunch of immoral, cash-hungry swindlers, it is also often credited with bringing into Chinese publishing a degree of professional savvy and business acuity. Forced to compete with or to use the second channel, the state-run publishing houses have learned to keep close tabs not only on the Party's and the elite's preferences but also on those of average readers. And they don't always converge: when the Party wants people to stay away from a certain book, or when the elite snubs it, that might just be the sort of book that average folks would love to read. It took no time at all for most people in publishing, especially for book vendors on the street, to realize that a potential ban was always good for sales, since forbidden fruit is almost always more enticing. What's more, because the government has never been able to contain pirated copies and illicit sales—both being hallmarks of the second channel—even after a ban is officially announced, it has become virtually impossible to effectively enforce it. With so many private bookstalls everywhere, there is no way to keep a good check on all of them.

"The government is much wiser these days," the head of a Beijing publishing house told me. "It has learned that the best way to deal with the intellectuals is not to deal with them at all, and the best way to cool a controversy is to put it on the back burner."

Still, tensions were acute in the gray buildings that house the Beijing Press. Tian Zhenying, the editor of *The Abandoned Capital*, told me that she and her colleagues at the press have been feeling a lot of pressure "from the top" since the book's publication. As of this writing, no official decision had been conveyed to them, but rumors had been running amok. As a rule, if a book is branded "reactionary" and banned, somebody at the publishing house must be held responsible and punished accordingly. The rumors were already taking a toll: to play it safe, the house decided to hold back the release of their second stock of the novel until they receive clear signals from their superiors. So far, the only clear thing is that the house is watching on the sidelines with their overstock of originals while private distributors are making loads of profit from the pirated copies.

Asked what the main reason behind the novel's commercial success is, nearly everyone—editors, critics, writers, and common readers—has the same reply: sex, of course it is sex. According to several surveys, some readers felt somewhat cheated after buying the novel, complaining that "it doesn't go all the way" on sex. But they bought it and read it—portions of it, anyway. Some critics noted sarcastically that if Jia intended to write a modern-day

Dream of the Red Chamber, he ended up producing a work closer to *The Golden Lotus*. These critics bought it and read every word of it—by their own confession, often more than once. A prominent filmmaker told me after reading the novel; "It doesn't have a high literary value, but Jia's an honest man— he wrote exactly the way he fucked." Somebody even made up a line parodying a famous rhyme from *Dream of the Red Chamber*: "Jia is not a fake: culture is his name, sex his horse." (In Chinese, Jia is a synonym of "fake" and also happens to be the surname of the hero in *Dream of the Red Chamber*.)

At a dinner in Beijing, I asked a well-known, arrogant novelist friend of mine for his opinion. He patted my shoulder: "I hope you won't go around fooling your American friends about this trash. Put it this way: if one day I decide to throw my face away for money, you'd get another hot and bothered best-seller. Anybody knows how to take his pants off if he wants to." Later, a newspaper cartoonist added his professional spin to this. "You see, it's a face and ass issue," he explained, showing me his spoof sketches of a bare-bottomed novelist. "Jia took off his pants and showed a not-so-pretty ass. Those critics can't bear the sight; it reminds them of their own ugly asses. So they cover their faces and yell, 'Shameless, cover your ass!'"

REMOVING ONE'S pants wasn't just a face issue in the Maoist epoch, even though face was just about all one could see those years in China. Sex practically vanished from sight in Chinese culture; people kept their Mao suits buttoned up tight all the time. It wasn't a matter of choice: viewing sex as a sign of bourgeois decadence and something that would erode revolutionary purity and military morale, the communists promulgated a stiffly antibody, antiflesh, antisexuality attitude. They systematically eradicated all palpable signs of bodily interest and institutions of carnal pleasure.

One of the first things the new regime did in its early days of power, around 1950, was to shut down all the brothels, opium dens, and gambling houses, which had been a lively, thriving part of old and cosmopolitan cities such as Beijing or Shanghai. To clean up the "dregs of feudal culture" and rejuvenate the "sick body of East Asia," the young government earnestly and ruthlessly implemented measures to wipe out pornographic trade and literature, to cure opium addicts, and to eradicate venereal diseases. There were campaigns for reforming prostitutes: they were treated as victims, given a political education, then assigned to healthy, normal jobs and welcomed back into the bosom of the proletariat because these poor women were our *jieji jiemei*, "sisters of our own class." In a nation that had been ravaged by decades of wars, poverty, and injustice, the Party's vigorously purist ideology sounded like a clarion call for a healthier, stronger, and more egalitarian society. This serious moral purpose, combined with "class compassion," worked wonders—not only on prostitutes and gamblers but also on many sophisticated intellectuals and old guards of traditional culture. Not simply cowed by the new regime's power, they were genuinely charmed by the new ideology. It was refreshing, irresistible, too good to question. It was a time dominated by the power of virtue. Nobody knew that Chairman Mao was in fact a great lecher, satisfying his thirst in the grand style of the great Chinese peasant emperors; nobody would have believed it.

With each following decade, the puritanical, ascetic nature of the Party culture intensified and climbed to new heights. In place of old brothels and pleasure quarters, the state built workers' palaces and public parks for the proper amusement of the masses. There, dressed in plain, clean, sexless clothes, the people gathered and celebrated revolutionary occasions, danced and sang innocent, joyful songs on holidays. The rest of the time they devoted to the work of constructing a new China. Women comrades worked like men, and were to be treated like men; love was mostly a comradely feeling, marriage a comradely union. In the language of the time, the entire process of courting, dating, and marrying was summed up in one standard phrase: *jiejue geren wenti,* "to solve one's personal problems." It sounded like a military phrase in the same league with, say, "to blow up an enemy's fortress" or "to overcome an obstacle at one's job": you dealt with your "personal problems" in the same way you dealt with other matters. In reality, nothing could be truly personal or private, none could be judged separately by ethics other than proletarian morality. To dwell on carnal thoughts was shameful, to flaunt one's sexuality was wicked, and to commit one improper sexual act (such as a man peeping into a women's bathroom, or an extramarital affair) could very well ruin your whole life. In the jargon of the time, it was referred to as "making a lifestyle mistake"—a crime second only to "making a political mistake."

By the seventies, not just sex but romance had altogether disappeared from Chinese arts and literature. Heroes and heroines in novels usually remained single and single-minded, displaying interest only in their revolutionary mission. Paintings, sculptures, and posters depicted fearless, robotic figures in work uniforms, always either raising a clenched fist against enemies or smiling happily and idiotically at Chairman Mao or at the nation's rosy collective future. Nor did the few movies the Chinese got to see in those years show any trace of sex, either: the screen was filled with war commandos and soldiers, class struggles unto death, workers and peasants too deeply engrossed in their noble jobs to bother with such trifles as the charms of the opposite sex.

My generation of Chinese were considered the red children of the Cultural Revolution. We grew up in a culturally vacuous environment, amazing for its sexual ignorance. In my elementary and middle school days, girls and boys almost never spoke to one another. We never so much as looked in each other's directions. Only when I turned nineteen did anyone explain the facts of life to me, and even then the way I learned about it was purely accidental: I was sharing a dorm room with an Irish student in my sophomore year at Beijing University, a rare opportunity to meet a foreigner back then. Seeing how frequently I was visited by a male classmate, my Irish roommate one day decided to "educate" me. Because of our language difficulties—her Chinese was shaky and my English nonexistent—she had to draw a series of sketches to communicate the idea to me. She told me afterward, "Enjoy yourself but be careful," and my face turned purple. To this day I still remember how she cursed the Chinese government for keeping its people in such ignorance: "Stupid! Inhuman!" she kept shaking her head. I sat there like a lump, churning with mixed emotions—excitement, embarrassment, humiliation, expectation. Over the years, many of my Chinese friends told me about their first moments of sexual enlightenment: a lot of them knew nothing about sex way into their twenties, and when they did learn something, it was often by chance. Some guessed from hints in the few classical novels one could get a hold of, others watched animals mating on the farm.

I remember an episode on the farm myself. After graduating from high school in 1977, we were packed off to labor with peasants for a year in a small village outside Beijing. Even though the Cultural Revolution had officially ended the previous year, this kind of reeducation program was still in place. One spring evening, the entire village gathered on the threshing ground by the wheat field to see *Lenin in 1918*, one of those Soviet films every Chinese had seen in those years. It was a rare entertaining reprieve from the heavy, tedious daily labor. Sitting on the ground on both sides of the screen, chatting in a balmy breeze and watching village kids running about, we were all enjoying ourselves immensely. The movie had a tender moment everybody was familiar with, between Lenin's bodyguard Wahili and his wife on the eve of his departure for the battle front. Just when the couple were about to embrace and kiss, though, a huge black hand shadow covered the screen, blocking the scene until the kiss was over. The young peasants booed and whistled so wildly it sounded like we were in a football stadium. It turned out that the village's Party secretary, a pipe-smoking, grandfatherly man, had been dutifully standing by the projector, waiting to black the scene out with his own hand.

After this kind of vigorous censorship, the craving for sex and romance took a while to resurface. In the early reform years of the late seventies and early eighties, romance and love crept back into literature on tiptoes. Zhang Jie's *Love Cannot Be Forgotten*, a genteel, sentimental short story about a platonic love affair between an educated woman and an older married man, elicited intense emotional responses nationwide without so much as mentioning a word about sex. Not until the mid-eighties did any fiction begin to explore the subject of sex more frankly, though still well within the boundary of official tolerance and public delicacy: the last layer of clothes was rarely shed, and no writer was accused of writing in bad taste. On the screen, sex popped up here and there, but it was usually handled even more discreetly than in print, since the state monitored television and film more strictly. Up until very recent years, precious few Chinese films would get an R rating for sexual exposure had they been rated, say, in Hollywood.

Yet outside official control and elite culture, things have not retained such modesty. A pornography trade emerged in the mid-eighties and grew rapidly, with the southern coastal towns and cities taking the lead. Benefiting from freer policies and geographical proximity to Hong Kong and Taiwan, the so-called Special Economic Zones in Guangdong, Fujian, and Hainan Island were the first mainland regions to develop a sort of market economy and to enjoy a boom. The same privileges, however, also led to the smuggling of porn videos and materials from neighboring countries and to a mushrooming of undercover sex joints that catered to local and foreign money. Shenzhen and Hainan, both having been transformed from impoverished fishing villages into glitzy star showcases of economic prosperity in a matter of five to ten years, have also developed in time their notorious belts of massage parlors, beauty salons, and karaoke bars—often establishments that thinly disguise their flesh trade. An old proverb describes this tactic aptly: "Hang a sheep's head in the front, sell dog meat in the back." It is all part of the new entrepreneurial daring. Where money is concerned, conventional pieties are quickly becoming old hat.

The centers for reproducing porn videos are usually small, less conspicuous places where the police system is weak and the officials corrupt or indifferent. Shishi, for example, is a little town tucked in the southern part of Fujian province, with only twenty thousand residents in about three quarters of a square mile. It had been a sleepy fishing village until market reform got there; now its chain of video pirating shops manages to churn out ten thousand illegal copies a day, of which roughly one thousand are pornographic. From various port cities in the southern region, all kinds of porn videos, tapes, and sex toys (from cards decks with copulating couples to cigarette lighters and ashtrays made in the shapes of sexual organs) flow in daily. Videos are quickly copied in large quantities and sold for a good profit on the local black markets. Business is done in a primitive, crass style: hawkers beckon and stop potential clients on the streets, whisper deals in their ears, then lead them to the private storehouses to pick up the goods. Once Shishi established its reputation as "the adventurers' paradise," thousands of tourists and porn peddlers flocked there every day from the heartland of China.

The porn products are also disseminated by wholesale mail order, often with postal and railway workers gladly lending a hand after taking a cut of the profits. Once reaching their destination in the interior parts of China, these tapes and gadgets can sell for prices ten times the price paid. Very often, as they circulate among friends, tapes are copied generation after generation until the picture becomes blurry. I have heard a number of my Chinese friends complain about the poor quality of these tapes. They are usually called *maopian*, raw tape, or *huangdai*, yellow tape. "Oh it's quite spooky," a writer friend once told me about a fuzzy raw tape passed on to him from other friends. "They ought to be called *guipian*"—ghost tape.

Yet no matter how cheaply made and remade, this is a lucrative underground industry like no other, for the public demand for porn seems as insatiable as it is invisible. In the absence of adequate public sex education, porn is likely to fill in a blank spot important to millions. So, under the government's nose, the trickle has turned into a flood: suddenly, every province, every city shows signs of its invasion and feels its impact.

Here are some of the incidents local investigative reporters found out:

- The policemen of a certain city failed to destroy porn tapes they confiscated; instead, they circulated the tapes among themselves for amusement, until the tapes made their way back into society.
- The video-cinema team of a certain county took six porn movies on the road and showed them openly in sixteen towns. Copulation took up 90 percent of the content of these movies, and children under ten were among the audience.
- A television station employee became so absorbed in watching a porn video on the job that he absentmindedly connected the wrong line and aired it on prime time news to an entire city.
- Some private companies in Hannan Island offered porn videos as bonuses to their clients in the interior parts of China: the more product order their clients signed on for, the more awards they get.

I myself encountered an incident like the last one, in the summer of 1988. I was invited to a conference in Shanghai to receive literary award; the host, a young, can-do editor of a fiction magazine, assured me that we would have loads of fun at this conference, because it was the first such event his publishing house had been able to arrange, through the joint sponsorship of several local commercial companies. He was not exaggerating: we were all put up in a four-star hotel, and, aside from the usual speech, discussion, and banquet routine, they scheduled a cruise on the Yangtze River for the afternoon and a dance in the hotel's fancy top-floor discotheque that night. One evening, we bused off to another location to view a special double feature — *neibupian*, our host announced with pride, movies for internal circulation. Five minutes into the first feature, a Mexican or Brazilian production called, I think, *The Tattooed Women*, sweaty nude bodies began to pile up and tangle into all sorts of positions, and moans and sighs poured through the small room crowded with stiff-backed, tongue-tied writers and editors. The air was suffocating, but nobody left. The second feature, a French one, went on pretty much in the same vein. This was indeed a conference of multiple rewards: afterward, I learned, the sponsors were repaid with ad pages in the literary magazine.

Incidents like this are embarrassing but harmless. The problem, to some people, is that pornography doesn't seem to stop at "visual pollution"; statistics suggest far more pernicious effects. Back in 1964, after fifteen years of rigorous campaigns, the Chinese government had proudly announced the virtual disappearance of venereal diseases in China. In December 1988, the official New China Agency made an announcement that staggered the Chinese public: venereal diseases had not only come back but, from 1982 to 1987, they more than tripled each year. There was also the rapid climb of teenage rape cases and other sexual crimes, extramarital affairs, even prostitution rings, all inevitably linked, in the public mind, to the rampant spread of pornography and the sex trade.

By 1987, the alarmed Chinese media began to talk about the most dangerous moral perpetrator that was poisoning our society, our youngsters, our education system: indeed it is a "yellow tide" which, if not stopped, could drown China.

FROM THE very beginning, sex was intertwined with politics, and politics with campaigns. When the Party decided that sex was linked to slackened morale, weak willpower, and private carnal pleasure, it meant that sex was politically bad — and the Party's way of getting rid of something politically bad had always been to mount a campaign against it. Campaigns worked in the fifties, and they worked in the sixties and seventies. There had been campaigns not only against the human enemies — ultrarightists, capitalist roaders, revisionists, and so on—but also against anything the Party deemed bad. When there were too many flies, for instance, there'd be a campaign against them and every good Chinese citizen would take out his swatter and chase the flies. When there were too many sparrows in the air feeding on the crops in the fields, there'd be a campaign against them, and the good citizens would take out their gongs and drums, drumming up a deafening storm to scare away the evil birds. Those were the glorious years, for the Party and for the collective will.

In the reformed eighties, however, campaigns became something else. The institutions were still in place: the Party documents calling for a campaign were read in political study sessions, and people dutifully expressed their support or turned in some required response in writing afterward. It was the same method, the same pattern; the difference was in the attitude and the atmosphere. As people turned their minds more and more to economic matters and daily life, political movements inevitably lost their hold. With each new campaign, there was less enthusiasm, less fear, less interest. It was all turning into a hollow echo of a bygone era.

By the time the Party decided to fight against pornography, the crowd appeal and mobilizing power of official campaigns had further dwindled. Official documents about *saohuang*, "wiping out the yellow," went to the security bureaus, the police received orders to storm some notorious dens on their list, and porn dealers with inside sources received warnings—but the rest of the population sat on their hands and ignored it. Nobody turned in their own yellow tapes, nobody reported anybody else as in the good old campaign days. Afterward, people read in their local papers about the arrests of pimps and prostitutes, saw on television news that porn merchandise had been confiscated, and, once in a while, they would hear about a big porn case, big enough that someone was executed for it. Yet none of this had any real effect anymore—neither on the public, nor on the porn dealers. The antipornography campaign came and went, like thunderstorms in summer, something you expect and get used to. And everyone knew that it would soon be business as usual. A popular ditty pinned down the public's jaded sentiment toward these periodic antiporn campaigns:

> Wipe out the yellow,
> Wipe out the yellow;
> The more you wipe,
> The more yellow it gets.

There was also the widely appreciated story about Li Ruihuan, a savvy politburo member in charge of ideology who launched the first major antipornography campaign in July of 1989. It was only one month after the Tiananmen massacre, and the hard-liners' purge of the dissidents had a real edge, infused with the sort of deadly potency that official campaigns hadn't had for years. As arrests and executions went on, old fears returned, informers and traitors emerged, and terror reigned in all the major cities. In this atmosphere, Li Ruihuan's vehement campaign speeches about the urgency of battling the yellow tide broke the political tension in Beijing like no other comic relief. Li convened meetings and called for sweeping actions: he put the propaganda people on the alert, got the security forces busy with investigations, sent the police on raids, and generally drove the entire porn underworld into a cold sweat. Yet for all its high moral tone and deadpan seriousness, politically seasoned people around the country could hardly suppress their chuckling at Li's rambunctious campaign. It was almost like watching a mock parade: the frills were there, the noise level high, but it was a theater of double entendre, and everybody who understood the game played along. This was tantamount to staging a full-scale antisparrow campaign while there were one million counterrevolutionaries in the country waiting to be rounded up. Back in the fifties, Li would have gotten a bullet in the head for playing smart with the Party; in 1989, he made all the porn dealers fear for *their* heads, while making himself the most popular politician of the year.

For a time at least, it looked as if politics had taken cover under sex—one might even say, liberty had ducked behind pornography.

TIAN ZHENYING, Jia Pingua's editor at the Beijing Press, helped to arrange my trip to Xian. It was no mean task to find the best-selling novelist, for he has a habit of periodically going into hiding, either to write or to avoid the media. He wrote *The Abandoned Capital* in a friend's cottage in some backwater village; not surprisingly, soon after its publication, he again disappeared. Some said he was hiding in the countryside, others said he had checked into a hospital. Tian, though, had been in touch with him: "He is in a hospital, very sick," she confirmed solemnly. "Normally he would not see anybody. He said if it was someone wanting to pick a fight with him about the novel, he would not be in the condition to do it." I had to assure Tian of my neutrality as a researcher before she told me that Jia had agreed to my visit.

A light snow was falling, the day I arrived in Xian. The drive from the airport to the city was nearly two hours of crossing a slow, brown river and a vast, desolate plain at the end of which the city loomed like a tired old animal wizened by the lonely landscape. Rows of graceless, slapdash new shops and restaurants crowded the main avenues toward the ancient drum tower, the center of Xian. Even in fresh snow, the streets looked listless and dirty, the styles of the houses utterly uninspired. The only magnificent sight was the old city walls: draped in snow and kept in perfect shape, the walls spread majestically, circling and towering over the city like a gray aura. Right underneath the walls was the famous Xian junk market: a long row of decrepit shops stuffed with piles of secondhand ware, everything from used cotton quilts and rusty hand tools to bits of rugs and wires. Most of the goods are stolen. One of Xian's nicknames is *zeicheng*, the "thief city." On a sunny day, with goldfish, birds, and flowers on sale, the scene might have looked more cheerful; but on that gloomy, cold day, I saw mostly idle shop owners huddling behind their junk piles, slurping huge bowls of hot noodle soup or staring out blankly, looking like bored thieves themselves.

Mr. Song, the executive editor of a Xian literary magazine where Jia is the nominal chief editor, showed up in my hotel room on time. As planned, he was to take me to the hospital to see Jia. Song is a native of Xian, a tall man with a tired, weather-beaten face, who could be anywhere between forty to fifty-five. He has the solicitous, watchful manners and the competence of a person accustomed to being second in command. We stopped by his home on the way, because he wanted to pick up his camera. It was one of those standard urban dwellings in all Chinese cities: a walled-in, rundown compound with rows of identical concrete buildings, the type Americans are likely to associate with public welfare housing. Not a single soul was hanging around. While waiting in the taxicab, I asked the driver what kind of neighborhood this was. In a thick Xian accent, the driver informed me that this was a pretty nice residential area when it was first built in the seventies—but "now it's become one of those dope places," he added casually. I asked him what sort of dope is going around these days. "*Dayan*, you know, big smoke, opium. Comes in ashes, rolls. You can sniff, smoke or swallow." He made a large, circling gesture with his hand, indicating the neighborhood generally. "A lot of people in those buildings are addicted."

Before I could inquire further, Song returned. For the rest of the drive, he gave me a tourist guide chat about Xian. Basically, it's a sad situation: the economy hasn't picked up, the central government hasn't offered any particularly favorable policies or special tax breaks like those given to the southern cities, the local mentality is conservative and obstinate, people talk about changes but nobody makes a move, and the best and the brightest—Xian has a lot of well-trained scientists—try to leave for the south. What about tourism? I asked. "That's been a major source of revenue, of course; we've got all these great imperial tombs around here," Song nodded with visible pride. "Still,

147

proper infrastructure around them has not been developed. That needs funding too. You'll see what I mean after nightfall. Aside from the historical sights, we have no entertainment in the city. No nightlife, except for some outdoor food stands and a few karaoke bars." I didn't know what to say, but Song didn't seem to be in a particularly sullen mood. A twinkle crossed his eyes as he offered me this tip of local folklore: "You know what the tourists say about coming to Xian? 'You look at tombs during the day, and sleep in a tomb at night.' And what does a hotel clerk say to a guest complaining about the flies in his room? 'But sir,' the clerk says: 'they're flies from the Tang dynasty!'" We both laughed.

The cab pulled into a side street, and Song told me the hospital was right ahead. I looked outside to what appeared to be a farmer's market. Herds of people drifted about with sacks and bags in their hands. Horses, mules, and people pulling carts were among the traffic. A funeral home jumped into view with its sign: COFFINS, MOURNING OUTFITS, FLOWERS. Then a few steps down, another boarded-up shop sign, brushed in dripping black ink: HEART-ACHE REMEDIES. Suddenly, the street looked so dire, so ominous in the dull wintry afternoon glow that it made my skin crawl. Tombs. Were we talking about tombs? What kind of spirits, I wondered, would hover around here after nightfall?

My head was still swooning a bit as I followed Song into the hospital. To get to Jia's ward, we had to pass a decaying courtyard covered with rotten leaves, take a creaky elevator, then follow a long, dark hallway that reeked of medicine and stale flesh. Song let me know that this was a prestigious hospital, for people with status.

Jia Pingwa looked as homely in person as in his pictures, which I had seen everywhere in Beijing. He is a short, slight man with soft, oily black hair, a big head, pallid skin, and nervous brown eyes. His sickly complexion and slow, listless movements made him seem much older than a man in his prime. In his unfashionable, unmatched clothes, speaking his thick country accent—so thick that Song had to translate for me several times—he could easily be taken for somebody's peasant cousin visiting the county seat for the first time. When talking to me, he often lowered his eyes or looked at Song; yet underneath this meek veneer and lackluster appearance, I could soon sense an observant, quick-witted man who knew exactly what ground he stood on. It may be shyness well served by smartness, or vice versa; in any case, he could certainly hold his own without showing it.

Jia had his private room, which is not easily available in Chinese hospitals; he had been staying here for the past few weeks on account of a mysterious pain he suffered in the stomach. The room was spartan and cheerless, save for large bundles of ripe bananas and tangerines strewn on the cold concrete floor. Jia offered me these bright fruits, adding; "They are *qigong* tangerines, good for your body." The tangerines did look very soft and fluffy, but I preferred the bananas, smiling at Jia's half-occult, half-bantering sensibility.

Everything about him had a touch of secrecy. He was registered under a pseudonym so that other patients in the hospital wouldn't know that the famous author of *The Abandoned Capital* was here, getting so many shots and pills every day that his face was all swollen. Nobody could reach him directly by phone, but there was a speaker wired on the wall to pass on every message addressed to Patient XX—the pseudonym Jia had taken. Yet all these precautions didn't seem to result in much privacy for him. In the four hours of conversation we had in his ward, visitors kept dropping in to see him. At one point, there were half a dozen workers from the Xian Butterfly Watch Factory, who seemed to have come all the way just to offer their greetings to the famous writer. To describe the scene more accurately, the factory delegates simply edged into the ward, gawked at Jia, while their chief, a man with a glossy black leather briefcase and jovial laughter, said a few pleasantries and promised to treat Jia to a banquet as soon as his stomach would permit him. Behaving like an honored hostage, Jia showed them that he was still wearing an earlier gift from them—a butterfly watch—and politely chatted until the group left. Just when I began to think of the episode as some innocent local celebrity worship, I heard Song whispering to Jia something about a deal between their magazine and the watch factory: the magazine needed money, and the factory needed publicity literature. "It's very, very difficult nowadays to keep a literary magazine running," Song had told me earlier on.

Our conversation dwelt largely on *The Abandoned Capital*. Jia patiently went over the circumstances under which he had written the novel, how he came up with the structure, the theme, the central characters. I'm sure he had done this a hundred times by now, but he was careful, even anxious, to reemphasize certain key factors where his image perhaps faced the most controversy. He had not (not consciously, at least) pulled any commercial tricks to promote the book, he said; the media did all the hyping on its own. He did think that sex would help keep the readers interested in finishing a thick novel, but that was drawn from common experience, and it was the only "commercial thought" that had crossed his mind. The self-censoring blanks on sex scenes weren't present in the first draft; rather, for fear that the book might not get printed, he made some cuts, and the editor made some more— then he put in the blanks to mark the cuts. And he did not, of course, have those affairs like the hero in the novel did—it's fiction, not autobiography . . .

If not based on personal experiences, I asked, rather bluntly, what then had been his sources and inspiration for the sex scenes? To my surprise, Jia answered without hesitation: "*Maopian*, chiefly." Porn videos? Not the erotic classics like *The Golden Lotus*, or perhaps *The Carnal Prayer Mat*? Biting deliciously into a banana, Jia said: "I've read those too, sure. In terms of language, yes, the classics had an influence on me. But I got a feeling for the sex scenes mainly by watching a bunch of videos. One time I borrowed a whole stack: Thai, Hong Kong, Taiwan—they aren't as good as the ones from Europe. The other source is some stories friends told. Of course, as an adult man, I've got my own experiences to blend in." Jia's marriage of thirteen years broke down during the writing of *The Abandoned Capital*—his wife wanted a divorce after reading the unfinished manuscript. But that is not a subject Jia wanted to get into.

Obviously impressed by Jia's candid admission, Song cut in, his face a bit flushed: "I wasn't aware of this situation; so many *maopian* are going around, eh?" Wolfing down another banana, Jia said: "Lots. And they saved a lot of families. An eye-opener. You know how little people know about sex? In my native town, if a husband asked his wife to change a position, she'd think he's gone mad."

Jia said Chinese readers are accustomed to the kind of fiction in which intellectuals are decent, sex is avoided, and things generally work out in the end. His novel broke all three rules: he gave the readers a bad literary type for a hero, wrote explicitly about sex, and offered no happy ending, not a ray of hope throughout. "Three reading obstacles! But that's what I wanted. When *Yearning* first put a bad intellectual character on television, the average audience loved it, the intellectuals hated it. I picked the literati as my main characters because I know them the best: they are a tragic class of people on their road to extinction. The thing is, if the elite of our country have degenerated this much, you can imagine the rest."

Jia insisted that he portrayed his hero as a sexual pervert. "With no power, no money, no influence, sex is the only thing he can escape to from this hollow life. So he sinks into it, can't pull himself out. He destroys others as well as himself—it's sick. Maybe I should have handled it differently, making it more of a normal case," Jia ruminated. "That way I might have written better on sexuality." Then, suddenly, all his worries seemed to disappear and a devilish expression escaped him. "Well, I didn't offer truth, kindness and beauty. People were expecting a lovely baby, but the baby came out with all the piss and shit. That's what some critics said about me. That's also reality."

Song told me that a lot of old Party cadres in Xian have called *The*

Abandoned Capital "the death toll our Party, our nation, and an immoral work that stirs up base passions." Jia cut in, "But every old cadre in this hospital has a copy by his bed." We all chuckled. He said: "The older Chinese have no way of getting out of our past, our history. Even my generation, people over forty—we can't get out. That's what I feel sad about. Not about myself, but about our nation, our race." He lifted his eyes and looked me in the face: "You know what I did when a young Xian guy came up to me and asked me to sign his copy of *The Abandoned Capital*? Well, he told me he got the visa to go to Japan to study, so I wrote on his copy: 'Well, you're getting out of the abandoned capital!'"

By the time we got out of the hospital, it was dark. Although the temperature must have dropped by ten degrees, the snow had turned into slush and sunk the street into a hopeless muddy mess. Rotten vegetable stems, animal excrement, and who knew what else had all frozen solid in the ruts left by grinding traffic. Garbage whipped by in the wind; trembling, shadowy, thickly bundled figures scuttled by. The farmer's market, along with the funeral home and the heartache clinic, had all shut down. Standing in an icy wind on the dimly lit, deserted streets, I was seized for a moment by the spell of the city's past: it was frozen into some prehistoric era, a primitive, claustrophobic town cursed with an odor of death and plague, forgotten by civilization. It was the world Jia tried to capture in his novel.

"THERE IS absolutely nothing perverse in this novel's sex scenes," Dr. Yang assured me emphatically during our conversation about Chinese attitudes toward sex and the controversy over *The Abandoned Capital.* A suave, well-groomed man in his fifties, Doctor Yang practices and researches at Beijing's Peace and Stability Hospital, a venerable medical institution for mental illness. He specializes in abnormal sexual psychology. "You must keep this in mind: we are not all that far from animals. We have retained a lot of sexual habits and impulses of other mammals. It's normal and healthy, for example, to have desires to lick, bite, and suck your partner. We are also prone to all sorts of positions and games in sex. What a lot of Chinese consider to be morbid or sick is often very normal foreplay—nothing to make a fuss over. It's just we have lived in this ignorance for too long."

I mentioned that some of the most indignant critics of Jia's novel were well-educated, literary people. The doctor laughed and said that when it comes to sex, Chinese intellectuals are by no means superior to peasants—as a matter of fact, they are often worse. He gave me a couple of examples. Once, he had a patient who was a well-established scholar living at Zhongguancun, the famous residential district on the northwest side of Beijing, most of whose residents are professors, scientists and scholars. Married for eight years, the scholar and his wife had been frustrated by their failure to have a child. They thought something must be wrong with their genes. The exam, however, showed everything normal. Finally, while answering the doctor's questions about their sex life, it came out that the husband had been entering his wife from behind. "Eight years of anal intercourse," Doctor Yang shook his head. "They just didn't know better." He told me about another couple, who, though "very learned people," were even more off the target: they tried to conceive by putting a piece of lean pork into the wife's anus every time they had sex—"Because they'd read somewhere in an old Chinese book about *rurou*, 'enter the meat.' It happens to be one of those very graphic characters, but they took it literally!"

According to Dr. Yang, Chinese peasants may have very conservative values, but when it comes to sexual knowledge and techniques, they are better than the factory workers, and the workers are better than the intellectuals. Why? "Because life in the countryside is very dull. The peasants don't have a lot of other things to talk about. So you have all those yellow jokes and sex songs, very brash, very colorful—some of them quite ingenious." He recited one to me; it was hilarious, but untranslatable. He went on to say, "Then, too, every commune has at least one breeding station, you know, a stud farm for horses, pigs, rabbits, and sheep. Peasants would take their own pigs and so on to the station, and pay to have it done on the spot. Well, they sit there and watch: it's an education."

Dr. Yang thinks that pornography has served as a substitute for the necessary sexual education that China has no adequate way of presenting. According to a sex poll conducted in 1990 among university students, only 20 percent of the students first learned about sex from school or parents. Although a number of pamphlets on the subject of healthy sex are out now, *maopian* is still a major eye-opener for today's urban youth. "But most of these tapes come from Southeast Asia and are poorly made. They're quite boring after a while. Put it this way: if you go to a soccer game, do you want to just watch the shots on goal?" He went on to talk of the importance of popularizing a cultural education about sex. "The young people these days think that sexual liberation means free sex with no restraint. From nothing at all, they flip over to anything goes. But we must talk about things both below and above the waistline." That was what motivated Dr. Yang and some colleagues last year to launch a magazine called *The World for Both Sexes*, which ran articles both instructive and cultural on the subject of sex. Unfortunately, the magazine didn't make money soon enough; after only two issues, its Hong Kong sponsor pulled the plug.

To Dr. Yang, a novel like *The Abandoned Capital* contributes to the kind of sex education that China sorely needs. He had no problem with the way Jia has portrayed sex, though he disliked the novel's ending. "Sexual indulgence ruins your life, that's how old Chinese novels always wind up. But some of our ancestors valued sex highly. Taoism, for instance; some Buddhist schools too. Only Confucianism was ascetic."

He discussed the famous Taoist obsession with *liandan,* "smelting the pill of immortal essence." "It's not just a form of alchemy, melting down herbs and so on; you practice it in sexual intercourse as well." Basically, it comes down to a set of rules that Taoist men should abide by when it comes to sex with women. Since Taoism views sexual behavior as a fundamental, integral part of the cosmic paradigm, these texts present the female and the male body movements as a mirror of the yin and yang forces moving in the universe. It is from this lofty perspective that many Taoist writings extrapolate their sexual concepts; at a practical level, however, it often comes down to elaborate devices for strenuous exercises of the male will, in which the central goal is never sexual pleasure but, instead, the attainment of a higher essence of being. Because this is achieved by preserving and enriching the yang by absorbing the best of yin, a man is advised to firmly hold his yang while enticing and teasing the yin out, so that in the end he comes out a winner—his masculinity is not merely intact but purer, richer than ever—whereas his female partner, her weaker will slowly cracking under temptation, succumbs to crude desires, ending up empty and spent. This is male supremacy with a twist, by a logic in which the winner, literally, should take all. Quite often, these Taoist extrapolations read like military textbooks, full of cunning battle deployments and relentless instructions for the hard-headed male warriors with their eyes cast forward toward immortality, certain that the last laugh will be theirs. One wonders how much Chinese women should complain about their inferior lot.

However, Taoists certainly weren't the only ones preoccupied with sex in ancient China. While the lowbrow porn trade and literatures were flourishing on the underground market, a scholarly book entitled *Sexual Life in Ancient China* also enjoyed quiet success as a cult item in Chinese bookstores. Its author, a Dutch sinologist by the name of Robert H. Van Gulik, had ploughed through valuable archives neglected by, or inaccessible to, Chinese scholars and had mapped out a sketch of Chinese sexual culture from ancient times up to 1644, the beginning of the Qing Dynasty. The book discusses everything from the high Taoist and Buddhist philosophies on sex to common social attitudes toward sex, from erotic paintings and porn literatures to "spring pills" (aphrodisiacs) and sex toys. Around the same time, a book by Chinese scholar Zhou Yimou, *The Health-preserving Sexual Life in Ancient China*, also came out; Zhou appeared to be something of a stuffed shirt, compiling old texts into "a brief guide to healthy and correct sex according to our wise though sometimes wrong ancestors." Both books are informative, for they suggest how the ancient Chinese had been much more open about sexuality, and how Confucian and neo-Confucian orthodox schools had gradually helped to develop prohibition and asceticism. Unfortunately, books such as these are too academic and specialized to reach general audiences.

"Ultimately," Dr. Yang said, "the growth of a more sophisticated sexual culture depends on a higher level of general culture. And that would take a long time to develop in China."

M. X. LI, a young medical researcher from Beijing now living in New York, agrees with Dr. Yang's assessment of the Chinese misunderstanding of sexual liberation. She too thinks that it has to do with a generally low level of sexual education and an overflow of pornography. Some of her gynecologist friends work in various Beijing hospitals, and they keep telling her how casually their young women patients take to abortion these days. "Because of the population control policy, the hospitals no longer request their names, place of employment, or marital status, and it doesn't cost a lot of money to have an abortion. So these unmarried young women, some very young, treat it all as a light thing. Some of them have done it three or four times before they turn twenty-five! I think they've lost more than frigidity."

When it comes to sexuality as portrayed in Jia's novel, though, Li has an entirely different view from Dr. Yang's. "It isn't a matter of perversity, and I do believe that Jia writes honestly. In fact, that's why I'm so stunned by how old-fashioned and male-chauvinistic this normal man, this honest writer, is about women and sex. In his eyes, women are coy playthings, having no business in life except being the object of male appreciation and pleasure. They cling to men, and men enjoy them the way they enjoy some beloved trinkets: a piece of delicate jade, say, or a snuff box. This is exactly like the attitude of all the old Chinese mandarin gentlemen of the last two thousand years. It's as if Jia has never stepped into the twentieth century."

Her remarks bring to my mind what a Chinese female singer once said to me: "You know what Chinese men's biggest hangup is? Sexuality. They never come of age sexually — not in a modern sense. So they either remain infantile all their lives, or they behave like dirty old men even when they are young. Sometimes both." I think of another rather popular novel by another famous male Chinese writer, Feng Jicai, with the revealing title *The Three-inch Golden Lotus*—the tritely traditional expression for bound feet. The novel came out several years ago, at the height of China's culture craze, and Feng's intention was to expose the backwardness of feudal Chinese tradition. As the novel paraded through extravagant scenes of "bound-feet beauty contest," however, it became obvious that our good author lost himself in the erotic beauty of it all. Controversial even back then, this novel has recently come in a fancier reprint, complete with the author's own detailed illustrations of a variety of sophisticated shoe styles for bound feet. "A wondrous book!" hailed the publishers and booksellers alike. It is much the same praise *The Abandoned Capital* has received.

"It's a naked male fantasy through and through," said Dai Jinhua, smiling as she stubbed out another cigarette butt in the ashtray. "The craving for, and fear of, women have always been there in Jia Pingwa's novels, but he was more evasive in the past." We were talking in my mother's living room, which by now was shrouded in smoke.

Jinhua and I were classmates in the early eighties at Beijing University, where she now teaches comparative literature. By appearance, Jinhua strikes one more as a rock star than a professor. Her fashion statement usually consists of faded jeans or big, billowy skirts, matched with a lean, body-hugging sports jacket or an oversized turtleneck pullover. The accessories, too, must make her quite a sight behind the lecture podium: a large digital watch with a wide black band studded with sterling beads, long dangling earrings, the Marlboros she puffs away on, one after another, and finally, a pair of black-rimmed, defiantly severe glasses. Some might say that she looks exactly the image of her chosen identity: a radical feminist cultural critic. Tall, handsome, and in her earlier thirties, she has established herself as a top scholar in her field with two books, one on cinema, the other on Chinese women novelists. Men grudgingly respect her, though sometimes with thinly veiled condescension. A young male literary critic, who claims to be her friend, once commented to me, "She has a brain that cuts to the point of an argument like a knife. I've never seen that in any other woman. But she doesn't socialize much—I guess it's out a lack of self-confidence as a woman." Jinhua is well aware of her oddball situation. "You know what it means to openly declare yourself a feminist in China?" she once asked me when we were drinking together in a conference hotel in Hong Kong. "It means you get a double treatment from men. Men in the northern half of China, being macho in a more uptight way, treat you as this god-awful, untouchable thing, as if you are no longer female. Men in the south, being more loose and practical-minded, instantly think that they can take advantage of you because you are this liberated woman, so anything goes. So, outcast in the north, goods for all in the south. You wonder why all the Chinese women writers firmly deny that they are feminists?"

Giving in to pressure is not Jinhua's style, though. Characteristically, she does not mince words about *The Abandoned Capital*: "It's a daydream, the psychological compensation of a man who is repressed both socially and sexually. In the past, Jia tried to sanctify his male characters by uglifying the seductive female. This time he confronts his ambivalence, but in an even more timid and weak way. It's a double fantasy: the hero first attracts the women with his status of a 'cultural star,' then conquers them with his sheer male potency. Through this imaginary success, he attempts to shore up his self-confidence as a man of culture, which has already begun to totter in reality. But it's a double-edged lie; deceiving others as well as himself. This demonstrates not only Jia Pingwa's own anxiety but also a widespread mental crisis among contemporary Chinese intellectuals and modern men."

A lot of university students, especially women, share Jinhua's opinion. In interviews, some of them used strong words to express their anger at the way women are debased in Jia's novel; others even spoke of it as a part of the trend in the nineties to return to exploiting women in China's new commercial climate. With the expanding industry of porn literature and prostitution, they worry that women are once again being turned into cheap sexual commodities.

Dai Qing, a prominent Beijing journalist and political activist, is a friend of Jia Pingwa. She was so upset by what she described as "the male sexual psychology" evident in *The Abandoned Capital* that she could not bear to finish reading it. "I'm really disappointed by Pingwa. All the female characters in this novel are conniving little creatures whose only ambition in life is to please men. It makes you sick after a while." Later, she said to me: "Come to think of it, maybe it's the circle he moves in. Maybe he only knows those little women in small counties and towns." Little woman is certainly not the word to describe Dai Qing: like Dai Jinhua, she too has been something of a thorn in many men's flesh. Articulate, fiercely competitive, and brimming with indefatigable energy, Dai has not only written numerous taboo-breaking political investigative reports but has also organized quite a few nearly all-male dissident activities and groups. Collaborating with another woman writer, she wrote a series of reportage pieces about "sexually liberated Chinese women." When the bold portraits of these bold women appeared in various magazines around 1986, she once again made a lot of hearts jump and a lot of Chinese men frown. For her, it was simply breaking another taboo.

Dai told me she was having second thoughts about being called a feminist. "I always rejected the label in the past. Now I take a more careful measure of myself, and I realize in some essential ways I am a feminist. The communist experience for Chinese women gave us something unique: it empowered us with a sense of equality with men, but then we found out that it was a fake equality—stiff, not humane—and that the real discrimination had never stopped. We now want to reemphasize the feminine part of us. But having once been empowered, we can never go back to the old, docile role that traditional Chinese society allocated to women. We want a full, multifaceted, humane female experience. Of course, it's going to take a long time to reach this goal."

At present, some Western feminist books have been translated into Chinese, some theories introduced, and a few academic forums take place now and then, but feminism as an organized political and social movement hasn't yet hit in China. Even in intellectual circles, there is little active discussion or even consciousness of feminism. More often than not, cases of sexual abuse and discrimination against women come out in the popular press only incidentally, with sex and violence treated simply as one of the many nineties-era sensational media topics alongside money, commerce, and extravagant lifestyles. The reporters themselves often reveal a sexist or utterly insensitive attitude toward women, which is quite standard among Chinese men, regardless of education or background. According to a brief, inconspicuous report in a recent issue of *Tianjin Daily*, the suicide rate among Chinese women has jumped to the highest in the world, and its main cause has been failed relationships with men. But as the number of suicides goes up year by year, women's issues have stayed largely on the margins of public attention. Seventy-some years after the May Fourth Movement (a large-scale cultural movement that began in 1919 and sought to teach people modern values) first brought the image of modern women and issues of gender equality to China, and forty some years after Mao's efforts at creating the "socialist new man," fresh evidence shows that many Chinese men have lapsed into their traditional attitudes toward the female half of the country. Scratch the new men's surface, and you'll find the old men. Old prejudices have returned, but this time it is riding on the tide of commercial capitalism.

Up until now, Chinese women themselves have not been able to organize well to advance their own rights and interests. Most are still either ignorant of or defensive about feminist sentiments. Not long ago I heard about a "single women's club" in Beijing organized by the Women's Federation, but before I went to find out myself, Jinhua warned me about such group activities. "It's not what you think," she said in her usual acerbic tongue. "I went to one of their gatherings, thinking it was some kind of feminist sisterhood stuff. But there I sat, among a roomful of divorced women and spinsters; you'd think the bonding topic would be how great and liberating it is to be single, but no, they all broke down in tears when somebody started whining about her rotten former husband! They were just socializing and venting grievances in their transitional phases until a good husband comes along."

I have nothing against a group like that, but Jinhua's descriptions did dampen my interest. After all, the Women's Federation has long been a bizarre subordinate part of the official Party machine; one can hardly imagine the federation launching a real women's movement. To this day, I vividly remember a 1989 interview in which I participated with two women officials from the federation: the subject was the then-increasing frequency of abduction of women for sale in certain rural areas. After giving us all the information and statistics about how this illegal trade was conducted, one of the women officials said,

> As much as we are against it, we also understand that this is useful commercial activity. In those poor backwater areas, people don't move for generations and there are a lot of inbred marriages, that produce a lot of idiot children. Or men far outnumber women because women get married off to better areas, whereas men have trouble getting women from elsewhere to marry into a poorer place. What's more, the peasants always prefer sons, and some get rid of their female babies. All of this produces an unbalanced ratio between male and female. That's why you have the extreme cases, in some villages, of brothers sharing a wife, or renting wives out for money. Under these special circumstances, some entrepreneurs saw their chance: they bring women from one region to another and sell them off for marriage. They're in it for profits, of course; but you see, there is a positive side to it as well. It helps to break up the vicious chain of incest and idiot children.

Her statement was quite clear, and her tone factual.

Next to this, it doesn't seem so surprising for some southern Chinese city officials to talk about prostitution from an economic point of view: a red-light district is always good for the local economy, they say, because "it provides a soft environment that attracts investment." Central government spokesmen have dutifully castigated such "mistaken views," but everyone knows that, realistically, the sex trade is just too profitable, too well organized and widespread to be stopped.

And after all those decades of being buttoned up to the neckline, can you really blame the incredible Chinese thirst for the body and flesh? It is evident not only in illicit, secretive indulgences, but also in a public voyeurism running wild. As early as 1989, what the Chinese press called the "great nudity craze" manifested itself in the huge boxoffice success of a special exhibit at Beijing's National Museum of Fine Art. The exhibit consisted of nothing but life-size, realistic nude portraits. Since then, every printing shop in China seems to have churned out its own batch of nude and half-nude beauty calendars. Wherever you go, you see these calendars hanging at bookstalls on the streets, and next to them you see the weekend tabloid papers flaunting photographs of titillating, lightly clad pop stars, and magazines chock full of stories about prostitutes, massage girls, "karaoke girls," drinking, dancing, swimming companions for hire. You read about "Big Cash" with his "Little Honey" (new slang words for the male nouveaux riches and their young mistresses). You buy a popular set of guide books on how to succeed in business, and it turns out the secret lies all in your groin—"For the arena of commerce has a striking resemblance to the arena of Eros," the worldly author informs you, "and those who succeed in chasing women will also succeed in making money." In Canton, during the performance of *The Lovers*, a Shanghai play, rowdy audiences threw fruit peels at the stage and demanded refunds because the expected bed scene failed to materialize.

"Our countrymen must be going crazy," someone active in media circles commented to me. "Nothing sells unless you give them some pretty women and sex. I think Jia Pingwa is the smartest writer around—he knows exactly what to tap into. Too bad we don't have a good copyright law or a good distribution system yet: he would have made more than a million bucks." In the next breath, this same man, married and in his mid forties, assured me that those sexy karaoke girls could really give a guy some good service. Grinning broadly, he confessed that he had been treated to such expensive great fun by his Big Cash friends. Then, encouraged perhaps by my amused teasing, he told me that once during a work trip in a lonely southern province, he had even enjoyed such an evening while being escorted by the local *cops*. "A very sleazy place," he said. "Every booth had a long curtain. You could just draw the curtain and do anything you wanted inside with the girl." They didn't have to pay, of course.

"Look, it's a novel, not a political treatise," says a European sinologist friend of mine who has been living in Beijing in the past five years. "The feminists put their finger on the sex and gender issues; their points are well taken. But the sex scenes are the least interesting part of the novel—Jia knows nothing about sexuality, except from old Chinese novels. What's fascinating and brilliant about the novel is that it describes so clearly and relentlessly how the Chinese social system works from inside out: the daily transactions of power, how people manipulate at all levels while carrying on with their little mundane chores of life, the bribing, the networking, giving and receiving favors... All that bustling mishmashing in a muddy nest."

"All that dirt," I say. He laughs, wagging a finger at me: "Uh-oh, now you sound like a romantic. The romantics can deal with the sort of dirt that is in some ways valiant and heroic, like gangsters or bandits. Shining dirt, you know, the stuff big Hollywood movies are made of. Jia disappoints you— he doesn't grant you any elevation. He gives you a wimp and a cheat for a hero. Nobody puts on a decent fight for anything. That's right: it's dirty and not even hard dirt; it's all soft, slimy, slippery, nothing really admirable. But it's got a pretty cozy feeling to it, too. It's a familiar lifestyle where people know all the invisible rules, the social codes. They know they can't beat the system, they also know they can play along with this old game. That's China! Now, no other contemporary Chinese novelist has painted that picture so well as Jia."

Over lunch, a Chinese business-lawyer friend agrees: "That's the way I feel about the novel, too." By his own admission, my friend is an avid consumer of various types of pornography (movies, videos, books), especially since he moved to the United States a few years ago. Jia has written nothing new about sex, he concludes, and is far less daring than *The Golden Lotus*. "But he's got Chinese society down in a nutshell." He tells me about his own encounters during his recent business trips to China: the twelve-course banquets billed on public money, the tips, the favors, all sorts of tricks to take advantage of the system. "Everyone does it, exactly like in *The Abandoned Capital*! It's as though the revolution never happened and the Chinese have lapsed right back to their old ways. Everything is rotten to the core, but the machine somehow putters along, and you never know what might become of it tomorrow. At the moment, it's a boom atmosphere. So all anyone thinks about is how to stuff his own pocket as fast as possible, before some awful disaster strikes." As for Jia's pessimism, my lawyer friend puts it this way: "It's a thing these cultural types in the cities feel. *The poor and sour literati*, as the saying goes: things are not going too well for them, you know, especially in a place like Xian. Why, the southern cities are quite different from the northern ones these days. You go to Guangzhou and Shenzhen, everyone is gung ho about the future. They think Europe had the nineteenth century, America had the twentieth century, and the twenty-first century belongs to the Asia Pacific rim, with China sitting at the top."

The changing economic disparities in recent years have indeed disturbed the traditional rankings of Chinese cities. Subtly or hotly, regional sentiments get rubbed into the controversy over *The Abandoned Capital*, particularly among the elites. For the most part, the Beijing elite panned the novel; the reviews from Shanghai and Nanjing sounded sarcastic if not scathing. Further south, the coastal cities didn't seem to care much one way or another, the rights and wrongs of a novel not being an urgent issue on the regional mental landscape. But in Xian, the entire literary camp closed ranks around Jia, raving about and defending *The Abandoned Capital* as if it was a matter of truth and honor.

"The Shanghai critics are always putting down writers from elsewhere," a Xian critic pointed out to me, knowing that I am a native of Beijing. "They've yelled and cursed at Wang Shuo two years ago because he was so popular and so *Beijing*. Now they're cursing at Jia Pingwa because he's written a great novel and it's based on Xian! They like to attack whoever is successful." He presented to me his own book of criticism: *The Enigma of Jia Pingwa*. I joked about Jia being treated like a national treasure here in Xian. He blushed slightly, then shrugged: "Well, he is the best Xian can offer. But, to tell you the truth, I don't think our great old northern cities have much hope. Not Xian, not Beijing. Actually, Shanghai might produce something new only because of its colonial background before the revolution. It was open to fresh air from outside. We have the roots, the tradition; you need that for great literature. But you need to get out of it too: you need a mix to stand above it, not lost in it. I think Hong Kong has more hope." I smiled and said, "Certainly, but they need to come north and search for roots first, right?" He laughed, running his fingers through his hair. Jia had made his name first in the "Search for Roots" literary movement in the mid-eighties, writing about the Shaanxi peasants' life in the mountain ranges. To a mainlander, roots meant old, rural, weighty matters, something deeply entangled in the Chinese unconscious—something the bubbling Cantonese are not supposed to have or care much about.

Back in Beijing, at a crowded dinner table, a critic leaned forward with a knowing expression. "They say Jia's written a city novel. What sort of city is Xian? A county seat, really." A novelist known for his "fiction of Beijing flavors" ruled simply, "It's urbanity, seen through the eyes of a peasant."

"Well, it is curious that *The Abandoned Capital* should be considered a novel about the Chinese city," my sinologist friend in Beijing mused as we discussed it. "It really portrays a very provincial way of life. But look, China *is* provincial—even if the elite in Beijing don't want to face up to it!"

Jia Pingwa himself has described to me the culture shock he suffered when he visited the United States in 1991. Usually a reclusive man, Jia dislikes traveling outside his home province and feels dislocated even when he visits Beijing. When he finally accepted an invitation and went on a one-month tour in the States, it was like landing on another planet. He visited many places—the east coast cities, the rural midwest, California. "The biggest problem was I was constantly starved. I couldn't eat the food: the dairy products turned my stomach." Jia made a wry face as he recounted this. "By the end of it, I smelled cream everywhere I went and couldn't wait to get to the next Chinese house to have some noodle soup. But I saw things. I realized that the countrysides in China and the U.S. are so different that there is no way we can communicate to each other through our literatures about rural lives. I realized Xian is a village by world standards; even Beijing is rustic. And frankly, even though I can't stand their food, I feel Americans are a large people, more big-hearted than us. Ever since then, I've been thinking to myself, 'We can't just stick to our old modes of writing, we must try to reach out further.'"

Jia's favorite reading had always been classical Chinese fiction: the Tang stories, the great Ming and Qing novels. *Dream of the Red Chamber* and *The Golden Lotus*, he notes, are both about urban life, set in Ming and Qing cities, respectively. He wondered why contemporary Chinese fiction about the city always seem false and shallow, and he decided that there is something wrong with the language they used. "I've always thought that our ancestors had a purer style, unlike our modern writers who have been too much under the sway of European languages since the twenties. It's a language that cannot touch felt experiences." Furthermore, Jia noticed that there have been novels about cities like Beijing, Shanghai, and Guangzhou, but nobody had written about Xian. Yet, with its peculiar mixture of the urban and the rural, the old and the new, isn't Xian a uniquely Chinese place? It dawned on him that, after living in Xian for twenty-one years, he himself has not produced a single story about the city, all the while dwelling on the Shaanxi peasant life he left behind at age twenty! Now, he decided, was the time to come to terms with his Xian experiences.

What he tried to achieve in *The Abandoned Capital*, he explained, was a combination of Western philosophical sensibilities ("because they represent the most advanced stage of human thought, and they are concerned with the eternal anxieties of human existence, not with partisan politics") with a restoration of traditional Chinese literary styles, in terms of language and narrative techniques. "I wrote about how Chinese people eat, drink, shit, piss and sleep—common things, plain language, realist techniques. But there is a metaphysical level: I painted a China both real and symbolic, in a specific historical moment. This is something I've thought about doing for many years. I wanted to find a way to convey in depth how the Chinese existence feels."

Has he succeeded or failed? Or perhaps both? Has he mostly conveyed the tortured ethos of a peasant son who is forever alienated in the city and nostalgic about the simpler pastoral life? Or has he created a complex, uniquely Chinese cityscape like no other? Has he revealed himself as a sexist and sexually insecure man painting a reactionary, demeaning picture of women and sexuality, or has he made a breakthrough on the subject? These questions still torment Jia Pingwa as he lies in his hospital bed, haunted by the critics' praise and disdain. He has some plans to write a sequel to *The Abandoned Capital*; but for the time being, he feels too sick and tired to write anything. He is divorced, living alone. His father died, and his mother fell seriously ill. His bad liver got worse. "This novel has brought me too much misfortune."

Before leaving Xian, I asked the cab driver to pass by the area where Jia used to live. The residents had all moved away and the buildings were mowed down: nothing was left on the site but broken bricks and concrete junk. Here and there, weeds popped out from the cracks and snow. I jumped out to snap a picture of the ruins—but just as I clicked the shutter, I realized the place wasn't totally deserted. A middle-aged man in a faded thick blue coat was peeing by a remnant of a wall. As he relieved himself slowly, he rested his head against the wall, as if lost in some idle thoughts; the man's whole posture suggested exhaustion.

Another memento of Xian was a cassette tape Jia gave me, of a group of Xian musicians playing what they called "ghost songs": melancholy, ancient mourning melodies played on ancient Chinese instruments. Jia himself sang a couple of songs in the tape. "When the musicians played these ghost tunes on top of the city walls at night," he told me, "you felt the chill in your bones. Folks took their kids home and shut the doors."

I brought the tape back to America, and in my room by Lake Michigan in Chicago, I let loose the specter of Xian. Here, mountains and oceans away, it doesn't sound so creepy, merely sad and alien. Perhaps the ghosts are a bit lost. They probably never expected to get out of the abandoned capital.

Postscript

IN LATE January 1994, as both the sales of and the controversy over *The Abandoned Capital* began to cool, Chinese authorities finally announced an official ban on the novel. The stated grounds were strictly antipornography: it was found to contain filthy, pornographic content in low, vulgar taste, which was harmful to the physical and mental health of the adolescents. The author's insertion of blank blocks accompanied by annotation was found to have played, in reality, a role of stimulation, and to have a very bad influence on society. Beijing News and Publishing Bureau ruled that the unsold copies must be confiscated, and that an amount three times the profits made from the novel be paid by the Beijing Press. The house was also to submit a written self-criticism.

The ban has not led to any political persecution of the author, nor to a new wave of publicity for the novel.

7

ISLANDERS

IS THIS Beijing or Hong Kong? The moment I enter CIM's vast central office, my mind starts roaming. With the year in which China will take back Hong Kong from Great Britain looming large on the horizon—1997—who is taking over whom here? Look at this bustling corporate scene at the heart of downtown Beijing: the bright, open floor, the dapper promotional posters lining the walls, the market strategy charts, the clients solemnly waiting to be ushered in, the long rows of glistening desks with computer terminals, fax modems, and young employees dressed in neat, hip clothes, talking briskly into telephones about satellite television and video distribution, MTV and laser discs . . . This is, literally, a piece of Hong Kong in Beijing: CIM is a major Hong Kong investment company that has set up offices here to do business with mainland China.

A large throng of Hong Kong and Taiwan companies have swarmed into China in recent years, but one single fact sets CIM apart from all the rest: its main target is the business of culture. As others play safe and fight over market shares in the good old "hard business" areas like real estate and manufacturing, CIM is the first major Hong Kong company that has stepped into the tricky waters of joint-venture media and cultural productions with China. What's more, the company is not conducting its businesses in the standard "remote control" way, in which junior executives or local representatives carry out orders from their headquarters outside of China; rather, CIM's two big bosses from Hong Kong, Yu and Chan, have both set up their offices and residencies *in Beijing*.

> Let 1997 come sooner,
> I wonder just how the clothes are at Babaiban?
> Let 1997 come sooner,
> So I can go to Hong Kong.
> Let 1997 come sooner,
> Let me stand at the Hongshi Stadium.
> Let 1997 come sooner,
> So I can go to the midnight movies with him.

These lines are from "My 1997," the title song of the first album recorded by Ai Jing, a twenty-four-year-old singer who tops the list of mainland

Chinese pop singers CIM has taken to "package." For the first time, suddenly, political walls melt, regimes and territories become irrelevant: what matters is fashion, sports, movies, and romantic love for a man on the other side of the border. You have your agenda, I keep mine. As the Chinese economy and Chinese nationalism surge, Ai's slickly packaged first album has also hit the music stores all over East Asia.

"My 1997" was an instant hit, and Ai Jing became a star overnight. But that was only a ripple, the floodgates have now opened: these days, there is a Hong Kong phenomenon in Beijing—Hong Kong stores, Hong Kong fashion, Hong Kong pop idols, Hong Kong action movies and kung fu novels, Hong Kong food, even the Hong Kong accent. Half of Beijing has a certain smell of Hong Kong. Ai, who based the song on events in her own life, is living evidence of the curious relationship between China and Hong Kong at the moment. Living out of a fancy Beijing hotel suite, always dressed in casual, chic clothes, she is constantly being flown in and out of Hong Kong and other East Asian countries for promotional tours or studio shots. She has been dating CIM's music division manager, Liu Zhuohui, a Hong Kong man. Liu has the clean-cut, stylish looks typical of young Asian yuppies: glued spiky hair, designer glasses, stone-washed jeans and a T-shirt. Before coming to China, he used to earn a good living writing sweet, soft lyrics for Hong Kong pop singers—but now China has gotten to him, too. In wintertime, he has taken to knocking around in a pair of padded cotton shoes of the Chinese peasant style, which has invited jokes about his "going native." Meanwhile, Ai—his mainland Chinese girlfriend with her long, straight black hair, her petite, exotic frame, and her fashionable clothes—looks more and more like a Chinese Yoko Ono. She is hosting a hip MTV program, the first of its kind here, on CCTV, the most official of China's television networks. She's even becoming fluent in Cantonese.

Already, their romance and collaboration have born impressive commercial fruit for CIM. The promotion campaign for Ai is a decisive success; CIM now has a star's name written on its China mission banner.

IN HONG Kong, all the top hotels are booked solid for July 1, 1997, the date when the British crown colony will be handed back to the People's Republic of China. People will fly in from all over the world to witness history in style, to watch the unprecedented turnover—a grand spectacle for all. Will they raise champagne glasses and cheer, or swallow bittersweet wine in silence? Will the crowds sing, or cry?

Ever since the Tiananmen massacre in 1989, or even earlier, since Margaret

Thatcher signed the joint treaty with Beijing in 1984 and wrote off the fate of six million people, the Hong Kong public has watched the clock ticking away with anxiety and gloom. Governor Chris Patten's democratizing proposals have stirred local hopes and debates; yet after emerging from several rounds of rough dealing with Beijing, Patten looks more than ever like a red-faced lame duck. Things on the mainland, on the other hand, have been moving along: Deng Xiaoping's call for deeper and wider marketization in early 1992 wasn't just another speech—when the Emperor opens his mouth, the Chinese tend to listen carefully. Millions stuck their noses in the wind, and acted. John Kamm, the high-profile American businessman in Hong Kong who has been a key go-between in efforts to gain the release of political prisoners in Beijing, confided to me at a local banquet: "The big game lies with Beijing and Washington, in the hands of Deng and Clinton. I'm so sick and tired of all these local chicken feathers. Maybe I've lived here too long." Perhaps it's all the wine and empty talk at another banquet function that got on Kamm's nerves. Perhaps, it's the shifting winds at large around the island.

Politicians bicker, opinion polls sway. Every month the local press throws a fit over another rumor about Deng (it's always from some high-ranking ears wired directly to the politburo inside Zhongnanhai). Is he cutting down on the meat in his diet? He hasn't appeared on television for three whole months! He's turning ninety and he wants to swim on his birthday? Even with all the herbs in China and the best *qigong** master, what if . . . But all along, businesses are booming, international monies are pouring in, and the Hong Kong stocks are going up and up.

This is not exactly a miracle, nor is it a catastrophe, even if the people in Hong Kong seem to possess a particularly stout attitude toward both. They had their own economic miracle in the seventies—transformed over night, as it were, from a cheap, gaudy tourist island to a rich, glittering international city, the pride of modern Asia. And if nearly a hundred years of living at another people's whim and grace, in the narrow crack of empires and history, would count as a form of catastrophe, then they've had that too. They have a way of taking what's inevitable in stride. Now it may be, inevitably, China's turn—and Hong Kong's turn with China. The ascending GNP figures are there for all to see: China is already the third largest economy in the world, only after the United States and Japan, and it is expected to be second largest by 2025. The Chinese economy has sustained a double-digit growth

---

* A popular Chinese cult of physical therapy.

rate over a decade, and the market is still expanding, almost exploding, in spite of all the political clouds hanging overhead. China is changing, and not just economically.

So is a generation of people. Both in Hong Kong and on the mainland, people are waking up to the new reality and the new opportunities ahead. True to traditional mystique, the pioneers, in particular, have acted fast: while others are still blinking off sleep and confusion in the early dawn light, they are jumping onto a new boat, following, sometimes fostering, new economic and cultural trends. Quite often, they are agile, action-oriented individuals, charting new courses quietly, unrestrained by old alliances and never with loud manifestos. "These bold, nimble creatures are worth watching," an anthro-pologist friend who has been visiting both Hong Kong and China once noted to me. "Because in their movements, we might find a piece of our own future."

That remark came to mind as I walked around CIM's Beijing offices, wait-ing for an interview with Yu, CIM's big boss. Is this a laboratory, a model cap-italist workshop for China's future culture industry? Didn't this scene look like a shrewd corporate drive to further commercialize Chinese culture, to upgrade its productions so that they would hook up first with the Asian and then the international market? Would CIM succeed? How long could they get away with playing a game of "cultural invasion" in Beijing, the heart of what is still Communist China?

One thing is clear: such a company in Beijing does not mean merely out-side investment for profit. These Hong Kong businessmen are also showing the Chinese a new way, a style of running cultural business. Along with their technology and staff, they've brought their vision and institution, and they are here to promote certain kinds of cultural tastes and trends, certain lifestyles and attitudes. At the moment, they are a small group of pioneers; but if they grow and expand, they may help change the color of China.

CIM's CHINESE name is Zhicai, meaning Wisdom and Talent; it was founded in 1985 by Yu Pinhai, a young Hong Kong newspaperman and entre-preneur. It had been a junior corporation until 1991, when it abruptly became very high profile, owing to a brilliant merger that dramatically increased its worth. The deal involved one of Hong Kong's legendary figures—Louis Cha, pen-name Jin Yong, who is among other things the spectacularly famous kung fu novelist and owner of the Ming Bao Group, one of Hong Kong's major newspaper corporations. Cha, who had been on the Basic Law Committee that helped to draft legal guidelines for China's rule of Hong Kong after 1997, was an old-school Mandarin patriarch who had always dreamed of retiring to the beautiful Hangzhou in central China. Yet at the news of the Tiananmen massacre, he wept and promptly withdrew from the Basic Law Committee. Further disillusioned by personal tragedies—his only son committed suicide, and rumors circulated that he had been ripped off by several former mistresses—he announced that Ming Bao would be auctioned. Fierce competition and negotiations ensued, because many big businesses coveted Cha's influential multimedia property. After much deliberation, Cha stunned the business community with his decision: he sold it to Yu Pinhai, a thirty-three-year-old unknown upstart. What's more, Yu managed to buy it from Cha with very little money up front: through an intricate three-tier corporate chain maneuver and a reverse takeover, he bought just enough percentage to gain effective control over a major media and real estate enterprise which was then worth a little over $100 million.

Fantastic. But why Yu? Was Cha becoming so old and foolish that he was outmaneuvered by someone so young? Or was the young man so impressive and smooth that Cha, always a bit of a romantic, wanted to give him a chance over other, more profitable suitors? Unfortunately, this sort of generational change theory was almost too banal and too noble to be taken seriously. Darker speculations and rumors ran around. Some suspected Yu's political background: How did he get all that funding? Even considering his brilliant business maneuvering, it still required quite a handful. Was he backed by Taiwan? Or maybe by mainland China? Certainly, both sides had reasons to want a hand in a major Hong Kong newspaper chain. The wildest of all rumors, however, had to do with a potentially scandalous relation: Yu was said to be Cha's illegitimate son! Kung fu novel fans even dug up a famously mysterious puzzle from one of the Jin Yong novels to confirm this: the key word in the puzzle, which involves an old emperor passing his throne to an illegitimate son, is none other than *Yu*!

By ancestry, Yu is supposedly a northern Chinese, with his family background going back to Shandong province—not to Zhejiang, the central Chinese province where Cha came from. Yu himself was raised in Hong Kong and had a brief Western education. In the late seventies, he went to a Canadian university to study political economy; while there, he did some journalism work for campus papers and for a local Chinese television station. Ever since then, journalism had been his passion. After returning to Hong Kong, he moved from job to job: reporter, assistant editor, entrepreneur, business broker. He was in real estate, hotels, and all manners of deals. In the early years of his striving and climbing, he traveled all over Asia: southern China,

Taiwan, Malaysia, Singapore, Japan. There are obvious gaps in his life story, about which there is plenty of speculation and gossip—all impossible to confirm. His reputation as a tough, reckless man, for instance, goes back to his student days in Canada: rumor had it that Yu got himself in a jam once and was busted by the Canadian police, but no one knows whether it really happened or why, if it did.

It was the same with all the gossip about the Ming Bao transaction. In reality, no one except Cha and Yu knows the real story. The facts behind the scenes would, as usual, remain behind the scenes. What everyone knew for sure was simply this: a new stud has appeared on the race course, and from here on, CIM was a force to be reckoned with.

Within a year, CIM launched a massive number of investment projects on mainland China. By mid-1993, it had set up branch offices and companies not only in Beijing but all over China, as far as Tibet even. The traditional businesses (real estate, autos) remained covered, but the company kept a special eye on culture. Here, its target range is staggering: film, television, cable, satellite, music, video, publishing, distribution . . . just about anything the company can get its hands on. There has even been talk about setting up bookshops, cafés, and movie theaters in a chain of "culture plazas"—an idea imported direct from Hong Kong.

By the end of 1993, nearly all of CIM's projects had moved onto mainland China, and Yu himself was spending more time on business trips to different mainland cities than in his Hong Kong headquarters. Meanwhile, the Ming Bao stocks had gone up to over $388 million U.S., nearly three times their value when Yu first took over. Until 1993 though, Yu himself had for the most part remained in Hong Kong.

THE POINT man of CIM's massive "mainland offensive," Yu's top adviser, and the general director of CIM's cultural projects on mainland China is a man named Chan Koon-Chung. "You should talk to this guy, by all means. He's been extremely active in the media circles here," a Beijing newspaper columnist advised me. "These Hong Kong businessmen . . ." he sighed suddenly. "Sometimes it makes you feel Hong Kong is starting to buy up mainland culture wholesale." It was early spring 1993. I was in Beijing, marveling more and more at the many signs of Hong Kong's importance to the local pop culture.

A friend in a senior position in the film industry informed me, "We call him 'Chan Xuanfeng,' Chan the Whirlwind, because he seems to have managed to meet everyone he wanted to meet in such a short time." She laughed affectionately: she herself was one of Chan's first recruits. He put her on CIM's payroll to coordinate joint projects in video and publishing.

I turned on the television, and there was Ai Jing, in her casual chic Levi's and booties, telling Beijing youngsters all about MTV cool. A rock musician friend said, "She's CIM's first starlet—but the big boss behind is this guy Chan Koon-Chung."

Early in April, a note came from Sanlian, a major Beijing publishing house, inviting me to join a forum on media and cultural criticism. There would be a luncheon afterward. The house editor told me on the phone: "It's sponsored by Mr. Chan Koon-Chung, an investor from Hong Kong. Our house is nego- tiating joint-venture projects with him." Then she added: "Mr. Chan's a cul- tured person, too—he edited a magazine himself in Hong Kong." I couldn't make the forum. But two weeks later, I made an appointment to have coffee with Chan.

He was nothing like what I expected. Tall, lanky, about forty, with very fine skin, pale complexion, and a pair of gold-rimmed spectacles, he looked neither like a Cantonese nor like a businessman; instead, an air of the intellectual hung about him. His clothes were a surprise too: casual, rumpled brownish jacket with sloped shoulders, of an intricate wool weave; a padded sepia colored vest over a white linen shirt with a round Indian collar lightly embroidered along the edges; soft, loose fitting trousers with dark pleats and stripes; brown leather shoes of a muted shine. No suit, no tie, no pressed shirt or glossy shoes. The overall effect was a softly silhouet- ted, richly textured elegance, almost a hint of a European dandy, but gently understated, purposely rumpled and aged. Together with the soft handshake, the pale skin, the long strands of hair brushed down along the cheeks as if they were his sideburns . . . Chan struck me like some romantic character from a nostalgic old movie about Shanghai in the thirties. Surely, if he had a gold-tipped opium pipe in his mouth at this moment, he would look just like one of those decadent Shanghai poets who had returned from Baudelaire's Paris!

Of course, none of this passed my lips. Chan was sitting down at a sun- speckled coffee table in one of Beijing's bright, cheerful new high-rises; I was there to inquire about his commercial deals. We exchanged pleasantries and got straight to business.

"Both economically and culturally, China looks similar to the Hong Kong of the seventies," Chan told me, "so I can see clearly where the market is head- ing, where China is going to end up. We know exactly what to do and what will work. It's a huge market and this is an exciting time to be here." Statistics came tripping off his tongue. Plans, tactics, prospects—but anecdotes too, and jokes. A whole pot of coffee vanished.

Chan was polite, obliging; his manners were very cordial but not rigid. He seemed quite candid, too. He talked softly in a measured, confident voice, and he punctuated his Mandarin with occasional perfect English phrases the way educated Hong Kong people often do. From time to time, his eyes would light up at a vivid, humorous detail, his face taking on an expression of boyish caprice. "Miss Zha," he gave me an affable smile. "More questions?"

"Thank you, Mr. Chan," I said, almost feeling as though I should bow. "Maybe another time."

Who is he exactly? An entrepreneur after a big profit, an efficient corporate instrument, or maybe just an intellectual trying to make it in the commercial world by playing culture broker?

"Chan is the founder of *Haowai*," a Hong Kong friend informed me. To the generation of educated Hong Kong readers who came of age in the late seventies, *Haowai* was a unique journalistic institution, a bastion famed for certain urban lifestyles and cultural tastes. "You might even say Chan was the first yuppie in Hong Kong," the friend suggested. "But you should talk to some of those *Haowai* guys."

Danny Yung, a distinctive character on the Hong Kong avant-garde scene, had been a central member in the *Haowai* circles and one of Chan's close friends back in the late seventies. Danny himself had founded Zuni, a Hong Kong performance art group, in the early eighties. A longtime cult guru who appears on local television a lot, Danny certainly has a look: he is short, soft-spoken, with a perpetually incipient beard and sideburns, and he is always dressed in rumpled, good clothes—usually in basic colors and very soft fabrics. A gentle, amused frown often hangs on his face as he listens to someone, but when he smiles or laughs, incredible wrinkles suddenly rush up around his eyes. The effect is extremely contagious—people tend to laugh with him. When I brought up Chan's name in our conversation, however, Danny frowned. There had been an incident between them not long before. Zuni had designed a cartoon spoof about 1997, which showed a big penislike organ pointing at Deng Xiaoping's face. The cartoon was sent to *Haowai*, but it was rejected on grounds of "poor taste." Zuni wrote a letter to *Haowai*, addressed to Chan, protesting privately what they saw as censorship. No reply. Zuni then held a press conference, protesting openly the beginning of Hong Kong journalists' self-censorship, even before 1997!

Danny seemed nostalgic about the good old days, when he wrote frequently for *Haowai* and Chan sometimes played parts in Zuni's performances. So much has changed since then—at least on Chan's part. "*Haowai* has turned into a teenybopper fashion display," Danny said; Zuni, on the other hand, has been trying to keep the avant-garde spirit and the protest tradition alive. Some critics say that Zuni's time has passed because, as one of them puts it, Danny founded it on one great idea ten years ago which Zuni has been repeating ever since: it was a breakthrough then, but it's old hat now. Danny doesn't think so, nor do any of his group of young performers who, despite the periodic change of members over the years, have remained fiercely loyal to their leader's artistic vision. Thanks to Danny's persistent, cunning fund-raising efforts, Zuni has come through many financial crises: it operates on small budgets, but the group is still there, an uncompromising presence in the public arena. At present, Zuni is preparing a project for the 1994 Hong Kong art festival. They are going to erect a five-story red star, tilted and partially cut deep into the ground, on the plaza in front of the Hong Kong Cultural Center. Nobody aware of China's 1997 takeover of Hong Kong would miss its political implication: the installation would be like a scene from *Planet of the Apes.*

Matthias, Danny's assistant and a young member of Zuni, was much more blunt about his opinion of the likes of Chan. "Chan used to be an important cultural figure in Hong Kong in the late seventies and early eighties. Now he's sold out for money, so typical of that generation. They've all got their Canadian passports or moved to Vancouver. My parents moved there too. Vancouver is the middle-class dream, a paradise for all the stuffy Hong Kong bourgeoisie: good food, nice weather, big houses." Matthias has heard about Chan's coming to China. Naturally: China means future market share. It's where the big money will be.

CHAN KOON-CHUNG is a man of curiously mixed backgrounds and qualities. Born in 1952 into a textile family in Shanghai, Chan moved with his family to Hong Kong at age four. Some of his father's past employees helped with their departure arrangements, and the Chans were lucky enough to get out just before massive political campaigns swept up China. After a Catholic prep school education, he graduated from Hong Kong University in 1974 and went straight to Boston University to study journalism. At that time, the counterculture movement had not quite ebbed within American academia; a third of the social sciences staff at B.U. either were or had been Marxists. Fascinated by American campus culture, Chan took various radical courses (with professors such as Anthony Giddens), drove back and forth between the coasts, and generally inhaled as much American urban cerebral esprit as he could. Returning to Hong Kong over a year later, he was armed more with Western leftist theories than with an education in professional journalism.

Journalism, though, was to be the first of his many career turns. For the first few months back in Hong Kong, Chan worked as a reporter for *Star*, a local English-language daily modeled on the British tabloids. The job didn't last long: as soon as he had scraped up a moderate amount of money, in 1976 he set up a small mezzanine bookstore in an attic in Wanchai, a central district of Hong Kong. Meanwhile, using the back room as an editorial office, he launched his own newspaper, a biweekly named *Haowai (The Extra)*. In essence, the founding editorial board and staff writers consisted of only two names: Chan, and Deng Xiaoyu, Chan's longtime friend who had just returned from America, studying cinema at Temple University. The newspaper soon changed into a monthly magazine with a new English name, *The City Magazine*. In time, the magazine would become a symbol in certain intellectual circles, a small cultural legend of late-seventies Hong Kong.

Hong Kong in those years was changing dramatically. On the mainland, Mao died in 1976, the Gang of Four was arrested, and the Cultural Revolution finally came to an end. The Maoists in Hong Kong, having made a lot of noise on the local political scene, were now left leaderless, with a bankrupt ideology. The camp dispersed, and throngs of radicals went into banking and business, turning their disillusioned energy to the pursuit of material wealth. The threat from Red China diminished significantly. An indigenous movement began to gather force: using Cantonese and English, not Mandarin Chinese, was the new form of radical chic.

Chan and Deng worked hard in their cluttered den, bringing youthful joy to everything they touched: as an original idea hit Chan, he was prone to become so excited that he'd jump up from his chair and hit his head on the low ceiling. In this attic of less than fifty square feet, though, the two young men cranked out innumerable articles under a dozen pen names: in-depth investigative reports, personal journalism, social critique, reviews of art films, fashion, food, music, architecture, tongue-in-cheek commentary on local beauty contests, serious ruminations over Hong Kong's identity, a splash of fiction, lots of satires and spoofs—every subject that would interest an urban, cultured person, and any genre that would fit the cosmopolitan, playful young. Chan and Deng got their friends to contribute pieces, and then got friends of friends to do it. The magazine had a distinctive style, the essays were punchy, and the authors experimented with a blend of Cantonese, English, and Mandarin in their writings in order to find their own fresh voices. They were carving out a sensibility, limning a new space. It was Hong Kong's first magazine on urban trends. As they set out, Chan and Deng had *The New Yorker*, *The Village Voice*, and *New York Magazine* on their minds.

Before long, a loose yet devoted core group of writers, artists, and readers congregated around the magazine. These "friends of *Haowai*" were united not by politics but by lifestyle and certain tacitly understood aesthetic preferences. It's not so easy to pin it all down, but in general, friends of *Haowai* tended to be well-educated, sophisticated, youngish individuals of generally liberal sympathies, with varying degrees of bohemian tendencies and aesthetic eccentricities. They wore fine clothes, but were contemptuous of custom-made tastes. None of them was against being rich, though style and originality were their forte. They had an epicurean attitude, a cool with rumpled edges, like their preferred fashion statement. Some of them were activists in artistic or social movements, others worked for banks or taught at schools. All cared about what went on in other major cosmopolitan cities in the world, for they considered themselves to be, or strove to be, a part of that scene and apart from the mainstream, middlebrow Hong Kong bourgeoisie. There was an excitement about Hong Kong among them: its potential to become a cultural and artistic vanguard city of Asia, as New York had become to the West around the turn of the century. *Haowai* was playing a role in defining that quivering new image. Later, they were to be called the first yuppies of Hong Kong. Among his circles of friends, Chan is often held responsible for—sometimes accused of—heralding and celebrating the inception of yuppie lifestyle in Hong Kong. It was a somewhat misleading label, for *Haowai* under Chan really displayed more of a bohemian bent than the sort of standard yuppie sensibilities that Westerners would associate with the term. But then, at that time, few in Hong Kong could tell the difference between the two.

Along with the indigenous movement, a more general change was taking place. Hong Kong was getting rich fast, and a younger generation was coming of age with more and more pride in being Hong Kong and keeping the poor and backward mainland China at arm's length. Meanwhile, the pragmatic local mindset, deeply entrenched to begin with, was finding new expression in the intensifying commercialism. "Western Marxists thought they had won the battle with radical Maoists," Chan would say years later, "but they didn't quite grasp that Hong Kong was already on the threshold of the post-ideological era. Late capitalism was setting in."

As for his own longstanding interest in Western Marxist theories, Chan gathered it all up in a book, *Marxism and Literary Criticism*, which came out in 1982. It contained well-researched, lucidly written essays on topics ranging from early Marxism, the Soviet avant-garde and Russian Formalism, to Walter Benjamin and the cultural industry, Jacques Derrida and French poststructuralism. It's a thoughtfully organized, insightful introduction to several of the major Marxist-related theoretical debates over ideology and language in the past one hundred years. It must have taken Chan years of disciplined labor to mobilize so many dense, esoteric intellectual sources and then to fit it all into such a comprehensive package. Unfortunately, it could not escape the usual fate of a trendy book that arrived only after the trend. The chance for this sort of book to generate a more general debate had slipped away: by the early eighties, interest in such highbrow topics in Hong Kong was confined strictly to the academy and to a tiny circle of intellectual readers. The majority of Hong Kong readers were picking up pocket-size, formulaic novels for their subway rides to work.

Chan was aware of this himself. Perhaps he wrote the book to fulfill an intellectual need within himself, to sort things out, and to bow out in a proper manner from an important and complicated period in his own life. Indeed, before the book was published, Chan's life and career was already taking a new turn.

Chan married in 1978, and his first son was born in 1980. Until then, he had been busy running his magazine and bookstore, observing and taking part in various urban counterculture trends, and dashing out brilliant, quirky commentaries for the circles of friends around *Haowai*. None of this brought him much of an income—but he was young, and with a loving, supportive wife who had a steady job in investment banking (as well as occasional loans from his well-to-do parents) they had gotten by. Now, though, things were different: he was approaching thirty and he was a father. It so happened around this time that some film people, having heard of Chan's literary reputation, asked if he could write screenplays; they would pay, of course. So it began: he would have coffee or dim sum with some film directors in the mornings and come home with script assignments. In the ensuing five years or so, he wrote some ten screenplays and adapted two plays from short stories. He worked with numerous leading Hong Kong directors. He even played supporting roles in a few movies. ("A dork who loses out to Chow Yun Fat, the romantic lead in *The Story of Rose*, for example," he told me.) Meanwhile, still keeping a guiding hand on *Haowai*, he picked a younger generation of editors and gradually passed the executive power to them. The essay-writing continued; he was as sharp and witty as ever, but he wrote more sporadically now. Then, after collecting some thirty pieces in a new book in 1986, he stopped altogether.

Later he would describe the period as "painful." For the sort of intellectual cult leader that Chan had been, it must have been a tough adjustment, what with the perpetual waiting for new projects and the frequent canceling of old ones (of the ten scripts he completed, only three were produced), the relatively low status of script writers in the film industry, the shock of realizing that being a creative intellectual could mean so little—indeed, nothing at all, outside certain small circles. In the larger picture of things, it seemed that what Chan and his cohorts had done in the past ("being an armchair radical intellectual, mostly" is how he puts it) was turning into a pale shadow, barely hovering on the edge of significance.

But Chan is a quick study and by nature an optimist. He proved himself to be one of those deft, open individuals who could sprint from a fall. And for a future "culture industrialist," he couldn't have fallen into a better, more fantastic training ground than the Hong Kong movieland—for here was an exuberant, ever-churning pressure cooker. Not only did action and dialogue on the screen move like lightning but everyone in the profession was wired on hard-nosed, fast-lane business programming, and hyperdexterity is an attribute taken for granted. Crushed into a tiny tract on a packed island, this is an industry with an annual output second only to Hollywood and India— and Hong Kong is the only place on earth where local audiences have consistently preferred their own movies to America's. Chan has come far from his smoke-filled intellectual attic, from his days of pleasantly involuted, dilettantish salons.

He learned his new trade from scratch, and then inside out. Never a slow one, he now moved faster than ever, doing everything: between the scripts and occasional acting, he familiarized himself with every phase and aspect of filmmaking, down to the last technical detail in the cutting room. He built up contacts in the industry; later, he even started a film directors' guild, the first ever in Hong Kong. Amid all these activities, he still found time and energy to host a music program on television and to start a major environmental group with two friends.

Then, in 1983, a crucial turn came: by a fluke, Chan won the rights to produce a movie, which he turned into a commercial success. From there on, he took the capital and his energies into movie and video production. He made all sorts of things: small art films (he co-produced Wayne Wang's *Life Is Cheap, Toilet Paper Is Expensive*), horror flicks (the last in this genre was *The Haunted Precinct*, a coproduction with an American studio), as well as action/romance movies. He flew on business trips to North America, Japan, and Taiwan. There were the flops and aborted projects, but there were more and more successful ones. Aside from film, he did consulting work for various Hong Kong business moguls getting into the media business, by setting up satellite television systems and obtaining radio licences. He put money into a joint-venture children's publication, which turned out to be a huge hit. By 1991, Chan had established himself as a successful movie producer and an affluent businessman; by then, he had also had a second son, and his family had moved to Canada to settle into a big, nice house in Vancouver. The boys were going to good schools. Chan's wife found her new passion in volunteer work for a Buddhist teacher there. A Shanghai maid lived in the house, cooking and cleaning. Every three months or so, the family would happily hop a trans-Pacific jet plane to spend their holidays in their old Hong Kong residence. By any standard, Chan was settled in life: approaching forty now, the oddball dandy had become a success story.

It was then, at the end of 1991, that he visited Beijing for the first time. Chan happened to be the 1992 chairman on the Hong Kong International Council of Young Leaders, the Hong Kong equivalent of the Washington, D.C.–based American Council of Young Political Leaders. To give its members more international exposure, the Council scheduled a delegation to visit various top-level mainland officials. The trip changed Chan's life.

YU PINHAI, now a rising star on the Hong Kong business scene, had a reputation for attracting and using talented, professional people to further his own game plan. He was said to have amassed his first big profits in real estate development by charming various specialists in key positions into helping him. Now with the powerful Ming Bao Group secured, Yu didn't lose any time in acting.

Chan Koon-Chung was among the first to get a phone call from Yu. Nancy Shi, the wife of Hong Kong's filmmaking genius Tsui Hark (*Peking Opera Blues, Shanghai Nights, Once Upon a Time in China*), also received a call. Shi is a media celebrity in her own right, famous not only for her versatile career in acting, movie producing, and half a dozen other artistic lines, but also for her personal charisma, spunk, and aplomb. Kelly Cheung, former general manager of Hong Kong Television Broadcast Ltd., the largest media corporation in Hong Kong, was also on Yu's wooing list. One by one, Yu did his personal charm number on them. As impressive as he was persuasive, the young, smart, and powerful businessman talked not merely about profits but also about a deep sense of mission, a bright long-term view of the twenty-first century. And he showed interest not just in buildings and plazas, but in arts and culture! Yu asked for their help. He saw their expertise and stature as invaluable to all of CIM's developments and its future. He pleaded for them to be his top advisers and directors, to board the ship; together, they could do great things.

Chan, Shi, and Cheung, being old friends (Chan co-wrote the screenplay for *Shanghai Nights*), compared notes and found that they were all quite won over. It wasn't the money: the six-digit salaries Yu offered them were generous enough as far as advisory fees went, but that was only about half of what they were already making—at least in the cases of Chan and Shi. Rather, it was the potential, the stimulating vibe of being a part of a great future which Yu had somehow infused in them. They decided to join. Yu got what he wanted: CIM could now boast a top-notch troika on the media culture front. The next day, everyone in the field heard the news.

Of course, ornament aside, Yu expected much more: above all, CIM needed new ideas—creative, well-grounded ideas. What should they put their money into? Where is the future?

"Mainland China!" Chan said. He had just returned from Beijing, and the excitement he felt was of an intensity he hadn't experienced for some time. Fired up with ideas and insights, Chan talked to his new boss and colleagues about China: the vast market, the increasingly liberal attitude toward commerce, the official hunger for foreign investment, and above all, the potentially huge and, at present, almost vacant space in the culture business. "Most people had their eyes on the real estate, transportation, the stock market, and so on," Chan tells me later on. "Culture was placed on the back burner because the state and most entrepreneurs had a mentality that was both pragmatic and shortsighted. As a result, these areas needed outside money very badly. Besides," he smiles, "I'm tired of flying to the U.S. just to make crappy videos. And what does building a couple more big office towers in Hong Kong matter? There are so many of them already. But China! You can do so much more here with the same amount of money. And what you do here has a bigger impact, a deeper meaning."

It wasn't very hard to convince CIM's leadership that the big game was in China. Yu himself had been to the mainland many times before. In 1986, a year after CIM was founded, when Yu was still hustling as a small businessman, he had opened a three-star hotel in the southern tourist city of Guilin, only to be forced to pull out after the Tiananmen massacre in 1989. Nancy Shi's husband Tsui Hark had also visited China, and was hoping to use the mainland's spectacular sights to shoot some of his upcoming movies. I happened to meet the couple at a dinner in Hong Kong around Christmas 1991. When I asked Tsui about his plans beyond 1997, if he might be thinking about moving to Hollywood, Tsui said, "No, I'm thinking about moving to Beijing."

And really, the timing couldn't have been better. Two months after Chan's northbound trip, Deng Xiaoping made his southbound trip to Shenzhen, where he gave his watershed speeches calling for greater market reform. It was the most significant signal from Chinese officialdom that more open economic policies were in the future. The wind was auspicious for the adventures.

Thus began CIM's mainland expedition. By mid-1992, Chan Koon-Chung had set up camp in Beijing.

THE POLITICS of collaboration has always been complicated in China. Ever since the government announced its open door policy in the early eighties, waves of foreign corporations and investors have been rushing in, hooked on dreams of fantastic fortune from a market of one billion consumers and cheap laborers. They were in for some cruel surprises. Many left in frustration after getting bogged down in the mud of red tape, murky laws, inefficiency, and shifty politics—but this was perhaps endemic to doing business in a third world, semicommunist environment. Foreign investors in things related to *culture* find themselves in even trickier waters. Typically, the state put out its palm for their money (and for greasing) but kept a very suspicious eye on the cultural goods they delivered. From the mid-eighties through the early nineties, numerous Western media corporations had made their overtures to China: some ended in a complete debacle, others with a measure of success, but the lesson had been invariable—caution, caution, and caution.

Aggressively expanding their programs all over China, Chan and the few CIM assistants he brought to Beijing watched their step. Chan knew they were economically strong but politically vulnerable. It didn't take him long to grow aware of the complexity of their situation, of all the stumbling blocks and traps around. His strategy, accordingly, was to find and to use as many able local insiders as possible, while he himself would keep a relatively low profile, quietly initiating, directing, and supplying funds from behind. He was good at this. CIM's money was almost always desirable, but Chan's personal charm and solid business sense were instrumental in enlisting the right kind of people, identifying the right kind of projects, opening up personal channels, and winning over many difficult joint-venture deals.

Liu Zhuohui and Ai Jing were two of the first "locals" Chan recruited. When Chan looked Liu up in Canton, he was already into his fourth year on the mainland, where he'd been running his small music studio, Great Land, on a shoestring and trying to promote new pop music talents. Chan parlayed the CIM vision, offered him monetary support, and moved him to Beijing to direct Great Land on a bigger scale, under the auspices of CIM. "I was impressed," Liu later told me. "I thought to myself: well, if a well-known cultural figure like Chan Koon-Chung is willing to work for CIM and Yu, it must be something good. So I let myself be bought off."

Through a Taiwanese publishing agent who had become an old hand on the mainland book market, Chan also bought from a major Taiwan publishing house the rights to reprint entire sets of popular and highbrow Taiwanese kung fu, romance, and history authors on the mainland; he also got a big Shanghai publishing house to copublish with CIM a fourteen-volume scholarly book series on market economy, which sold very well. He appointed another local expert, a former Red Guard turned entrepreneur, to bring out a more inventive, broader newspaper in Guangzhou, and he did the same with two Beijing papers. He sponsored Sanlian's effort to revive *Life Weekly*, a venerable lifestyle magazine from the thirties. He registered new joint video and television production companies in different cities. He even contributed his own money toward printing an overseas version of *Dushu*, China's most prestigious monthly review of books.

Yu and CIM's other senior directors, who still resided in Hong Kong, gave their input to their mainland projects whenever they were called on. As a business team, CIM was quite unmatched in the field. Somewhere in 1992, for instance, Chan heard about a new policy change that made foreign investment in cable TV possible. As soon as he learned from a Chinese friend about an opportunity in the central Chinese city of Wuhan, he flew there at once. Through Wuhan Cable TV Network Ltd., a company Chan had just brought into partnership with CIM, he set up a series of meetings with all the municipal officials who had some say about the cable TV programming rights. Yu and Nancy Shi flew in from Hong Kong: wearing their elegant clothes and sunny, confident smiles, the trio went from meeting to meeting, talking and shoulder-patting their way through banquets and drinks. The city officials and media leaders were so impressed by their business acuity, their easy style and amicable charm, that in a matter of a few days they rejected a previously favored investor and handed the cable television coproduction rights to CIM. CIM committed nearly three million dollars right away. The new cable television network expanded Wuhan's television channels from four to sixteen, and brought in many new, refreshing programs from Hong Kong. Not long after the deal, the central government's policy reverted, blocking any such cooperation in the future—but CIM had already gotten into Wuhan, and they were there to stay.

There was, of course, more to CIM's initial success than swift action and personality. After several business dealings, the head of a big Beijing publishing house described to me his impressions of the CIM people at the negotiation table. "They seemed a strikingly young bunch to represent such a major corporation. You'd be first struck by their casual clothes and easy manners, then you'd be all the more impressed by how sharp they are. They have a much better understanding of the unique Chinese ways of doing business under the current circumstances. Much better than, say, the Americans." Among others, *Time* magazine had once approached his house with joint-venture proposals. "It didn't get anywhere because the American representatives insisted on us putting absolutely everything on the table and following everything through by written law. They refused to bend or deal with anything unclear. It's quite touching to see such principle-abiding people, but you know how things are in China." He shook his head softly. "Nothing is simple and clear. So they left empty-handed." The CIM people were different: they were flexible. While discussing the terms of a joint publishing contract for a magazine, the Chinese side raised problems of official censorship. Without hesitation, Yu and Chan suggested that an overseeing committee be formed, chaired by an appointee from the Chinese side, to monitor the direction of the magazine. "They knew perfectly well," the head said, "that as the principal financier they'd have a strong influence on the direction of the magazine, no matter how subtle or indirect the influence. We knew that too. What's important is they too understood that we needed to deal with our official superiors in an appropriate way, or the whole deal would be off." He said that CIM was also generous on financial terms, willing to give more of a percentage of future profit to the Chinese side than the other foreign investors were. "It's pleasant to work with someone who can appreciate the unusual Chinese ways. After all, we all want to change and improve things here."

The first year after Chan moved to Beijing went by quickly; his life was hectic but rewarding. Circumstances were not always congenial, yet Chan felt that coming to China broadened and deepened his vision of life: because he had been raised and had grown up in Hong Kong, it had never quite occurred to him that another kind of Chinese people existed in this world. Even though he had met some overseas Chinese during his stay in Boston, they had not seemed to him all that different. Chan's vision and, indeed, optimism, about life had been shaped by his own basically happy experiences: growing up in seventies Hong Kong meant growing up with a belief that today is better than yesterday, and tomorrow will be better than today. His generation of Hong Kong youths had been blessed with that sense of infinite opportunities and self-confidence: as children of affluent and middle-class parents, they had a good education, talent, and family support, they could be whatever they chose to be. And most of them did just that: they've become winners in the top echelons of today's Hong Kong society.

Seeing the realities of life in China changed all that. On business and sometimes on pleasure, Chan has traveled through the mainland's provincial towns as well as its vast, dirt-poor countryside. Often, it has struck him as a journey in time: the landscape and the people seem to recede into history, withdrawing into remote epochs that linger into the present. Chan had never before dreamed of this China, these Chinese, this startling, live manifestation of his own ancestral roots. These people with features much like his own were alien: young men who looked so old, so defeated by life already, and women turning forty who looked like grandmothers. It is a harsh, sometimes primitive life; and with a shock of pain, Chan realized that to a lot of those living this life, it was also devoid of hope, without a way out.

But Chan's temperament, though sensitive and touched by compassion, even a shade of melancholy, is finally not of the sort given over to cosmic despair. There is a lightness about him, a buoyancy that constantly turns him to the brighter side of things; a positive resolve nearly always carries the day. And so far, he has had more than enough reasons to feel hopeful, even proud, about his mainland adventures. To meet all there is to meet, the best and the brightest of the Beijing cultural scene, or perhaps of China, is an honor he found unparalleled—and, in a way, things worked out better even than he had expected. Step by step, he was coming closer to realizing all he had ever dreamed of—a minirenaissance of major and minor arts and letters. Even the constant uncertainty about whether such labor can come to fruition became a part of the excitement.

Along the path of his numerous career shifts, Chan realized that if one could not control the medium or come up with the right institution, the fate of creative and moral people would be at the whim of those who are in charge. "Bad institutions beget bad 'content,'" he explained to me. "I want an environment that makes 'let the good guys win' possible." Since then, he consciously suppressed his urge to write in order to focus his energy on "systems-building." Privately, he calls his approach "institutionalist," meaning that he tries to build the right kind of institutions, media, and companies, believing that with them in place the right kind of "content" will naturally follow.

His approach remained essentially the same after he went to China. He secured newspapers and magazines, set up distribution systems in print, audio, video, and movie media, and tried to participate in television station operation. "I can pull that off because the financiers see a huge dollar sign somewhere down the road," Chan told me, his face shining with urchinlike satisfaction. He didn't tell me until much later that, time and again, he had also been reminded by his backers that he was too indulgent with culture; he had to keep reminding himself to play the game more skillfully. He cites a Buddhist motto: "Train thy vision as high as the sky, thy action as fine as the flour." Buddhism, he has insisted, has made him at once more spiritual and more worldly. In 1989, while researching and fund-raising in India for a film project, *The Thirteenth Dalai Lama*, Chan encountered a charismatic young Tibetan Buddhist teacher from Bhutan. The film project, to be coproduced by Francis Coppola's Zoetrope, was terminated when Coppola's company filed for bankruptcy protection in 1990, but the Buddhist teacher stayed on in Chan's life. Chan's wife afterward became a devotee, helping the teacher to run his programs and retreat camps in Canada. Chan himself remained on the periphery of the teacher's circle of followers from all over the world, though he confesses to have learned a good deal about the wisdom of life from the teacher.

I asked him for an example. A mischievous expression again crept over his face. "The wrathful face, for instance—Buddhism emphasizes skillful means in doing things. The great lotus master, as you might know, has eight faces, with expressions from kind, serene, to wrathful. Why? Because the Buddha cannot merely rely on peaceful means; sometimes it must use a wrathful face to subdue, to draw attention to its words, to influence. Working in an environment like Beijing, sometimes I have to exercise my 'wrathful face' to be effective. I can't just be the goody-goody type I'm usually prone to be." This brought a smile to my face. By and by, Chan told me a bit more of these Buddhist wisdoms, about meditation, restraint, and internal harmony. He also spoke about expatriate hardship, and how he can now "turn poison into nourishment." As a matter of fact, he let me know that, just before I walked into this hotel café, he had been meditating by fixing his gaze on the single rose on the table, which filled him with a feeling of supreme serenity.

In a gentle way, Chan's character riveted my attention.

ONE DAY, late in the fall of 1993, while Chan was vacationing with his family in Vancouver, the phone rang. It was Yu Pinhai. He was on a business trip in Toronto and he wanted to see Chan. Before Chan could suggest anything,

Yu said he was on his way, flying in to Vancouver: Let's just meet in a bar and have a chat, nothing formal, he said.

The two men had a drink in a local bar, and the chat was over within an hour. Yu flew back to Hong Kong right afterwards, but Chan went home realizing that something very important had just happened. Yu had asked about Chan's holidays and his family, then he had talked about how busy CIM's business in Hong Kong was getting these days, and that he would like to see Chan helping out more in Hong Kong. Of course, he would send more CIM staff to Beijing to help run the business there. What Yu had really meant, it occurred to Chan now, amounted to this: Chan would be relieved of some of his duties on the mainland.

Two weeks later, Chan flew back to Beijing. At once he saw the change: Yu had sent in four men from Hong Kong, each to supervise a business section in CIM's Beijing office. Technically, they were lieutenants under Chan, dividing his previous business responsibilities, which indeed had grown a good deal because of the rapid progress he had made within a year and a half. The new section chiefs were ensconced in their individual cubicles at CIM's new office compound, which Yu had just leased in order to meet CIM's increased need for office space. Yu himself now had his central office there, a big room with locks and windows so that he could either take the entire staff on the open floor into his view or shut himself behind the doors. Chan still had his office in the old CIM quarters on the other side of the city, but it was clear that Yu intended to move more and more operations over to the new, more modern compound, which would become the headquarters. Yu himself now visited nearly every week. Now that the company's mainland business looked not only promising but perhaps even long-term, CIM had also arranged permanent housing for all its Hong Kong staff in the cozy apartments at the Asian Games Athletic Club. No slot was slated for Chan, though. Up until now, Chan had been living out of a suitcase, either in some temporary rental suite or simply checking into a hotel every time he arrived in Beijing. This time, his secretary booked him into another plush hotel. The company would continue to arrange his accommodations and, of course, would cover all of Chan's expenses as usual.

With a sinking heart, Chan realized that what he had only vaguely expected in a distant future was really happening. Some of his Hong Kong friends who knew Yu had warned him about Yu's past record of periodically changing the senior staff and dumping top lieutenants; they had discussed a certain ruthless, suspicious streak in Yu's character, a taste for concentrated power. Someone had even compared it with the late Chairman Mao. But

Chan hadn't paid much mind to it. To him, Yu was a kindred spirit in some ways and in other ways not, which was fine with him. What mattered was the China mission, and in this he had had Yu's full support. With Yu's backing, he had opened all the local networks and laid down the first tracks for CIM; the Beijing cultural circles had learned about CIM with Chan as its human face. But perhaps, the moment had come to remind them who the real big boss was: it had come time for Yu to take things into his own hands. Chan's contract with CIM would not end until the following April; now he was not so sure he wanted to renew it, and even less sure that Yu would want him to renew it. Yu had put Chan to very good use, and now he was getting rid of him.

YU PINHAI is a strikingly good-looking man. He is about five feet eleven, well built, with thick black hair that grows low on his forehead. His face is lean and masculine, his features cleanly chiseled. He has expressive, uncommonly penetrating eyes, which he likes to fix directly on whomever he happens to be talking to. Usually but not always, one finds him dressed in his hip designer suits (Krizia has been a recent favorite, and its Hong Kong store keeps Yu informed on all its latest styles). His leather shoes always have a good shine. Instead of a dress shirt and a tie, he normally wears a polo shirt or a turtleneck underneath, and leaves his suit unbuttoned. The matching styles and colors set each other off neatly, indicating at once power and informality. In a crowd, his swift, resolute movements and forceful speech, bordering occasionally on stagecraft, easily mark him as the leader. When necessary, he can be extremely suave and patient, but sycophantic dimwits don't get anywhere with him. On the whole, Yu exudes the air of someone who is absolutely secure in the power of his own intelligence and masculinity.

For a smart, handsome, and elusively self-made young millionaire, Yu's character fascinates the people around him; behind his back, they simply can't stop talking about him. CIM's Beijing offices are filled with gossip about the big boss. Is he worth three billion Hong Kong dollars, or just seven hundred million? Has the national security bureau approached him? Which top official is secretly backing him in the government? Is he going steady with his girlfriend? Were he not so rich and powerful, would he still be considered such a hunk, or just another "little white face"? Who are his favorite staff members at the moment? Who is getting the cold shoulder? These questions consume people: they talk up a storm about Yu at dinner tables, at parties, on the phone. Everyone's heard about Yu's relationship with a famous mainland pop idol, but they still love to go on and on about his reputation as a womanizer. Yu is supposed to be quite proud of his virility—especially since he became rich and came to China, away for long stretches of time from his supposedly unhappy early marriage. People say that Yu has a little honey in every port city he stops in. They say that to him flirting is as natural as breathing: he turns his charm on every good-looking woman who comes his way—businesswomen, hotel clerks, waitresses. His energy is boundless, his charm (perhaps doubled by his money) irresistible, and he can take a good "high" any time of the day.

The moment Yu took charge of CIM's mainland ship, everything got escalated. He drove all the employees at a faster pace, loading them with new projects, new directions, new executive orders. The section chiefs were always in a sweat now: Yu drew up brilliant, ambitious blueprints, he wanted them to set up new distribution systems, open new joint-venture fronts, put out more products, and promote more singers, more newspapers, more everything. The scope of his vision was grand and far-reaching: he saw a powerful conglomerate, a multimedia empire rising up before his eyes, its glory shining into the next century. Generations of Chinese would benefit from his cause and remember CIM. Feeling the thrill of all great visionaries, Yu wanted expansion, expansion, and expansion, as quickly as possible.

The work environment changed dramatically too. The old CIM office headquarters under Chan had been rented directly from a Chinese office building, with the standard, old-style layout of separate rooms. At state enterprises, a typical socialist working day in this kind of office would be spent in a general atmosphere of lethargy: sipping tea, reading papers, and gossiping. The rooms, shared and blocked by thick walls, breed habits of spying and secrecy. However, CIM employees under Chan had an inspired attitude toward their jobs, not to mention incentives like higher salaries and commissions. They did work and got things done in those old offices. Never a fan of big, concentrated corporations, Chan also didn't mind scattering his teams for convenience and special needs. The offices of Great Land, CIM's music branch headed by Liu Zhuohui, for one, had been located at Huawei, a downtown commercial plaza away from the CIM headquarters.

Yu apparently had a different philosophy about corporate work spirit. For the new offices he rented, he wanted completely open floors: long rows of desks laid out in the style of assembly-line machines in a large workshop; everyone could see everyone else, the phones, the faxes, the computers—the faint, rigorous electronic buzz goes on all day, along with the lowered voices engaged in business conversations. Yu placed his own office at the heart of all this activity: from his seat the young general had an unobstructed view of his entire business battleship. The intensity of it all invigorated Yu, and he certainly hoped that it would do the same for his employees. He loves to play hardball in everything he does; and when it comes to business, he'd like everyone under him to do it his way.

AI JING and Liu Zhuohui are not very happy these days. They miss their old offices at Huawei terribly. There, scattered in several suites, the musicians, technicians, and administrators all worked efficiently in their separate capacities. It was easy to call a small staff meeting or to take a television interview in one of the suite rooms without interfering with others' work. Sometimes, Ai, Liu, and Huang Xiaomao, Great Land's senior Chinese staff and a veteran Beijing pop lyricist, would be on such a roll they would keep working, talking, and smoking into the night, turning out new songs or new marketing strategies. Ai and Liu had their apartment suite right next door. Occasionally, Huang would work with them till dawn, curl up on the couch for a nap, and then go home in the morning to sleep some more. They loved the dim lights, the cozy, informal atmosphere: it made them feel like more than hired employees—they felt like artists, creative producers.

All that vanished after the move to Yu's new centralized office. On the open floor, they were no more than a small part of a big business machinery, chugging along with neighbors like real estate development and automobile imports. Drenched all day long in the unrelentingly bright fluorescent light and ceaseless telephonic buzz, it was hard to listen to a trial recording unless they put on earphones; sometimes it was hard to hear yourself think. Everyone punched their time card at nine A.M., and at five P.M. sharp, the building janitor came in to switch off lights and heat. One glance at Huang Xiaomao and you could see he didn't belong here, didn't belong to the nine-to-five job in an airy, open office: with his long ponytail, nicotine-brown fingers and casual, artistic clothes, he fit much more comfortably in an underground rock club, which is exactly where he came from. However, since Chan had enlisted Liu, Ai came with Liu, and Liu enlisted Huang, all of them now found themselves in the same boat—it's just that no one quite expected the boat to swell so quickly into such a large corporate ship!

At the moment, however, Ai and Liu fret about a more immediate quandary. As part of the expansion plan, Yu just announced that he would like all his singers on the promotion list to sign a six-year contract with CIM. During these six years, they will not receive a salary but Yu plans to pour a lot more money into marketing, packaging and promoting every one of them. He wants to put their blow-up photos and albums in the windows of every video shop in China; he is going to pack them and their bands into large van trucks, sending them on national tours. They will become sensational hits and make millions of dollars—and so, naturally, will the company. From Yu's point of view, he is offering a gold mine to these starlets (some of them merely twenty-year-old upstarts) for which their reaction can only be gratitude.

Not Ai Jing. Now twenty-four, Ai ran away from her home in Manchuria at a very early age and has remained something of a free spirit ever since. Indeed, it has been part of her musical image and appeal: she is widely admired as a young vagabond rebel who cherishes nothing more than her freedom and individuality. "It's flattering to know Boss Yu has such faith in our artistic cachet and commercial potential," she says to me. "But he wants exclusive rights on us for six years: all concerts, all products, and no rights in choosing agents or terminating contracts. How can I sign something like that?" So far, everyone else on the list has signed. After Ai indicated that she might not sign, Yu half threatened to cut off all promotion efforts, even to stop her current recording. Also at stake is Liu's job: in case of a breakup, could Liu stay on with CIM after Ai walks? And if Liu says good-bye, Huang would probably pull out right after him. There wouldn't be much of a Great Land left. What could they do after that? Back to their shoestring budget and small operations? Ai Jing is famous and in demand now. Still, given the primitive and chaotic state of the Chinese art market, it's not easy to find a big backer like Yu, who actually cares and believes in investing so much money in Chinese music talents. And after all, CIM did make Ai a star in the first place. Fiercely independent, Ai does have her vulnerable traits, not to say conscience and loyalty.

"Blackmail me? I won't have it," Ai says, pacing the apartment. Liu takes a long drag on his cigarette, drinks a beer, and mumbles: "He wants more products, more records. Where is the great distribution chain in China? Sooner or later, our offices will be stacked up with so many records, along the walls, on the floors, that we won't be able to walk in." Yet, can they really afford to break away from Yu's hook now? The corporate maw may appear monstrous from a certain angle, but if you ride with the beast, it can carry you far, very far—and who knows, you may even get there all in one piece, with heart and soul intact.

Ai makes a phone call. "What should I do, Ah John?" John is Chan Koon-Chung's English name. After all, he was the one who got them all into this in the beginning.

FU ZUNJIE is one of the four section chiefs Yu brought from Hong Kong. After a decade of climbing up the editorial-management ladder at Ming Bao newspaper, Fu is now slated to take charge of CIM's mainland publishing and distribution business. He is thirty-five, short, and scrubby, and he speaks Mandarin with a thick Cantonese accent. Totally a product of Hong Kong, he confesses that China has hit him on the head with its sheer size, its immensely diversified regional cultures and customs—the generally chaotic state of affairs and the often-wayward ways of people have all but shocked him out of his previous illusions about a great, unified China. "I used to think that way from Hong Kong. No more. The differences—in economy, ways of thinking, lifestyle—are too great; we shouldn't have a forced unification. A lot of countries nowadays have just trade relations, why must China impose integration over so many things? It's all because of the idea of a unified nation-state." But his boss, Fu tells me, wants to establish a nationally unified distribution company, so that the same publications and books would arrive in every province in China through a great chain. The problem is that the market needs vary a great deal between the north and south. This became clear in the case of a theater- and film-oriented newspaper that CIM has put out this year: the southern regions wanted something light with a lot of photo illustrations, whereas the north is much more interested in good writing. Besides, Fu has had so many headaches in working with mainlanders. He admits the current Chinese distribution system is a big mess. "But getting anything done here is a time-consuming struggle. China is a long way from the kind of professionalism we're used to in Hong Kong. People don't understand law or contract, nor do they respect them. Instead, they stress connections, human relationships. Especially the older people, they always say, 'You don't understand, this is China.'" Fu has discovered that the Cultural Revolution was a watershed experience for the Chinese: the young, under thirty-five, are still capable of learning new things, he says, but the children of the Cultural Revolution, now in their late thirties and forties, learned always to safeguard themselves first. "They are shortsighted, out for their own interests, taking advantage of you when they can, and breaking with you the moment something happens." Fu himself is a competent, diligent person, and he hates his Chinese employees' habit of always gossiping and blurring the line between the professional and the personal. "At first I socialized with them after work, wanting to understand the locals more. But you give them an inch, they take a foot: they are no longer afraid of you as the boss at work. You can't *move* the Chinese to work hard, you have to *whip* them." Scratching his chin, Fu grins puckishly: "I've always had a tendency to lecture my employees. China has certainly made my bad temper worse."

Those on the receiving end of Fu's periodic office wrath have not taken it all in good humor. One of his Beijing staff members speaks of it as a manifestation of the general tension and cultural gap between the people from Hong Kong and the Chinese. "They have this condescension," she says in a tone between bitterness and contempt. "Just because they're richer now, they assume they are superior in general and know the right ways to do everything." She misses the days of working under Chan. "He's much more gentle and understanding. He made you feel like an equal member of the team, and the job seemed so much fun. Not like now, all rigid and formal." A Beijing playwright who has had dealings with CIM is even more bluntly antagonistic. After sarcastically describing to me how a young CIM staff member, a native of Sichuan Province, has taken to wearing three-piece suits and emulating a Hong Kong accent, he blurts out: "Who cares about their stinky money anyway? What culture does Hong Kong have? The cultural center is here in Beijing, and it will always stay that way."

Meanwhile, they move in separate worlds within the same city. The Hong Kong expats live together in their plush hotel apartments, take cabs to work in modern office towers, and hang out together at night in expensive karaoke bars; the Chinese squeeze into their squalid homes, bicycle or fight on the buses to work, and watch cheap TV shows at night. If, as people often say, Hong Kong is the "last emporium" of British colonialism, then its shop clerks may be, unwittingly, exacting a premature revenge on their future colonial masters: they are having a royal time in their capital, while the royal subjects of the empire can only grit their teeth under the whip of their . . . masters, or slaves?

"HERE IS what I think of the basic difference between Chan's approach and Yu's," the chief editor of a Beijing economic newspaper sums it up for me over a cup of coffee. "When the Japanese devils entered a Chinese village in the forties, they first looked for the collaborators who knew the local situation well—this is Chan's way. When Americans want to conquer a foreign territory, they send their choppers and drop their parachuters from the sky, armed to the teeth with the best weaponry—this is Yu's way."

The Chinese local situation, in the eyes of some of the most politically seasoned and foxy natives, is one of the most dangerous, unstable, and tricky grounds in the world. Groping through an unprecedented, messy transition between "communism, Chinese style" and "market economy, socialist style," the country reveals its ambiguities, contradictions, and contrasts at every moment. The rules of the game are never very clear, and policies change all too frequently. Connections are always important in doing business, but for foreign investors in China, cultivating the backing and favor of certain top officials can sometimes be the key to winning the game. And the natives watch. They are well practiced at reading signs, adjusting to winds, instinctively distrusting those from the outside. This modus operandi, now deeply ingrained, is as automatic to the Chinese as a reflex.

So far, CIM has made its share of errors and misjudgments. They have sometimes underestimated the shifty nature of things, the unreliable, complex character of certain Chinese partners they chose to cooperate with. Since then, they have learned to pick out those institutions with less entangled staffs, feuds and factions, and partners with simpler histories. They are getting better at the game.

Still, the top Chinese leadership has not sent clear signals about CIM's presence in China. Perhaps the government hasn't made up its mind about where Ming Bao stands since Yu took over. In Hong Kong, it's generally considered a politically neutral newspaper, with critical as well as supportive coverage on China. However, rumor has it that Mr. Cha, the patriotic patriarch whose kung fu novels have found a fan in Deng Xiaoping, and who still has an influence over Ming Bao, tries to block overly negative reporting on China. And everyone now knows about Yu's heavy investment on the mainland. Recently, when the Ming Bao editors decided to print the prison notes of Wei Jingsheng, China's most prominent political prisoner of the last fifteen years, they notified Yu in advance. Yu said it was their decision; the notes were printed. "Personally, I didn't like Wei's notes," Yu commented afterward. "But I'm pleased not to intervene with the paper's editorial decisions." For some time now, Yu has set people to work on getting official Chinese endorsement. Words have been passed up through the inside lines. A top-level official reception at the Great Hall of the People was tentatively arranged at one point, for the occasion of presenting funds that Chan and Yu helped to raise from Hong Kong for the famous Project Hope, a major campaign for Chinese schools in poor rural areas. At the last moment, though, the expected top official didn't show; his deputy came instead. Rumors circulated that Yu had donated funds to the Tiananmen students in 1989, and is a good friend of Christian Loh, who is Governor Patten's appointee in Hong Kong's Legislative Council and a high-profile advocate for democratic reforms. It was also said that Chan Koon-Chung and Tsui Hark had been two of the three people who initiated a petition in support of the Tiananmen students, which was signed by many Hong Kong film luminaries. Soon afterward, a million Hong Kong people marched on the streets.

Then, in November 1993, news spread that both *Life Weekly* and *China Business Times*, two of the major publishing projects backed by CIM, had gotten stuck in the process of getting official approval. To start up the projects, Yu has already paid out a few hundred thousand yuan. Workers have begun to renovate the office buildings, new teams of journalists have been formed, consultants' fees paid out; banquets, drinks, debates into the nights; the heat, the excitement, the general anticipation that real professional newspapers, perhaps a Chinese *Times* and a Chinese *Wall Street Journal,* might be born. All stranded for now—all may turn out to be money thrown into the water.

One of the editors who had joined the new *Life Weekly* team pulled out with an excuse and went back to his old state job. Privately, he draws this conclusion about Yu: "He's either the greatest genius in the world or the biggest fool under the sun. We'll see."

ABOVE ALL this churning water, the atmosphere at CIM's central command is strangely calm, orderly, and cheerful. Nothing has ruffled the feathers of the young helmsman. From where Yu sits, which is on high, the view appears clear, unobstructed, quite magnificent. He is almost always in a good mood, determined and optimistic about the future course he has charted out for CIM and, by extension, for a good portion of China. Although still without a holding company in China, CIM has registered over forty joint-venture companies on the mainland and carved out seventeen business territories. The goal is to establish a new multimedia system across the nation, and for this Yu plans to throw in roughly $200–300 million over in the next five years—not much at all to him, considering the end results. It is his firm conviction that China is approaching a cultural renaissance in the coming decade, and he himself will do all he can to help lay the basic infrastructure for it. He thinks he can get the job done within two to three years. By a method of leverage, he will build the system up level by level, with wedges linked to or driven into the existing system. Yu is the architect, the designer; his staff is left with the job of minute implementation, of building it all up brick by brick, block by block, following his blueprint. Yu is the helmsman, the captain; his crew is expected, with their skillful maneuvering, to avoid the reefs and overcome the obstacles along the charted route. A few minor botched operations won't deter them—and Yu has perfect confidence in his chosen followers.

My interview with him takes place after many phone calls to his secretary. It begins with my joking that he's as hard to see as Chairman Mao, and ends with him glancing at the clock: he has a plane to catch. When not talking or working, Yu always has a plane to catch—he's always on the run. "He's flying in the air all the time." This has been a remark from several CIM people under Yu. They marvel, sigh in admiration, then they wink.

In point of fact, the interview turned out to be much longer than scheduled, for Yu gets rather carried away by the beauty of articulating his grand project. Looking sharp as usual, he rams through all the points from behind his big, shining desk. Why culture in China? Because he has always had a personal interest in culture, particularly in news and print media. It's hard money, but it's a very hopeful area in China. And the Ming Bao Group has the most advanced technologies in this field in Hong Kong. Chaos in the Chinese market? But it produces two things: what's bad is the bureaucratic jungle; what's good is you can get very big very fast. His models? CBS, Sony, TCI, Time Warner. Of course, China is much closer to Japan and Singapore than to the West. Politics? The Chinese waste too much energy in trying to figure out the complicated threads of their political scenes. It is unnecessary to second guess in the dark; one need only focus on what one wants to do, and do it well. Deng's health and 1997? I take the long view, I think in terms of twenty years. I don't care when Deng dies. Anyway, my basic goal is the same as the majority of the Chinese leadership: I want to build a better and stronger China, and I believe a socialist market is the way. Yu shakes his head, excited again. "There are so many talents in this land. Sprinkle a little manure, and so much will grow."

But what if things don't work out? What if, due to some unpredictable shift of wind, the great ship sinks? I insist rather stubbornly, probing him with a problematic, darker vision. This is not Hong Kong. Here in this vast land, history has knocked millions on their faces over and over again; the past has not left many people on a high plane of idealism. Too much blood and tears may not make them stronger; they are more likely to grow weak in the legs, to see shadow before light. And they've lost trust in grand missions. In case of a shipwreck, or just at a sign that it might happen, they'll be the first ones to jump off.

"All right," Yu looks calmly into my eyes, unflinching. "If they know how to swim, they've got nothing to fear. If they don't, they shouldn't have come onto my ship in the first place."

ON A cold day toward the end of 1993, I meet Chan Koon-Chung again in a Japanese restaurant in Beijing. As usual, he is wearing his discreetly elegant clothes and his gentle, sweet smile. His manners, as in the past, are civil, almost courtly. We order sashimi and sake. He has just returned from a visit to Hong Kong and is quite happy about the business agreements he made there with various financiers. He has been extremely busy, traveling in and out of Beijing, between China and Hong Kong, both on CIM's business and, increasingly, on his own projects. He has tried to persuade Ai Jing to sign the CIM contract, believing that the terms will not stay as rigid as planned.

He smiles as I mention his being pushed aside by Yu. "It was *bei jiu shi bing quan*," losing the power over a cup of liquor. This is an allusion to the most famous banquet in Chinese history: Zhao Kuangyin, the first emperor of the Song Dynasty, grew uneasy with the powerful top generals who had helped him to win many bloody battles on the way to his throne, so he invited them to a banquet, where he stripped them of their military powers over a cup of liquor. Chan shakes his head softly. "It's a shame, really, because I would have stayed on to do my best for CIM. Yu is a businessman with a sense of mission. I guess what I'd been doing in China is Yu's passion too, and it's hard to see others taking your passion away from you."

But he is not giving up on his vision either. He wants to stay on in China. Aside from his own money, he has found some new major backers. ("My apologies, business secret not yet to be disclosed.") He will do exactly what he has been doing, in his own way: start small, put things on track so they can each grow on their own, set up model ventures and institutions to inspire others to follow and compete. Guerrilla strategies, grass-roots approach, mobile and pliable, no big corporations, no set formulas. Like hundreds of snowballs rolling, gathering momentum along the way. ("Do you know about 'Chaos Theory'? How seemingly unrelated things will eventually cause a systematic change in the environment?") He aims at a reasonable balance between the commercial and the cultural; he is after the profit but also a good cause.

What is he doing at the moment? Well, a thousand things: he has just sealed a laser video joint-venture deal, has made headway on a CD-ROM computer book publishing project, has bought the renovation rights to save a famous colonial building in downtown Beijing, is working on some children's animation and comics software imports, and is looking for ways to set up a new cinema chain in major Chinese cities. He has been thinking hard about how to reform the existing Chinese distribution system. "China is not doing well in upstream production or downstream retail. I won't bore you with all the technical details, but distribution is key: right now readers can't find books, and books can't find readers. Whoever figures out a solution is worth millions. After that, a good, best-selling novelist like Jia Pingwa can make a lot of money. It will inspire others. Talented writers won't have to be poor anymore." Oh, by the way, he has just come from a meeting on a new magazine called *Beijing Chronicle*. The first issue will be out next April. Chan is supporting it with his own money, and hoping that this previously stuffy, moribund publication might transform itself into the first comprehensive, lively monthly about urban trends and lifestyle in Beijing.

"Because of its high tradition, its unparalleled concentration of literary talents and publishing houses, only Beijing has the potential of skipping over the Hong Kong model to become a center of more refined culture. It shouldn't be like now, with the night taken over by Hong Kong–style karaoke bars. So, you see, I'm a real unlucky man: I'm one of the first few from Hong Kong to realize how contemptuously Hong Kong culture is regarded by the Beijing elite, and yet here I am, using everything in my power to promote Beijing, trying to make it a real cosmopolitan center of culture." I ask if he has found an abundance of gifted, open, and competent people in Beijing. "You really want the truth?" I nod. He shakes his head, smiling. "Sometimes, intelligent conversation is more difficult to build than a communications conglomerate."

Chan is equally candid about Hong Kong's strengths and limitations. "Hong Kong has two unique creations: its movies and its entrepreneurial spirit. The first has just begun to hit the international market, the second has only regional impact. Not much originality in other areas. On the whole, Hong Kong is not a vanguard on the world scene—but, I think, China can learn a thing or two from Hong Kong."

Yet in the face of today's massively complex, ever-changing global cultures and political economy, can one really assume that good institutions will beget good contents, or that, with the right kind of effort and money, the good guys will win? What does "good" mean anyway, and by whose definition? Can something good stay good? Can a small handful of noble warriors clothed in proper suits, speaking proper business jargon, with their sense of a "save the culture" mission carefully tucked under their money belt, make a big difference? Or does it merely comfort them to think so? Since commercial success and intellectual integrity don't always come happily together, to think of oneself as a "defender of the culture from inside the enemy camp" may at least help to ease one's conscience.

Thinking of people like Danny Yung and Matthias who have chosen a different line to fight for arts and culture, outside the mainstream, outside the corporations, I wonder whether such splitting of paths has caused irrevocable damage to old friendships and alliances. I ask Chan about the spoof censorship that Danny charged. He is stunned: Zuni's protest letter never reached him—he heard about the rejection only afterward. *Haowai* has been edited by younger editors for years, during which time he has taken a back seat; he hasn't been involved in direct ways. It has become a teenybopper type of magazine and, personally, he doesn't find the new format very interesting—but he understands the shift. The audience has changed, and the magazine wouldn't have survived with the old style. In any case, "purist" is not the word he would use to describe himself or his career; he is more of a mixture, a hybrid, he has crossed camps. So he understands why some of his old friends might see him as a traitor; he has been called names before.

For a brief moment, a pained expression comes onto Chan's face. "But it's a shame with Danny. Such misunderstanding. It's too bad." Then he is back to his usual good cheer. "Danny doesn't know how much I owe him. I'll never forget seeing him in those rumpled, loose-fitting trousers for the first time. It was in the seventies, when everyone in Hong Kong was still wearing tight pants and jeans. Stiffness was in. Danny's trousers made me understand something very important. It's not just fashion, it actually changed my whole attitude toward life. For that, I'll always be thankful to him."

I think of Chan as a sort of chameleon: his image resists reductionist clarity. At every phase in his life, he is full of contradictions and contrasts. He smoked and drank while organizing a Green movement. He has had equal commitments to Western Marxism and Tibetan Buddhism. He wrote intellectual essays and film scripts with one hand, business proposals with the other. Talking about profit percentages during the day, he thinks about art at night; he starts a journal, a group, then walks away to something else. Nothing is unambiguous: his impulses, his choices, his clothes, even his looks—they take on an androgynous quality once you observe him closely. This can be frustrating, especially to those who have admired him for one particular set of qualities he demonstrated at one phase; Danny and Matthias are not alone in their judgments. Hong Kong has many small, tight-knit artistic or political cells, each with its charismatic guru, a small, devoted following, and idiosyncratic codes of politics and sexualities. These cells exist and move on the margins of the highly commercialized mainstream center, and they tend to have intense in-group bonding, to follow their own rigidly purist patterns and rules, enduring for long years by resisting change. Chan has betrayed such patterns by blurring boundaries, crossing frontiers. Yet isn't that precisely what pioneers and vanguards in all eras have done? And in some ways, isn't Chan doing in nineties Beijing exactly what he did in seventies Hong Kong? For one thing, he has just launched another "city magazine"— for Beijing! What would Danny say if he had heard about that?

On the other hand, there is Yu and his brilliant, large corporate machine. In a 1982 essay entitled "People Like Us," Chan humorously described people like himself as akin to a Hobbit, one of J. R. R. Tolkien's fictional dwarfs. Toward the end of the essay, he quotes Tolkien's depiction of one of the Hobbit's traits: "Disappear when large folk whom they do not wish to meet come blundering by." Then he added: "But we shall return. Although people like us are essentially not eye-catching, we are probably a sizable bunch, and there must be more people like us. Please do not be converted by Hong Kong."

He was a romantic then, and is still a romantic now. He *has* returned, and perhaps can count people like Ai Jing and Liu Zuohui as, in some ways, his own kinsmen. They trust him, treat him as a friend, turn to him in moments of distress and laugh with him in moments of joy. ("Ah John is a fabulous dancer," Ai Jing once told me, "and he really saves me at the discotheque since he's the only man whom Ah Hui—who doesn't dance—doesn't mind me dancing with!") But they are going with Yu. Chan has made many friends in Beijing, Chinese invite him to their homes for a simple bowl of noodles, find him sympathetic and interesting to talk to. But they are more obsessed with, and scared of, Yu: in his concentrated, driven, and ruthless way, and with his big money and big vision, Yu inspires awe in others. And he has little patience with the sort of fine sensitivities Chan so often displays. Before their falling out, the two men had once gone to Tibet together. Standing before a profoundly graceful statue of Wenshu Buddha, goddess of knowledge and wisdom who holds a book in one hand, a sword in the other, Chan's eyes had turned misty. "He's a Buddhist," Yu tells me later. "And years ago, he was a Marxist. I'm also interested in both, but neither is my belief." I ask if "no belief" *is* his belief. Yu says coolly, "You may say so." There is a force about Yu that at once draws people in yet keeps them at a distance. He will never be just another guy at your dinner table. "Who knows, he may be just the kind of man who will force open what seems unbreakable in China," speculated someone who doesn't like Yu's high-handed way of doing business. "He may make things happen by sheer will." Compared to the older generation of Chinese business giants, legendary moguls like Gordon Wu, An Wang, or even Louis Cha, Yu is, at thirty-five, similarly charismatic, tight-wound, and authoritarian. His manners are also quite Westernized and smooth. He is very Chinese, yet commanding in a modern, international business style. He would never have the humor or the humility to compare himself with a dwarf. Dwarfs don't count.

It is a fact of history that, in China, little people have never mattered. Yet history is also full of ironies and surprises, and China is going through a juncture where it is the aggregated commercial might of the little people which drives the nation ahead. It is, as well, an era in which nobody knows what will come next.

In March 1994, news came to me that Ai Jing had refused, after all, to sign the six-year CIM contract. Yu Pinhai immediately suspended all the company's promotional activities for her music. The bridges haven't been burned, but this squaring off is bound to take a toll on both sides. Unexpectedly, the battle within has begun.

Around the same time, Chan Koon-Chung moved into his new apartment in Beijing. "*Jiao tu san ku*" is an age-old Chinese adage: "A shrewd rabbit always has three holes." Between Hong Kong, Vancouver, and Beijing, Chan has three homes now.

EPILOGUE

IN THE wake of the 1989 Tiananmen massacre, a famous Chinese dissident writer, living in exile in the United States, predicted on a major American television network that the Chinese regime would fall within two years "because it has lost its mandate to rule."

Three years later, the same writer predicted again, this time in a leading Hong Kong magazine, that China was "on the eve of mass uprising," because of widespread corruption, injustice, and oppression.

He was not alone in these opinions. Many people I have met in China at different points have privately predicted, perhaps hoped, that something like this would happen. As late as 1993, a Chinese journalist reporting on certain impoverished rural areas assured me that "the peasants are ready to rise up as soon as a charismatic figure emerges to lead them." And, of course, the rising number of labor strikes at state plants is worrisome too. Even now, with the deepening of economic reforms, the growing private sector prosperity, and the relative stabilization of Communist Party rule, I continue to encounter Chinese who are utterly pessimistic about the country's future, people who foresee either dark storms on the horizon or a sort of slow, fin-de-siècle degeneration. The difference is that nowadays most pessimists seem to be alarmed by such prospects rather than hoping for them.

Chinese history is littered with disasters, both natural and man-made; and disasters have often struck suddenly. Over the past one hundred years, so many revolutions and coups d'etat in China have been followed by the most ironic shifts and turns. As a result, catastrophe and sudden eruptions have come to seem like something cyclical and overdetermined, something lurching in a dark corner ready to leap out anytime. People have learned to expect and prepare for the worst. To some extent, the national mentality is shaped—warped, maybe—by such fears or expectations about the future. This has a double effect: it can make people strong and resilient, but it can also make people think and act in a short-sighted, rash manner or lapse into a resigned passivity. One way or another, it seems to be a trauma-tized mindset, burdened by too many historical upheavals: you fear for a shipwreck or you hope for a revolution, but you are not accustomed to the messy normality of slow, gradual change. You can't quite believe that it will last.

Nevertheless, as I have tried to convey in this book, things have changed tremendously in China over the last few years, as have the general moods and outlooks of many people. The economic reforms have created new opportunities, new dreams, and to some extent, a new atmosphere and new mindsets. The old control system has weakened in many areas, especially in the spheres of economy and lifestyle. There is a growing sense of increased space for personal freedom, partly because, by now, everyone knows the basic boundaries of freedom: as long as you don't engage in overt political protest, the state will more or less leave you alone. After decades of venomous campaigns and failed protests, a sense of fatigue and cynicism about politics seems to pervade Chinese society. So, for the time being at least, the majority of the population have happily turned away from politics and geared their energies to making money and living better.

This is a limited, compromised freedom. As one of my Chinese friends sarcastically put it, "Sure we're freer than before—we have the freedom to gyp our fellow men now." Still, it also seems to provide the kind of free space that a lot of Chinese have been craving and are fairly content with, at least for now. Thanks to the shift from politics to economy, the old paranoia and depression about the state and the Party have subsided a good deal. Even in Beijing, where central control has always been the tightest, the gloomy mood after the 1989 massacre has gradually given way to a general acceptance of reality and a more positive outlook on the future. Waves of imported pop culture vogues and consumer products have captured the popular mind. The smart, cool, and rich businessmen and pop stars visiting from Hong Kong and Taiwan offer examples for the local youth. The new sensibility, especially among the younger generation, focuses increasingly on money, lifestyle, and professional success.

It is against this background—with an economic boom now in its second decade, a vast market of seemingly infinite potential, and the temporarily stable political situation—that more and more Chinese are inclined nowadays to speak of a brighter future and a stronger China. Even though the situation remains volatile in many ways, and the possibility of unrest, triggered by uneven development, corruption, or a leadership shake-up still haunts many people, the population tends to sound more hopeful than before.

Fan Gang, a young economist at the Chinese Academy of Social Sciences, who is a rising star in his field, has talked to me with a strong sense of optimism about China's future. "For a while, the situation was precarious: you never knew if the reform would collapse in a period of crisis. But after all these years of groping in the dark, with the old and the new clashing, rubbing, and fusing with one another, I think now the economy has entered a new phase." As an example, he points out that in 1992, in Beijing *alone* one thousand new private companies were officially registered, whereas in the prior ten years, only two hundred had been registered. "Even though the current leadership is still trying everything to revitalize the state enterprises, ultimately it's an impossible mission: they are moribund. Meanwhile, the private sector is growing very fast." He also had some ingenious things to say about the rampant corruption, swindling, and cheating:

> A lot of Chinese lament about the current state of affairs as moral degeneration, but that's because they assume human nature is kind and decent, which is simply not true. It's only natural that people take advantage of each other, and of the loopholes in the system, when they have a chance. At the present, the market economy is not yet well regulated; there aren't enough laws, and there isn't enough legal transparency—so people have taken advantage of the situation. But gradually, they are bound to find out that all this cheating and protecting yourself from being cheated consume too much time and energy, and that the best way to do business is playing by a set of mutually respected rules. New rules and laws will be passed, and people will be ready to abide them. So you see, maybe we will *cheat* out a new system!

Liu Ge feels equally confident of China's future. A former Red Guard and a law graduate from the elite Beijing University, Liu came to the United States in the mid-eighties. After getting another law degree from the University of Florida, he was hired by an American law firm as a point man to expand business with China. Liu resides in Chicago with his wife and young son, but he travels regularly to China on business. When last we met, our conversation turned to the release of Wang Juntao, a dissident activist who received a thirteen-year sentence in the official trial after Tiananmen. His early release obviously had something to do with China's efforts to get the most-favored-nation trade status renewed. I joked with Liu, "So big lawyers like you and your colleagues in China are too busy making money to represent political prisoners, eh?"

Liu took this seriously:

> That's not true! It's just that we take another approach: we are helping China's "peaceful evolution." What we've been doing is to help China set up new economic laws, to help our clients to do business by market rules. In 1989, China had few economic laws. Over the last few years, many new laws got set up: so many bills came out each year. This is extremely important

because, you see, capitalism boils down to two basic things: private ownership and fair competition. Why are so many things in China so chaotic
today? Because it's in transition from the old to the new. You have private
ownership disguised as public or collective enterprises. You have people doing
business in wild, primitive ways. But gradually, there will be more laws
and rules; the market will be more mature, more compatible with international standards, the competition more fair and open. Then, China will have
been structurally transformed! Political change will come after that. Look
at Taiwan: for decades they had no political freedom, just a free market.
But the economy took off; they also raised their educational level. Then a
new generation came to power and the time was ripe—now they have
democratic reform.

A lot of the educated, urban Chinese I meet in China nowadays echo this
way of thinking. For them, the plight of the state factory workers and poor
peasants indicates the difficulties China faces in transforming Soviet-style big
industry and traditional agriculture into more modern, more market-oriented
modes of production, but it does not negate the general direction of the
reform. Even though it isn't easy to predict where this all will go, and the government has yet to demonstrate its abilities to navigate through the many
potential undercurrents, many feel that the Chinese economy is already
hooked into the international market so deeply that whoever is in power must
follow the current course; the stakes are too high to turn back. Many involved
in economics, history, and law like to talk about Taiwan as a model China is
likely to follow or to learn from. Many have dropped their previous hopes of
changing China by radical means, opting instead for slower, gradualist
reforms, for a "peaceful evolution."

Liu said that Tiananmen had slowed this development a good deal because
so many Western investors pulled out of China after the massacre. "I know
so many big American companies who canceled their China projects."
He said only Motorola went in after the massacre, and now they have
big factory buildings in Tianjin that make beeper and cellular phones for
the huge Chinese market. "Look, Deng Xiaoping must also know it's not
right to shoot the people. But the Party, just like the students, was not cool-
headed back then—they didn't handle it well." There are others who think
Tiananmen did more damage than merely slowing down the economic development. "If the young radicals and the old hard-liners hadn't pushed it to
such an extreme confrontation in 1989," one Chinese scholar said to me,
"the reformist government under premier Zhao Ziyang would have stayed
on. Then we'd have the economic *and* the political reforms." He threw up
his hands in frustration: "But the students got carried away by the street

theater! They got so hot-headed and stupid by the end, they refused to pull out of the Square when they ought to have. Oh, it was such an unfortunate mistake."

Liu and his Chinese friends had predicted after Tiananmen that China's reform would require roughly five years in order to overcome both domestic and international pressures; the difficult period, they believe, is over. "If China could pull through such a crisis, the course of reform is not likely to be reversed again—even if Deng dies. It's hard to imagine a bump bigger than Tiananmen."

Discussing how the prosperous local governments in the south have established laws to protect local businesses and to resist taxation by the central government, I asked Liu what he thought of the rising regionalism and potential division of China that some predict for the future. Liu shook his head. "That's only possible if the army stands by a regional government, since regional government alone won't have substantial enough power to go independent. But such alliances between civilian regional governments and the army are not easy or likely to form. Fighting between armies over conflicting material interests is a more real scenario. But that also depends on the convergence of a lot of factors."

Liu himself was inducted into the army in the seventies. His regiment was stationed in the northern province of Shanxi when some troops were sent to crack down on a minority uprising in the southern province of Yunnan. "It was an extremely bloody battle, but none of us stationed in the north knew about it at the time—as though it was just some little ripple." Experiences like that gave him a sense of the Chinese reality:

> Rebellion and unrest always occur in parts of China. Tibet, for example, has had several episodes over the years. But as long as the country maintains relative stability, the Chinese economy will take off like a rocket for a long time. Longer than Taiwan or Japan, because the market and the population are huge. Mao was right: the more people, the better. Take Japan and Taiwan, the boom span is usually in proportion with the population, because it will move like waves from region to region. Investors will gain both ways by coming to China: there are 1.2 billion consumers, and 1.2 billion cheap laborers. No other country in the world can beat that.

There is a feeling of excitement among many Chinese these days about the economic surge. When a group of Chinese gather and talk about the economy, the word *qifei* often pops up: to take off and fly. The Chinese have used this word to describe the postwar economic miracles in countries like West Germany, Japan, and Taiwan. Now they are using it to describe their own.

"The next century belongs to Asia and the Pacific rim" — I heard this pronounced everywhere, in the economic newspapers, at business conferences, at banquet tables among friends. "It's about time the world looks China in the eye," a Beijing sports writer said to me once, referring to both China's bid to host the Olympics in the year 2000 and the country's continuous economic boom. "It hasn't since the eighteenth century."

I once had a sumptuous dinner with three Cantonese businessmen in Guangzhou. They were the kind of fortiesh, suit-and-beeper-wearing, masculine and confident-looking men you'd see in a lot of new fancy Chinese restaurants these days. The three men at the dinner table that evening also happened to be former Red Guards from the same middle school. Later, they were all sent to the countryside for years. Now they were successful and rich: Hu owned a chain of cosmetic factories, Gao opened his own trading company, and Zhang, also in trading, was on his way to immigrate to the United States. From time to time, they lapsed into reveries about their Cultural Revolution days, even joked about an incident in which one of them had almost betrayed another. But most of the time, they talked about making money, making business deals, making connections. Several times, a beeper went off and all three at the table looked down at their own belt; one would pick up the call, start talking about some deals, and the others would go on eating and chatting. Gao said he was totally disillusioned by politics, and he was interested only in money and business now. The moment of truth for him came in the mid-eighties, at a business banquet with a delegation from a northern European country. Next to him sat a high-ranking statesman, and they had a chat. At one point the statesman told Gao: "I believe in Marxism too. But I have a question for you: we work to turn our proletarians into bourgeois, why do you Chinese want to do it the other way around?"

The other two men chuckled as Gao recounted this to me: he was clearly expressing the way they all felt. Hu, for instance, was proud of being "a red capitalist" — a Communist Party member *and* rich. At one point he leaned forward with a knowing expression and said, "Trust me — I've been places. The twenty-first century is China's, and twenty years from now, we businessmen will be the backbone of this country."

In contrast to the older generation and the fortysomething former Red Guards, younger Chinese don't seem to care to ponder such weighty issues as the future of the country. Those in their twenties whom I've talked with tend to focus on their career and lifestyle. "Older people have a sense of mission," a young Beijing video artist said to me. "They are used to worrying about the country, to talking about the big things. We live in the present and for ourselves. What's the use of guessing when Deng is going to die or what might happen then? I've got nothing to say about the national fate. I'm busy enough getting my own life together." My twenty-four-year-old cousin, who works for a Beijing advertising agency, aggrees that his generation is more self-centered and pragmatic, but he says that's because they feel confused and powerless about the larger issues. "We wouldn't even know where to *start* to analyze China's problems, and since they aren't in our hands anyway, we might as well keep minding our own business."

People in the cultural industry, in general, tend not to display the same kind of booming confidence and optimism about the future as do people, say, in the business sector. Small wonder, considering the widespread view among them that in the rush for material wealth and economic success, China and the Chinese have put culture on the back burner. "For the intellectuals and the literati," an educated, wealthy Chinese entrepreneur recently assured me, "there are only two words: *meixi*—'no show.' The state will have less and less money to support culture. Cultural enterprises need our donations and sponsorship, and that won't happen on a large scale until the next century."

"China's problem is cultural, not political," said China's most famous rock and roll singer, Cui Jian, at a press conference for Western reporters. Cui's rebellious, lyrical songs have made him a national icon for the young generation—and, as usual, his music has been viewed in the West as a form of political protest. Cui, however, has insisted at different occasions that his main concern is with culture, that culture is at the root of all China's political problems. "The basic theme in my music is freedom, the rights of the individual who wants his freedom."

"Political movements didn't solve China's problems," a Chinese historian said to me in 1993. "Money is not going to solve them either. We've been having a deep, fundamental cultural crisis ever since the Opium War, and we are still in it. The May Fourth Movement started the cultural enlightenment process in the 1910s and was overrun later by the nationalist and communist movements. The consequences were inevitable because the cultural soil was the same. Now we opt for a new approach. But until the cultural soil changes, the old China will keep creeping up on us."

To a lot of "cultured" Chinese, changing the cultural soil means changing the national character. "The general quality of the Chinese population is too low." "Unlike the Americans, the Chinese cannot think independently." "The Chinese are accustomed to obeying an authority blindly." Statements such as these would be considered racist were they not spoken by educated Chinese—and I hear such remarks made frequently. An eminent Chinese architect told me flatly that Tiananmen was a mistake precisely because the students failed to understand the Chinese character. "They were too radical and naive. The Chinese still need an emperor figure; constitutional monarchy would be good, too. This is the same all over East Asia: Japan, Singapore, Taiwan—it's part of the traditional Oriental culture. Too bad Deng is so old; if he were in his sixties, everyone below would rest assured and keep to their respective duties. The key is that someone from the top must hold court and set the tone, or the people below don't know what to do. If there are one hundred opinions, Americans can have a debate and come to a consensus, but the Chinese would lose direction completely. If the country gets divided up into many states, in America you can have a federal system, in China, you'll have warlords and warring states!" Such sweeping assessments of "the Chinese character" or "the Oriental tradition" may sound alarmingly like the elitist rhetoric Asian conservatives and neoconservatives have often used to justify a centralist political system or the rule of a strongman. And in places like Hong Kong and South Korea, it is obvious that people do not need an emperor or a monarch in order to prosper. Nevertheless, considering the traditional mission of China's educated class—to serve the state and to assist the emperor—and considering Chinese intellectuals' grand old habit of *youguoyoumin*—"worrying for the country and the people"—I am not at all surprised to hear so many of them express such sentiments and opinions.

For some, China's future still lies with its intelligentsia. A noted Chinese columnist, for one, has recently expressed such a hope at the end of a scathing article in which he scolded Chinese intellectuals for having been "lost" over the past 150 years. However, most Chinese intellectuals, at least those who aren't too "lost" to face reality, seem to have accepted that deep social and cultural changes will take generations. Bespeaking a distinctively Chinese cast of mind, many are placing their hopes on a good emperor and the gradual enlightenment of the Chinese leadership. So when a fifty-year-old prominent Beijing professor offered me his bit of "future theory" in December 1993, it struck me as quite similar to what I had heard from many other educated Chinese: "The current leaders under Deng," he said,

> are mainly those students who returned from the Soviet Union in the fifties; they will not want to change the old system completely—they'll try to save what they can of the central planning legacy. There is also a chance of a comeback of Zhao Ziyang and his more reformist entourage. But then, the next generation of leaders will be the former Red Guards and the students who returned from America and Europe. Their way of thinking is radically different from the older generation: they've gone through the Cultural

Revolution and rejected all that. They really want to go all-out capitalist. Only then will China change completely. Such fundamental changes happen slowly. The general mood at present is too rash and anxious. This is merely a time for fast-food culture.

I have already described in this book many divided feelings and opinions about the current state of Chinese culture and what the future might hold for it: some emphasize the importance of a benevolent leadership, others stress the gradual building of a Chinese version of multiculturalism and civil society; some see hopes in a fast growing, depoliticizing commercial culture, others feel alarmed by it, perceiving in it a new form of tyranny. Perhaps it is appropriate for me to end the book with two remarks about the "cultural soil." They were from two separate conversations I had during my last visit to Beijing.

The first was with Xu Hong, chief editor of Beijing's *Consumers' Gazette*, a small weekly newspaper that has become rather popular in recent years. Xu is in his late thirties. A former Red Guard, he had labored on a farm during the Cultural Revolution, so as our chat turned to the issue of cultural change in China, it was not surprising to hear him use farming metaphors: "If you've been to the farm, you must know the difference between the winter wheat and the spring wheat. With the spring wheat, you don't have to worry about severe climate, and you can have a quicker harvest. But it's a coarser grain, sometimes only good enough for fodder. Winter wheat takes longer to grow; it has to overcome a long winter, you have to put in more labor for it, and have a late harvest. But it's of a higher quality: finer, tastier. So there you go, which one do you want? If we want good stuff in culture, we must be patient and overcome a long period of rough weather."

The other remark came from Zheng Wanlong, the novelist who co-wrote the script for *Yearning*. We were discussing Hong Kong influences on the current mainland Chinese cultural scene, and the fact that Hong Kong has long been nicknamed "the cultural desert." Zheng shook his head at the sweeping prejudices among mainland Chinese intellectuals about Hong Kong. "We dismiss it before we even take a good look at it." He has been to Hong Kong several times in the past few years. "It's not always of high quality, but for such a small island their cultural scene has a pretty good range. They are more professional and competent than us in a lot of things. There are quite a few interesting things in this 'desert'." Then he came up with the metaphor. "I think it's like this: for ages we lived on *yanjiandi*, the saline-alkaline soil, and we grew nothing but corn. It was required that all corn must come from the same family, and come out exactly the same size, with the same taste, and so on.

209

That demand is no longer upon us—and what happens? Well, now we end up with a desert; nothing much grows on it. Maybe this will go on for years and years. But it may take a desert to change the soil. And who knows, in the future we may have not just corn, but wheat and rice growing out of it!"

Cheat out a new culture? A new world? In fin-de-siècle China, perhaps that is the hope the optimists are living in.